My Facebook® for Seniors

Michael Miller

que®

800 East 96th Street

My Facebook for Seniors

ISBN-13: 978-0-7897-5166-9

ISBN-10: 0-7897-5166-6

Library of Congress Control Number: 2013943644

Printed in the United States of America

First Printing: September 2013

Trademarks

Warning and Disclaimer

Bulk Sales

Que Publishing offers excellent discounts on this book when ordered in quantity for bulk purchases or special sales. For more information, please contact

U.S. Corporate and Government Sales

1-800-382-3419

corpsales@pearsontechgroup.com

For sales outside of the U.S., please contact

International Sales

international@pearsoned.com

Editor-in-Chief
Greg Wiegand

Acquisitions Editor
Michelle Newcomb

Development Editor
Charlotte Kughen

Managing Editor
Kristy Hart

Senior Project Editor
Lori Lyons

Indexer
Ken Johnson

Proofreader
Kathy Ruiz

Technical Editor
Sheila McDermott

Publishing Coordinator
Cindy Teeters

Compositor
Bronkella Publishing

Graphics Technician
Tammy Graham

Contents at a Glance

Table of Contents

About the Author

Michael Miller is a prolific and popular writer of more than 100 non-fiction books, known for his ability to explain complex topics to everyday readers. He writes about a variety of topics, including technology, business, and music. His best-selling books for Que include *My Windows 8 Computer for Seniors, Facebook for Grown-Ups, Easy Facebook, Easy Computer Basics, Absolute Beginner's Guide to Computer Basics,* and *My Pinterest*. Worldwide, his books have sold more than 1 million copies.

Find out more at the author's website: www.molehillgroup.com

Follow the author on Twitter: molehillgroup

Dedication

To my grandkids, who make my life fun and meaningful—Collin, Alethia, Hayley, Judah, and Lael.

Acknowledgments

Thanks to all the folks at Que who helped turned this manuscript into a book, including Michelle Newcomb, Greg Wiegand, Charlotte Kughen, Lori Lyons, Tricia Bronkella, and technical editor Sheila McDermott.

We Want to Hear from You!

As the reader of this book, you are our most important critic and commentator. We value your opinion and want to know what we're doing right, what we could do better, what areas you'd like to see us publish in, and any other words of wisdom you're willing to pass our way.

We welcome your comments. You can email or write to let us know what you did or didn't like about this book—as well as what we can do to make our books better.

Please note that we cannot help you with technical problems related to the topic of this book.

When you write, please be sure to include this book's title and author as well as your name and email address. We will carefully review your comments and share them with the author and editors who worked on the book.

Email: feedback@quepublishing.com

Mail: Que Publishing
ATTN: Reader Feedback
800 East 96th Street
Indianapolis, IN 46240 USA

Reader Services

Visit our website and register this book at www.quepublishing.com/register for convenient access to any updates, downloads, or errata that might be available for this book.

Sidebar menu

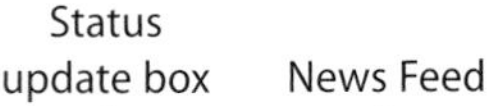
Status
update box
News Feed

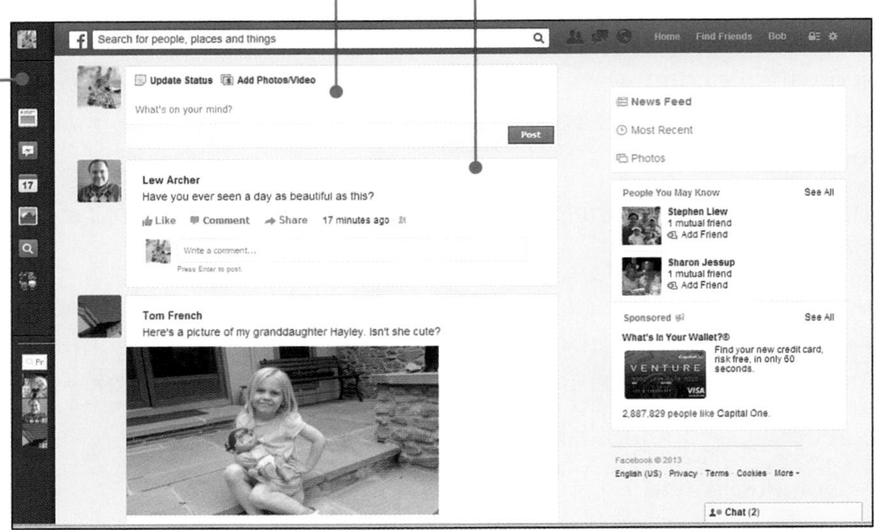
Search for people, places and things
Home
Find Friends
Bob
Update Status
Add Photos/Video
What's on your mind?
Post
News Feed
Most Recent
Photos
Lew Archer
Have you ever seen a day as beautiful as this?
Like
Comment
Share
17 minutes ago
Write a comment...
Press Enter to post.
People You May Know
See All
Stephen Liew
1 mutual friend
Add Friend
Sharon Jessup
1 mutual friend
Add Friend
Tom French
Here's a picture of my granddaughter Hayley. Isn't she cute?
Sponsored
See All
What's In Your Wallet?®
Find your new credit card, risk free, in only 60 seconds.
VENTURE
VISA
2,887,829 people like Capital One.
Facebook © 2013
English (US) · Privacy · Terms · Cookies · More
Chat (2)

In this prologue you find out what social networking is, and how Facebook works.

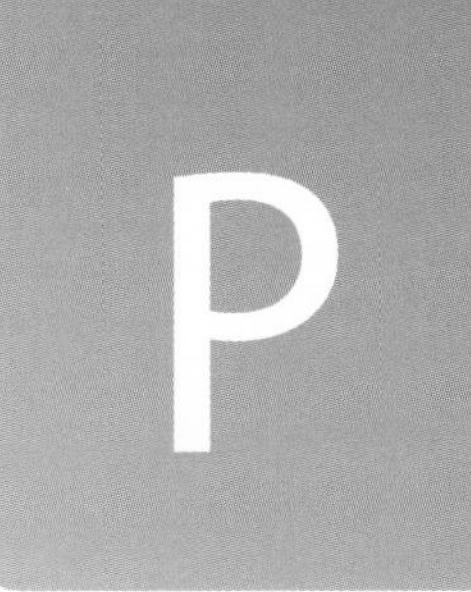

Understanding Facebook and Social Networking

If you want to keep in touch with family and friends, Facebook is the place to do it. Facebook is a social network, a website that enables you to share what you're doing with other people you know on the site.

What Is Social Networking?

A *social network* is a large website that hosts a community of users and makes it easy for those users to communicate with one another. Social networks enable users to share experiences and opinions with one another, and thus keep in touch with friends and family members, no matter where they're located.

The goal of a social network is to create a network of online "friends," and then share your activities with them via a series of message posts.

These posts are short text messages, called *status updates,* that can be viewed by all of that person's friends on the site. A status update can be text-only, or contain photos, videos, and links to other web pages.

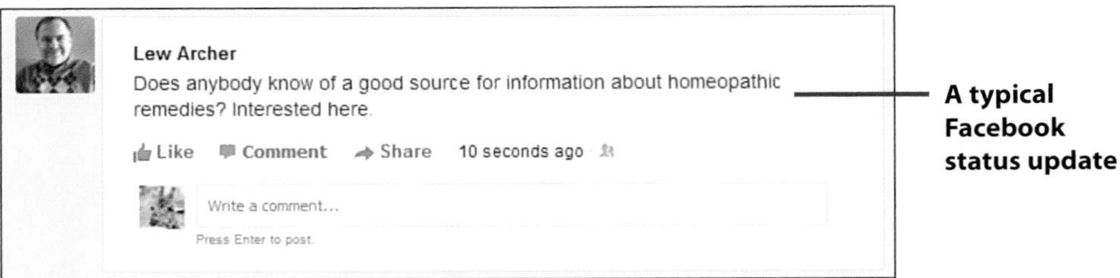

A typical Facebook status update

All your online friends read your posts, as well as posts from other friends, in a continuously updated News Feed. The News Feed is the one place where you can read updates from all your online friends and family; it's where you find out what's really happening.

Posts in the Facebook News Feed

The biggest social network today is a site called Facebook; chances are many of your friends and family are already using it. Other popular social networks include Twitter, LinkedIn, Google+, and Pinterest—but Facebook is the biggest, and it's the one where you'll find most of your friends.

Who Uses Facebook—and Why?

Facebook is the brainchild of Mark Zuckerberg, an enterprising young man who came up with the concept while he was a student at Harvard in 2004. Facebook (originally called "thefacebook") was originally intended as a site where college students could socialize online. Sensing opportunity beyond the college market, Facebook opened its site to high school students in 2005 and then to all users over age 13 in 2006. Today, Facebook boasts more than 1 billion members worldwide.

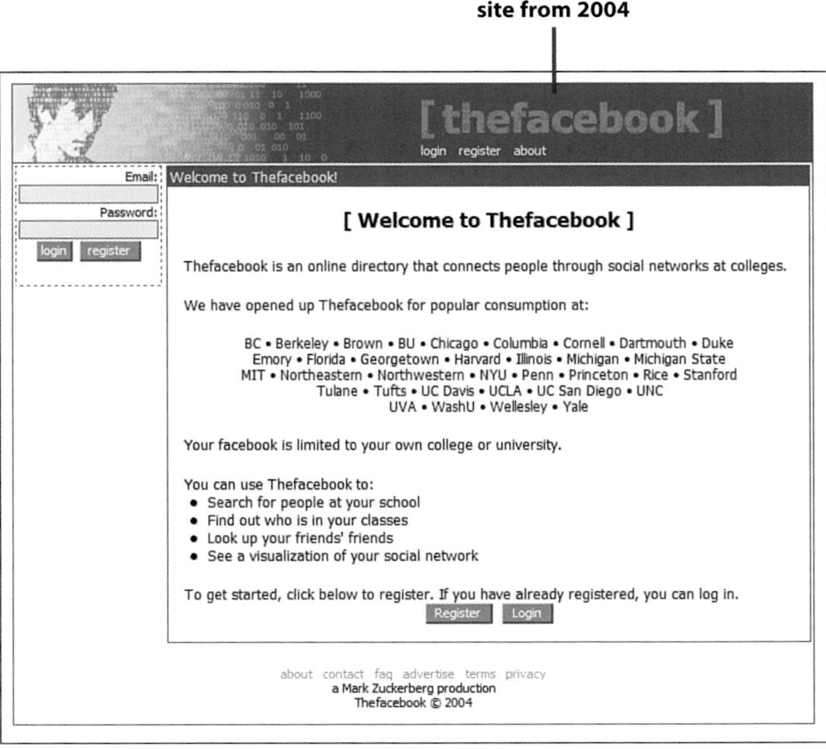

The original Facebook site from 2004

Even though Facebook started out as a social network for college students, it isn't just for kids anymore. Today, fewer than 10% of Facebook users are college aged. According to the Pew Internet & American Life Project, a higher percentage—14%—of all Facebook users are aged 55 and up.

Facebook is tremendously popular among older users. According to Forrester Research, about half of all online seniors use Facebook on a regular basis. That makes Facebook one of the most popular websites of any type among older users.

Why are seniors using Facebook? Most seniors (40%) use Facebook to connect with family and old friends; 30% use Facebook to share digital photos; and 20% play social games on Facebook. That makes Facebook both useful and fun—a great combination for users of any age.

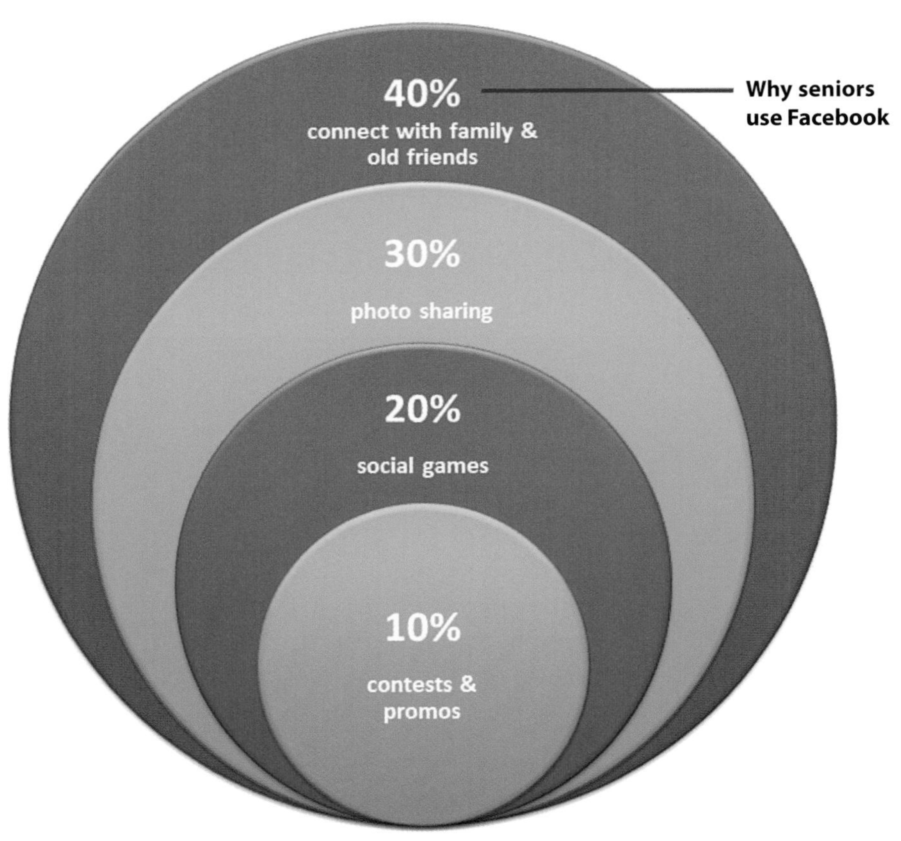

Why seniors use Facebook

How Does Facebook Work?

Facebook is a website with a variety of features. In fact, Facebook does so many things for so many people, you might not do them all. That's okay; use those features that best suit what you want to accomplish.

Social networking on Facebook is all about making "friends." On Facebook, a friend can be an actual friend, old or new, or just someone you know. Your family members become Facebook friends, as do your neighbors, people you used to work with, and people you used to go to school with.

After you make someone a friend on Facebook, all the status updates they make appear in your News Feed. This is a scrolling list of updates from all your friends, consolidated into one place on the Facebook home page.

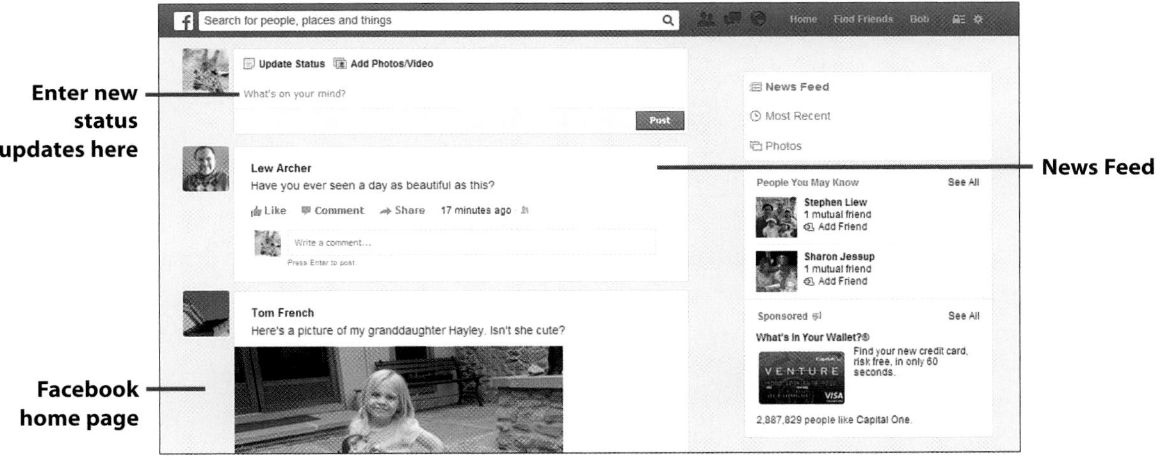

At the top of the home page is a text box you can use to enter your own status updates. A Facebook status update can contain text, images, videos, and links to other websites. You create new status updates to keep your friends informed as to what you're doing and thinking about.

Every Facebook member has his own personal profile on the site, or what Facebook calls a *Timeline*. Your Timeline page displays all the status updates you've ever made on Facebook, as well as your personal information and links to those photos and videos you've uploaded. Your friends can view your Timeline page to see what you've been up to, just as you can view theirs for the same reason.

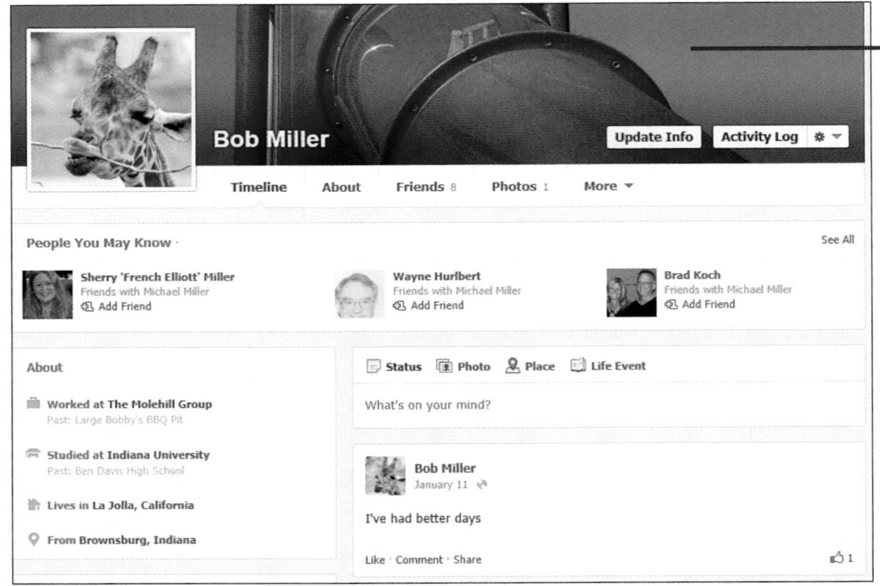

A Facebook Timeline page

In addition to the normal status updates, Facebook enables you to conduct live text-based chat sessions with any of your friends who are online. You can also use Facebook to host video chats, so you can talk face-to-face with distant friends and family.

To get the most out of Facebook, you have to actively participate. That means logging in regularly, at least once a day. That way you can keep tabs on what your friends and family members are up to. And when you post your own status updates on a regular basis, your friends and family will know what you're up to, too.

Sign in to your current Facebook account

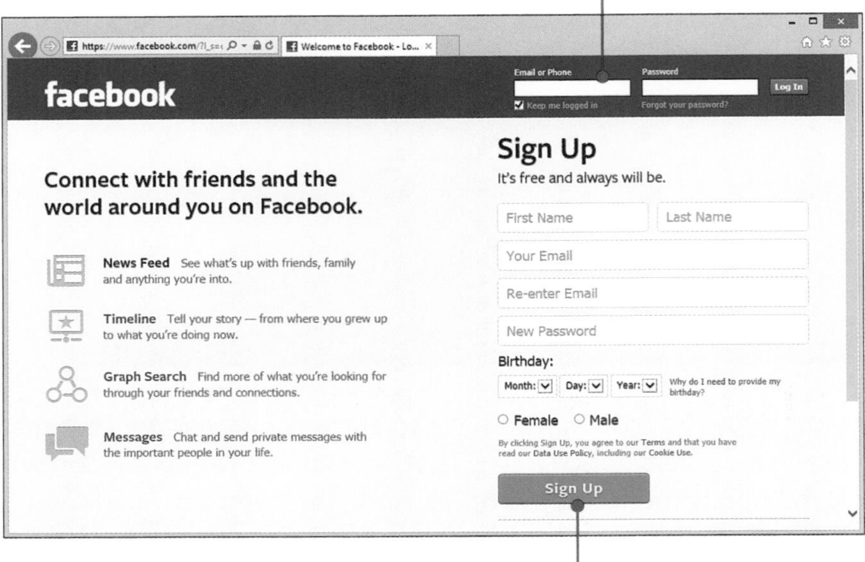

Sign up for a new Facebook account

In this chapter you find out how to create a new Facebook account and start using the Facebook site.

- → Signing Up for Facebook
- → Signing In—and Signing Out
- → Finding Your Way Around Facebook

Signing Up and Getting Started

When you're signed up as a Facebook member, you can post your own thoughts and comments, upload pictures to share, and even share your favorite web pages. Likewise, you can see what your friends and family are posting—their activities, photos, web links, and the like. That's why half of all online seniors make Facebook their hub for online social activity and check in at least an hour each day.

Signing Up for Facebook

Facebook has more than one billion members online, of all ages and types. Chances are your children and grandchildren are already using Facebook—and you'd be surprised how many of your old friends are Facebook members, too.

Create a New Facebook Account

To use Facebook, you first need to create a personal Facebook account. A Facebook account is free and easy to create; there's no fee to join and no monthly membership fees.

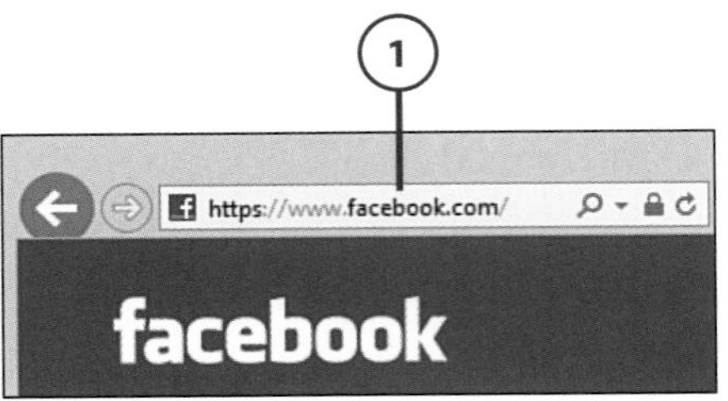

1. Use Internet Explorer, Google Chrome, or another web browser to go to Facebook's home page at www.facebook.com.
2. Go to the Sign Up section and enter your first name into the First Name box.
3. Enter your last name into the Last Name box.
4. Enter your email address into the Your Email box and then re-enter it into the Re-enter Email box.

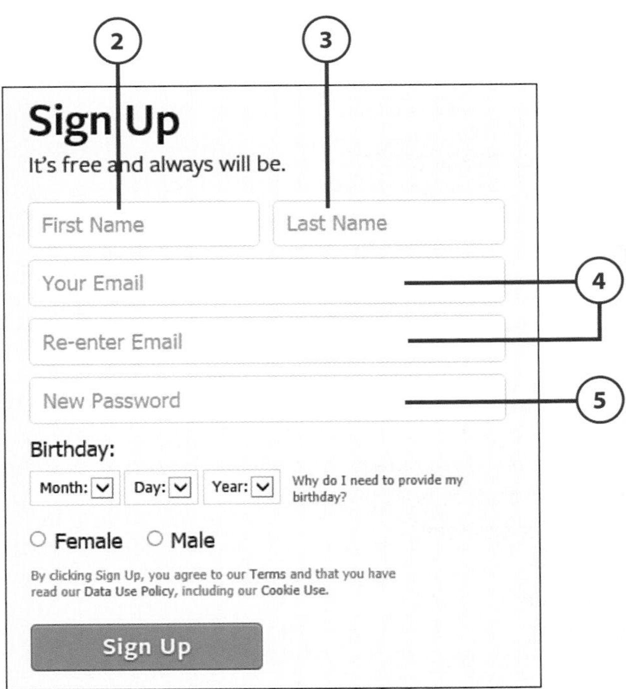

Email Address

Facebook uses your email address to confirm your identity and to contact you when necessary. You also use your email address to sign into Facebook each time you enter the site.

5. Enter your desired password into the New Password box. Your password should be at least six characters in length—the longer the better, for security reasons.

>>>Go Further

PASSWORD SECURITY

To make your password harder for hackers to guess, include a mix of alphabetic, numeric, and special characters, such as punctuation marks. You can also make your password more secure by making it longer; an eight-character password is much harder to crack than a six-character one. Just remember, though, that the more complex you make your password, the more difficult it may be for you to remember—which means you probably need to write it down somewhere, just in case.

6. Select your date of birth from the Birthday lists.
7. Check the appropriate option for your gender.
8. Click the Sign Up button.

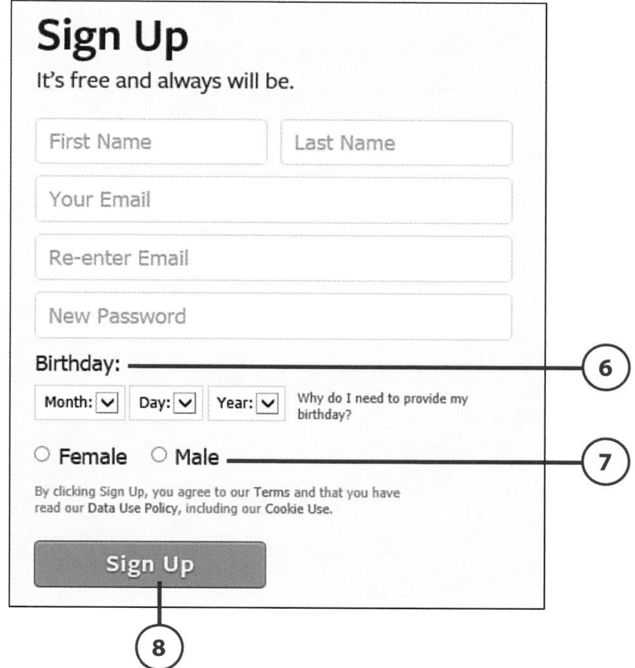

CAPTCHA

When Facebook displays the Security Check page, you're prompted to enter the "secret words" from the CAPTCHA into the Text in the Box box. A CAPTCHA is a type of challenge-response test to ensure that you're actually a human being rather than a computer program. Websites use CAPTCHAs to cut down on the amount of computer-generated spam they receive.

>>>Go Further

EMAIL CONFIRMATION AND MORE

After you click the final Sign Up button, Facebook sends you an email message asking you to confirm your new Facebook account. When you receive this email, click the link to proceed.

You'll then be prompted to find friends who are already on Facebook, and to fill in a few personal details for your profile page. You can perform these tasks now or at a later time, as we'll discuss later in this book.

Signing In—and Signing Out

After you've created your Facebook account, you can sign into the site and start finding new (and old) friends. You sign in at the same page you created your account—www.facebook.com.

Log Onto the Facebook Site

You use your email address—and the password you created during the signup process—to log in to your Facebook account. When you're logged in, Facebook displays your home page.

1. Use Internet Explorer or another web browser to go to Facebook's home page at www.facebook.com.
2. Enter your email address into the Email or Phone box.
3. Enter your password into the Password box.
4. Click the Log In button.

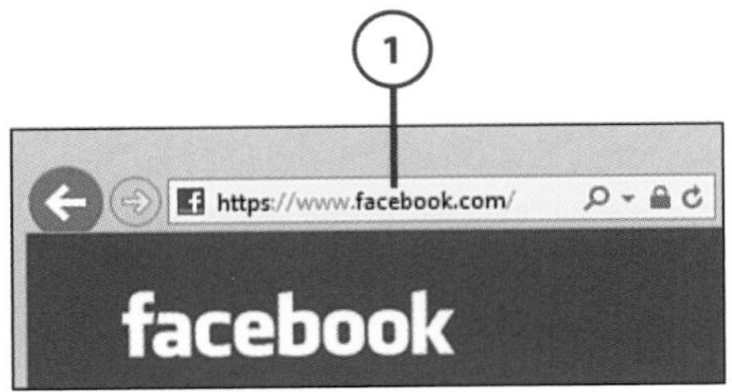

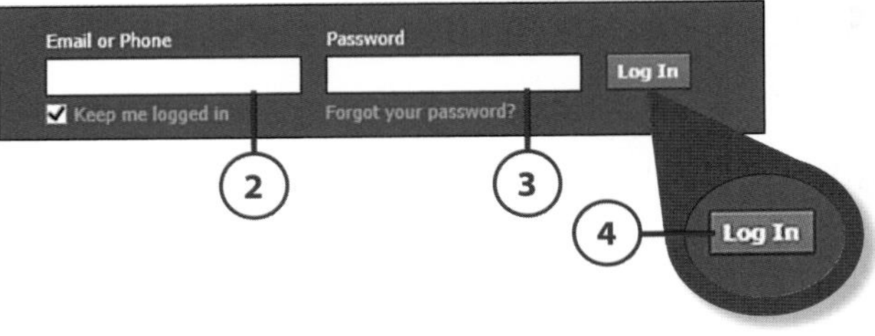

>>>Go Further

STAY LOGGED IN—OR NOT

If you don't want to enter your email and password every time you want to use the Facebook site, check the Keep Me Logged In option when you're signing in. This keeps your Facebook session open, even if you visit another website between Facebook pages.

You should not check the Keep Me Logged In option if you're using a public computer, such as one at the library, or if you share your computer with other users. Doing so makes it possible for other users to use your personal Facebook account, which you don't want. So if you share your PC or use a public computer, don't check the Keep Me Logged In option.

Log Out of Your Facebook Account

You probably want to log out of Facebook if you're not going to be active for an extended period of time. You also want to log out if someone else in your household wants to access his or her Facebook account.

1. From any Facebook page, click the Settings (gear) button at the far right side of the toolbar.
2. Click Log Out from the drop-down menu.

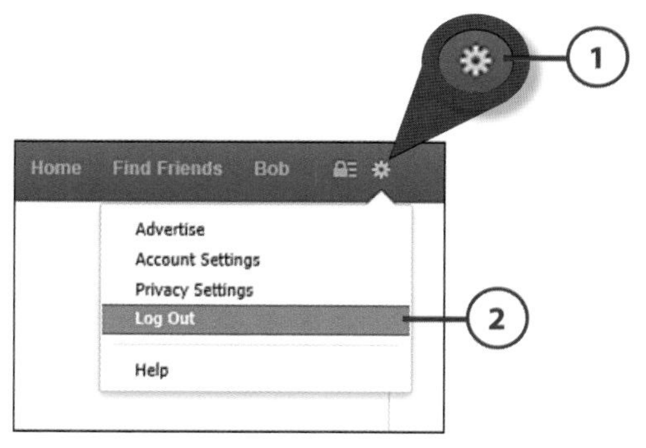

Sign Back In

After you've logged out, you need to sign back in before you can access your Facebook content again.

Finding Your Way Around Facebook

You discover more about using Facebook throughout the balance of this book, but for now let's examine how to get around the Facebook site. When it comes to moving from place to place on Facebook, you have two choices. You can use the Facebook toolbar that appears at the top of every page, or the navigation pane that displays on the left side of all pages. Not all options are found in both places.

Navigate Facebook's Home Page

After you sign into your Facebook account, you see Facebook's home page. This page looks a little different for each user, as it displays content personalized for you.

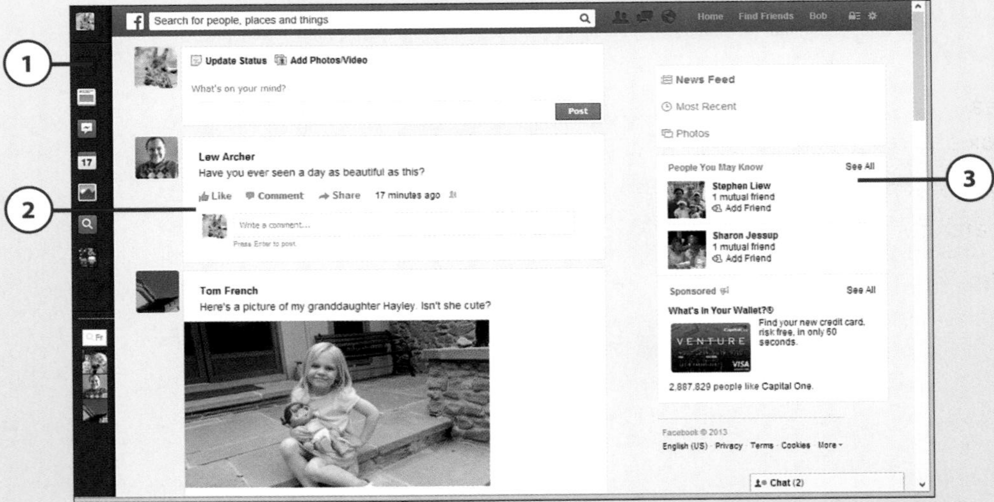

1. On the left side of the page is the *sidebar menu*. You use the options here to go to various places on the Facebook site.
2. The large column in the middle of the home page displays your *News Feed*, a stream of posts from all your Facebook friends. At the top of this column is a box you use to post your own status updates.
3. The column on the right side of the page displays various Facebook notices and advertisements. It also displays the *Feed List*, which enables you to display different types of feeds beyond the default News Feed.

Use the Facebook Toolbar

The toolbar that appears at the top of every Facebook page is your primary means of navigating the Facebook site. The toolbar also provides notification when you have messages waiting or if a friend engages you in a specific activity.

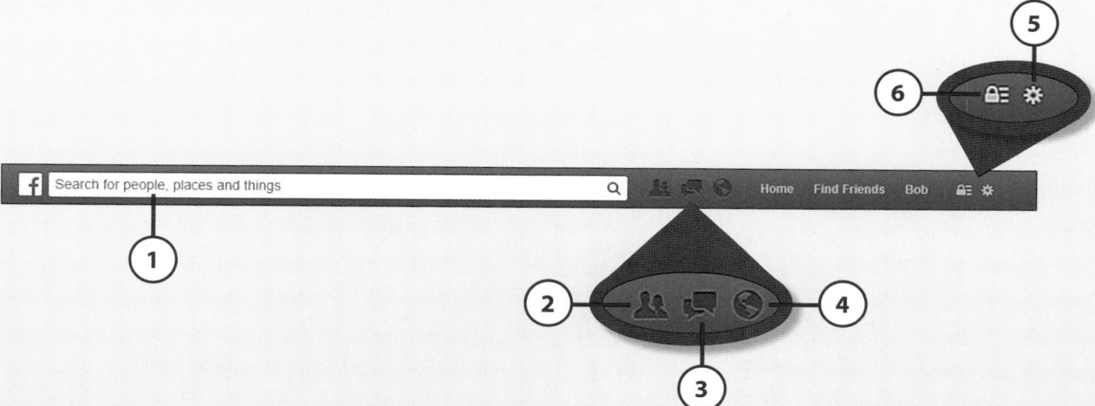

1. Search the Facebook site for people or things by entering your query into the Search box and then press Enter on your computer keyboard.
2. Click the Friend Requests button to view any friend requests you've received and to search for new friends on the Facebook site.
3. Click the Messages button to view your most recent private messages from Facebook friends.
4. Click the Notifications button to view notifications from Facebook, such as someone commenting on your status or accepting your friend request.

Counting Requests and Messages

If you have pending friend requests, you see a white number in a red box on top of the Friend Requests button. (The number indicates how many requests you have.) Similarly, a white number in a red box on top of the Messages or Notifications buttons indicates how many unread messages or notifications you have.

5. Click the gear icon to access all sorts of account settings. This is also where you sign out of Facebook when you're done using it for the day.
6. Click the lock icon to access important privacy settings.

Navigate with the Sidebar Menu

You can get to even more features on Facebook when you use the sidebar menu on the left side of the screen. Click any open area to expand the menu to display text labels for each icon, then click any item to display that specific page.

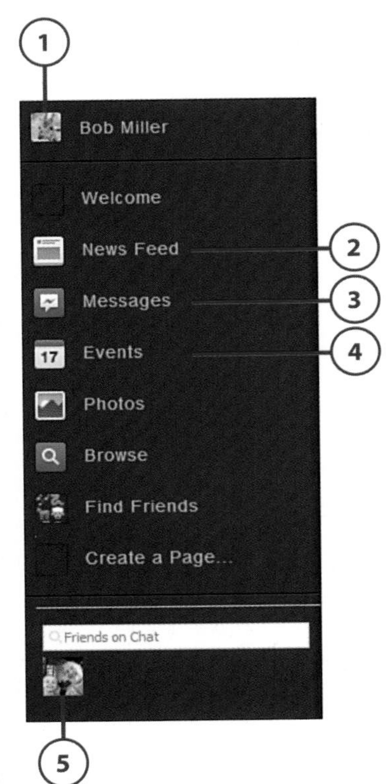

1. To visit your personal timeline page, click your picture at the top of the menu.
2. To read your News Feed, click the News Feed icon.
3. To view messages in your Facebook inbox, or send a private message to another user, click the Messages icon.
4. To view pending events or schedule a new event, click the Events icon.
5. To chat with any online friend, click that person's picture in the chat area at the bottom of the menu.

New News Feed

This book is written on what Facebook is calling the New News Feed, and the screenshots represent this latest version. As you read this book, however, Facebook may still be in the process of rolling out this new interface to all users. If your version of Facebook looks a little different from what you see in this book, just wait awhile—you'll get the New News Feed soon!

Filter suggestions by location and other factors

Facebook's friends suggestions

Click to send a friend request

Find friends from different parts of your life

Use the checkboxes below to discover people you know from your hometown, school, employer and more.

Mutual Friend
- Alvy Singer
- Lew Archer
- Michael Michards

Enter another name

Hometown
- Brownsburg, Indiana

Enter another city

Current City
- La Jolla, California

Enter another city

High School
- Ben Davis High School

Enter another high school

College or University
- Indiana University

Enter another college or unive...

Employer
- Large Bobby's BBQ Pit
- The Molehill Group

Sherry 'French Elliott' Miller
Office Manager at Higher Standards Inc.
Michael Miller is a mutual friend.
Add Friend

Sharon Jessup
Works at UPS
Michael Miller is a mutual friend.
Add Friend

Reeves Cary
Professional Vocalist at Self employed
Add Friend

Anne Yastremski
Randolph-Macon Woman's College
Michael Miller is a mutual friend.
Add Friend

Mark H. Dixon
Ohio Northern
Michael Miller is a mutual friend.
Add Friend

In this chapter you find out how to find people you know on Facebook and add them to your friends list.

→ Finding Facebook Friends
→ Accepting Friend Requests
→ Unfriending Unwanted Friends

2

Finding Old (and New) Friends

Facebook is all about connecting with people you know. Anyone you connect with on Facebook is called a *friend*. A Facebook friend can be a real friend, or a family member, colleague, acquaintance, you name it. When you add someone to your Facebook friends list, he sees everything you post—and you see everything he posts.

Of course, before you can make someone your Facebook friend, you have to find that person on Facebook. That isn't always as easy as you might think, especially when you're looking for people you went to school with or worked with several decades ago. People move, women change their names when they get married (or divorced, or remarried, or some combination of the above), and it just becomes more difficult to find people over time. It might be difficult, but if they're on Facebook, you can probably find them.

Finding Facebook Friends

Because it's in Facebook's best interests for you to have as many connections as possible, the site makes it easy for you to find potential friends. This process is made easier by the fact that Facebook already knows a lot about you—and the people you might know.

Facebook automatically suggests friends based on your personal history (where you've lived, worked, or gone to school), mutual friends (friends of people you're already friends with), and Facebook users who are in your email contacts lists. You can then invite any of these people to be your friend; if they accept, they're added to your Facebook friends list.

Facebook Friends

As far as Facebook is concerned, everyone you know is a "friend"—even family members. So when we talk about Facebook friends, these could be your children or grandchildren, people you work with, casual acquaintances, or even real friends.

Accept Facebook's Friend Suggestions

The easiest way to find friends on Facebook is to let Facebook find them for you based on the information you provided for your personal profile. The more Facebook knows about you, especially in terms of where you've lived, worked, and gone to school, the more friends it can find.

>>>Go Further

HOW MANY FRIENDS?

Some people like to assemble a large list of Facebook friends, to keep in touch with everyone they've known throughout their lives. Other people find a large friends list somewhat overwhelming, and prefer to keep a shorter list of close friends and family.

Either approach is good. It all depends on what you want to get out of Facebook, and what you're comfortable with. Don't feel obligated to accept every friend suggestion or request; add to your list only those people you really, truly want to keep in contact with.

1. Click the Friends button on the Facebook toolbar to display the drop-down menu, which lists any friend requests you've received and offers a number of friend suggestions from Facebook in the People You May Know section.
2. Click the Add Friend button next to a person's name to add that person to your friends list.

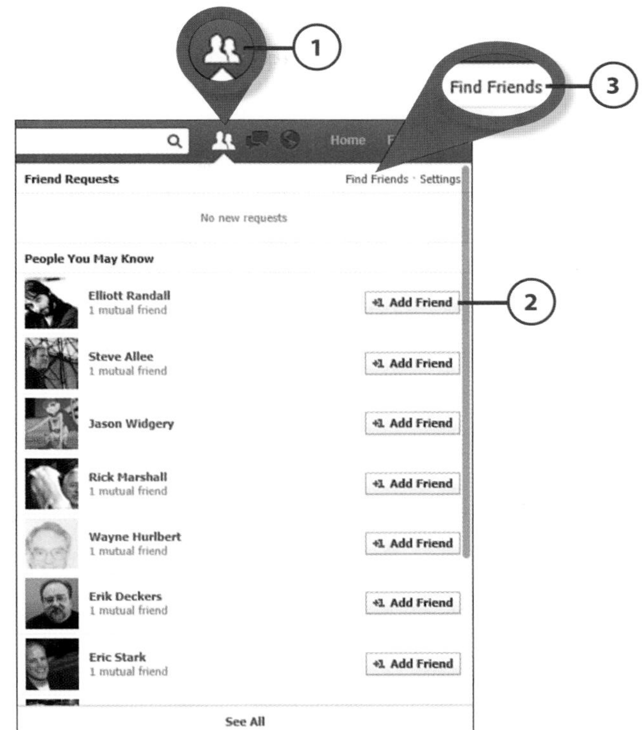

Suggested Friends

The people Facebook suggests as friends are typically people who went to the same schools you did, worked at the same companies you did, or are friends of your current friends.

---

3. Click Find Friends at the top of the menu to display your Friends page to continue searching for friends.
4. Scroll down the page to view other suggested friends from Facebook in the People You May Know section. Click the Add Friend button for any person you'd like to add as a friend.
5. Click the See All link to view even more friend suggestions.

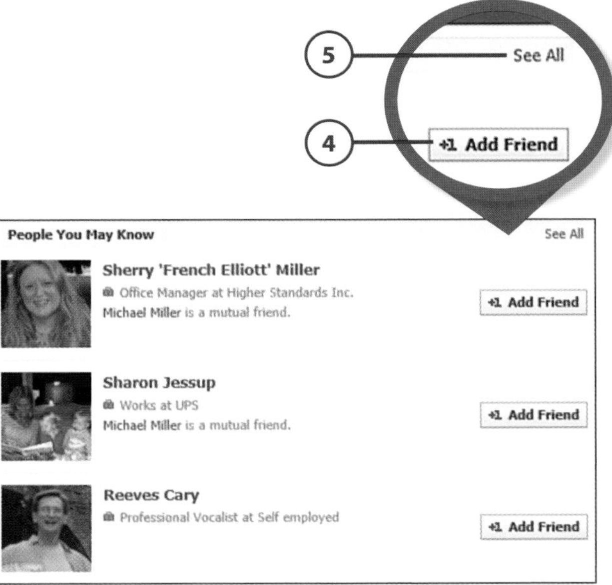

6. Go to the Mutual Friend section and check the names of one or more friends to see only those people who are already friends with your friends. (If a particular friend isn't listed, enter his or her name into the text box first.)

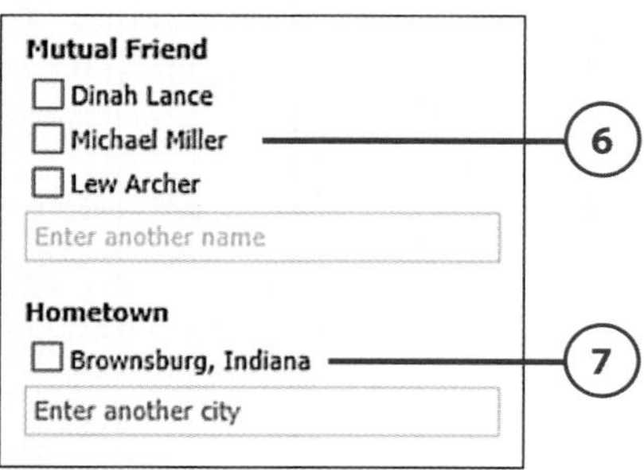

7. Go to the Hometown section in the left sidebar and check your hometown to see only those people who come from your hometown. (If your hometown isn't listed, enter it into the text box first.)
8. Go to the Current City section and check your city to see only those people who live in your current city or town. (If your town or city isn't listed, enter it into the text box first.)

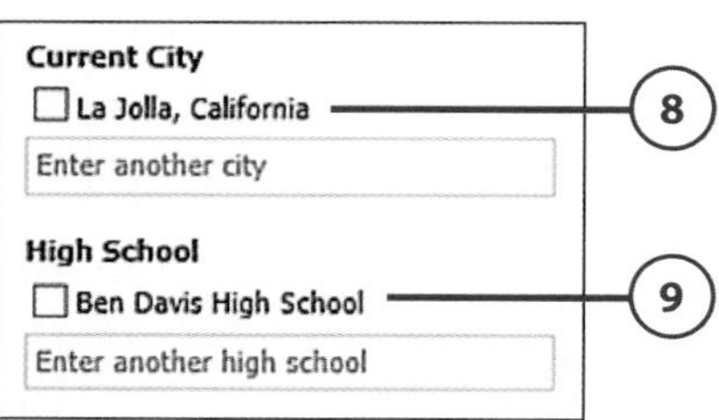

9. Go to the High School section and check the name of your high school to see only those people who went to the same school you did. (If your high school isn't listed, enter it into the text box first.)

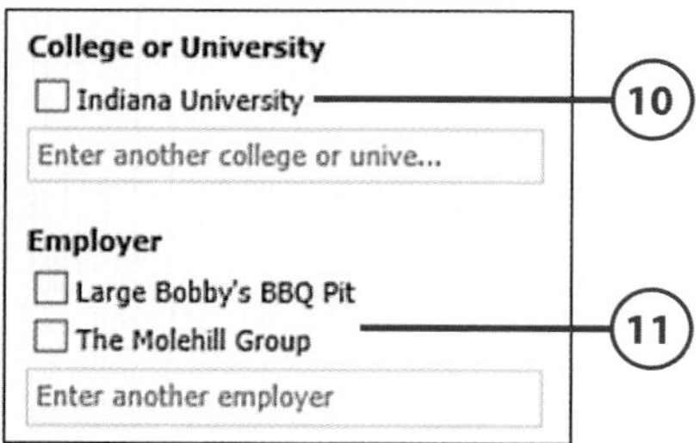

10. Go to the College or University section and check the name of your school to see only those people who went to the same college or university you did. (If your school isn't listed, enter its name into the text box first.)
11. Go to the Employer section and check the name of a company to see only those people who worked there. (If a company isn't listed, enter its name into the text box first.)

12 Click the Add Friend button for any person that you'd like to have on your friends list.

>>>Go Further

INVITATIONS

When you click the Add Friend button, Facebook doesn't automatically add that person to your friends list. Instead, that person receives an invitation to be your friend; she can accept or reject the invitation. If a person accepts your request, you become friends with that person. If a person does not accept your request, you don't become friends. (Nor are you notified if your friend request is declined.) In other words, you both have to agree to be friends—it's not a one-sided thing.

Find Email Contacts

Another way to find Facebook friends is to let Facebook look through your email contact lists for people who are also Facebook members. You can then invite those people to be your friends.

>>>Go Further

CONTACT SEARCHING

Facebook can search contacts from a variety of web-based email and communications services, including AOL (mail and messenger), Comcast, Gmail, sbcglobal.net, Skype, Verizon.net, Windows Live Hotmail, and Windows Live Messenger.

This process works by matching the email addresses in your contact lists with the email addresses users provide as their Facebook login. When Facebook finds a match, it suggests that person as a potential friend.

Finding Email Contacts

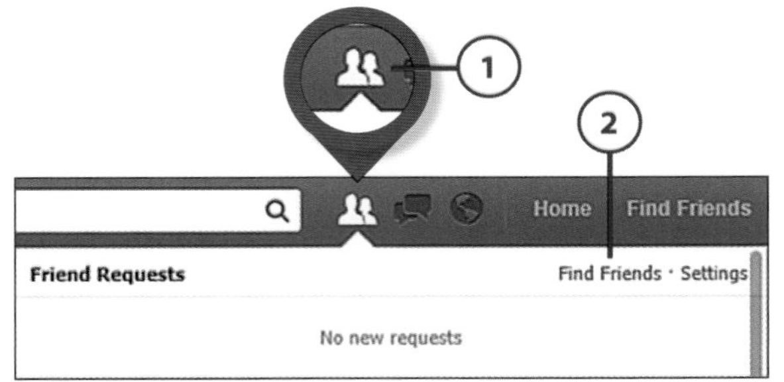

1. Click the Friends button on the Facebook toolbar to display the drop-down menu.
2. Click Find Friends at the top of the menu to display your Friends page.
3. Scroll to the email or messaging service you use and click Find Friends.
4. Enter any requested information (typically your email address and password).
5. Click the Find Friends button.

Sign In

At this point you might be prompted to sign into your email account or to link your email and Facebook accounts. Enter the required information to proceed.

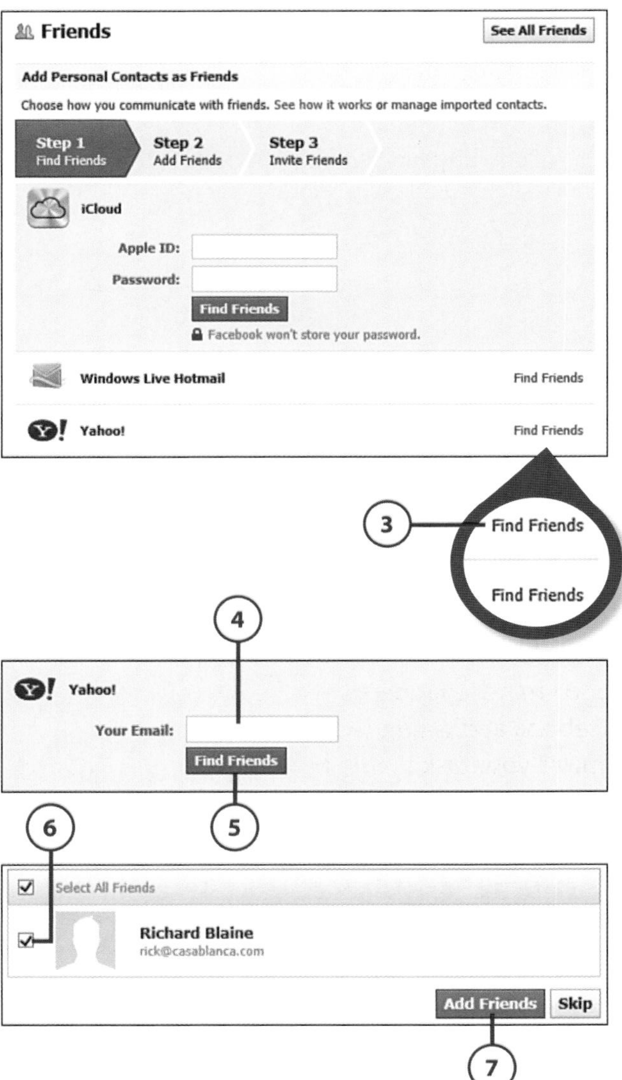

6. Facebook displays a list of your email contacts who are also Facebook members. Check the box next to each person to whom you'd like to be friends.
7. Click the Add Friends button to send friend requests to these contacts, or click Skip to go to the next step.

8. You see a list of your other friends who are not yet Facebook members. Check the box next to each person you'd like to become a Facebook member (and join your friends list).
9. Click the Send Invites button.

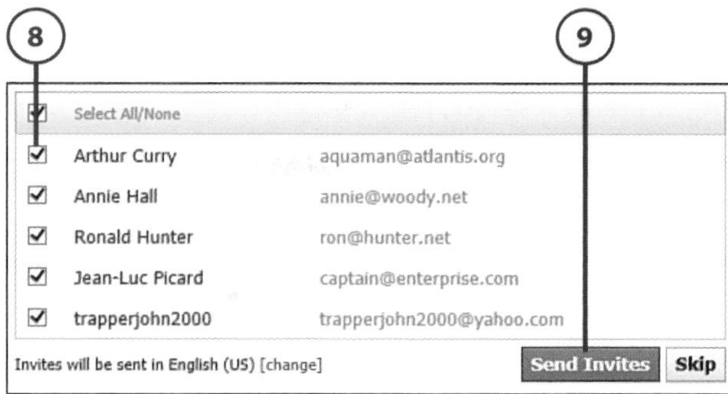

>>>Go Further

EMAIL PROGRAMS

If you use Microsoft Outlook, Outlook Express, or another email program to check your email or manage your contacts, you need to import those contacts from your email program to Facebook. It's a little more complicated.

Start by going to Facebook's Friends page. Scroll down the page, click Other Tools, and then select Upload Contact File. When the page changes, click the Upload Contacts button. This uploads your email contacts list to Facebook and displays a list of those contacts who are also Facebook members. Check those people you'd like to add as a friend and then click the Send Invites button.

Search for Old Friends

If Facebook doesn't automatically suggest a particular friend, there's still a good chance that person is already on Facebook and waiting for you to find him. It's your task to find that person—by searching the Facebook site.

1. Start to type a person's name into the search box. As you type, Facebook displays a list of suggestions.
2. If your friend is listed, click the person's name to go to her Timeline page.

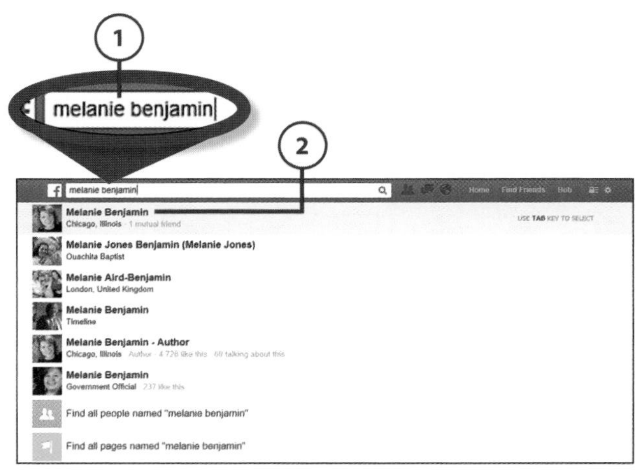

3. Click the Add Friend button to send an invitation to this person.

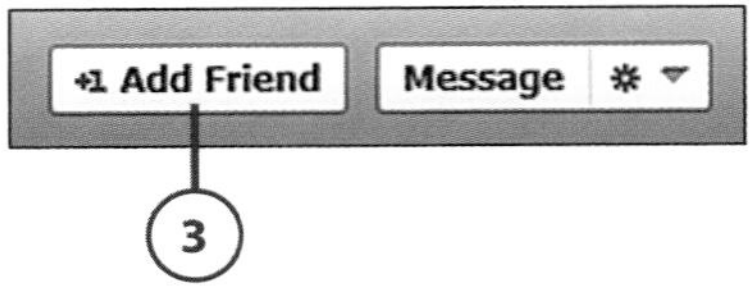

4. If the person was not listed in the search suggestions, click Find All People Named to display a list of people with that name. (You might need to click the See More link to display this option.)

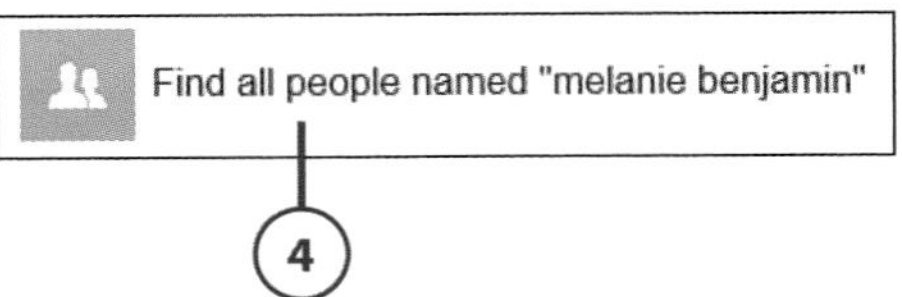

5. You can filter this list to display people who live in a specific location, work or have worked at a given company, have attended a specific school, and so forth. Go to the Refine This Search box on the right, click the Add button for the filter you'd like to apply, and then select an item from the list.

6. Click the Add Friend button to send a friend request.

>>> Go Further

FINDING HARD-TO-FIND FRIENDS

When it comes to tracking down old friends on Facebook, sometimes a little detective work is in order. It's especially tough to find women you used to know, as names get changed along with marital status. Some women have enough forethought to enter their maiden name as their middle name on Facebook, so the Cathy Coolidge you used to know might be listed as Cathy Coolidge Smith, which means her maiden name actually shows up in a Facebook search. Others, however, don't do this—and thus become harder to find.

You can, of course, search for a partial name—searching just for "Cathy," for example. What happens next is a little interesting. Facebook returns a list of people named Cathy, of course, but puts at the top of this list people who have mutual friends in common with you. That's a nice touch, as it's likely that your old friend has already made a connection with another one of your Facebook friends.

Past that point, you can then display everyone on Facebook with that single name. But that's going to be a bit unwieldy, unless your friend has a very, very unique name.

One approach to narrowing down the results is to filter your search results by location. For example, if you're looking for a John Smith and think he currently lives in Minnesota, use the Search Tools section at the top of the search results page to display only people who live in Minnesota. You can also filter by school (Education) and employer (Workplace).

Beyond these tips, finding long-lost friends on Facebook is a trial-and-error process. The best advice is to keep plugging—if they're on Facebook, you'll find them sooner or later.

Look for Friends of Friends

Another way to find old friends is to look for people who are friends of your current friends. That is, when you make someone your friend on Facebook, you can browse through the list of people who are on his friends list. Chances are you'll find mutual friends on this list—people that both of you know but you haven't found otherwise.

1. Click your friend's name anywhere on the Facebook site, such as in a status update, to display his Timeline page.
2. Click Friends under the person's name to display his Friends page.
3. When you find a person you'd like to be friends with, click the Add Friends button.

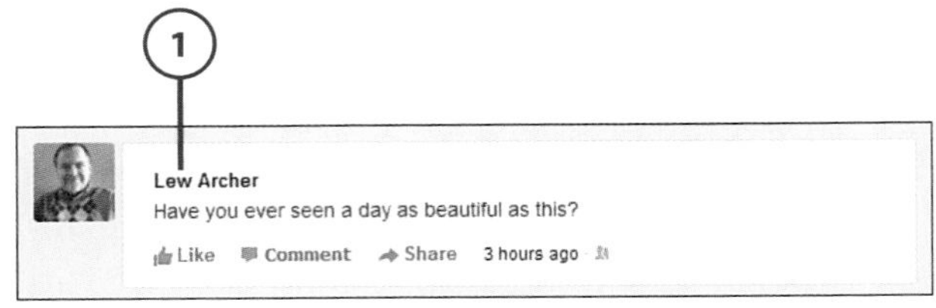

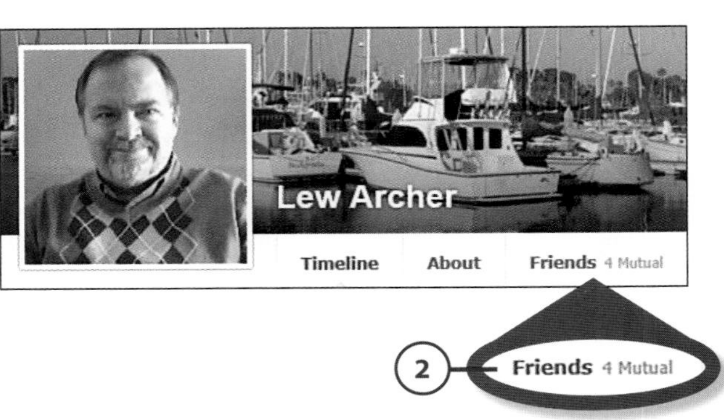

Accepting Friend Requests

Sometimes potential Facebook friends find you before you find them. When this happens, they will send you a friend request, which you can then accept or decline. You might receive a friend request via email, or you can view friend requests within Facebook.

Accept a Friend Request

You can also access all your pending friend requests from the Facebook toolbar—and then decide whether to accept or decline the request.

1. Click the Friend Request button on the Facebook toolbar. All pending friend requests are displayed in the drop-down menu.
2. Click Confirm to accept a specific friend request and be added to that person's friends list.

Decline a Friend Request

You do not have to accept all friend requests. If you receive a request from someone you don't know (or someone you don't like), you can decline the request.

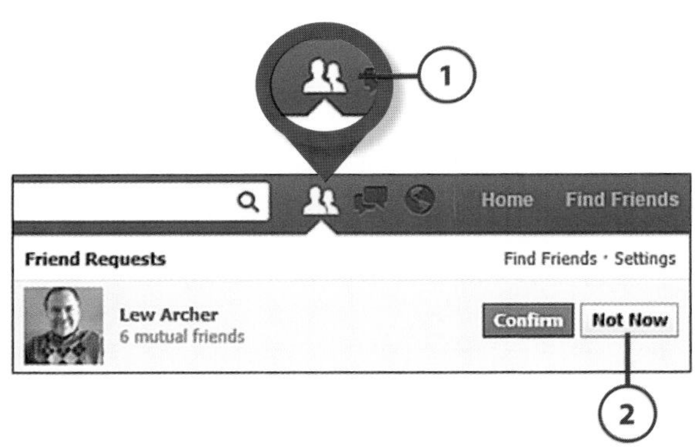

1. Click the Friend Request button on the Facebook toolbar. All pending friend requests are displayed in the drop-down menu.
2. Click Not Now to decline the request and continue to ignore that person on Facebook.

No One Knows

When you decline a friend request, the sender is not notified by Facebook. That person doesn't know that you've declined the request, just that you haven't (yet) accepted it.

Unfriending Unwanted Friends

What do you do about those friends who you really don't want to be friends with anymore? It happens; sometimes people drift apart, or you find you just can't stand that person's political views or inane posts. Whatever the reason, you don't want to read any more of that person's posts—which means you need to delete him from your friends list.

Unfriend a Friend

You can, at any time, remove any individual from your Facebook friends list. This is called *unfriending* the person, and it happens all the time.

No One's the Wiser

When you unfriend a person on Facebook, that person doesn't know that he's been unfriended. There are no official notices sent.

1. Click your profile picture in the sidebar menu or on the toolbar to display your Timeline page.
2. Click Friends beneath your name to display your Friends page.
3. Scroll to person you want to unfriend and mouse over the Friends button to display the pop-up menu.
4. Select Unfriend.

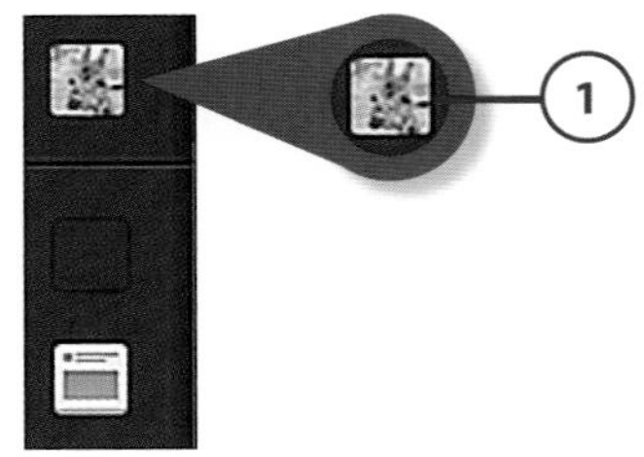

5. When the Remove as a Friend? dialog box appears, click the Remove from Friends button.

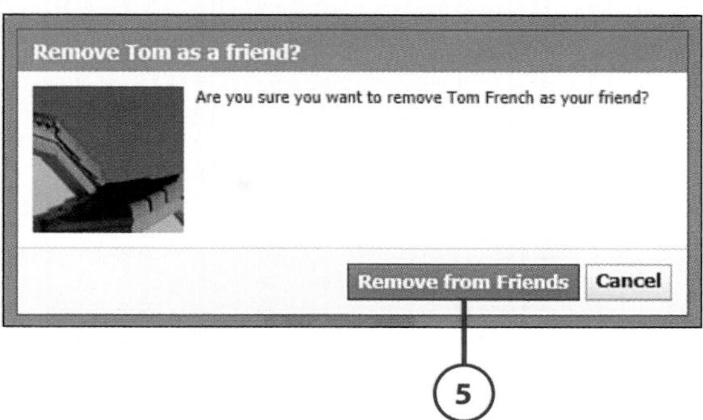

Refriending

If you've unfriended someone but later want to add them back to your friends list, you can do so. All you have to do is go through the add-a-friend process again.

Display Fewer Posts from a Friend

Maybe you don't need to completely unfriend a particular person. If all you want is to see less of that person's posts in your Facebook News feed, you can do that.

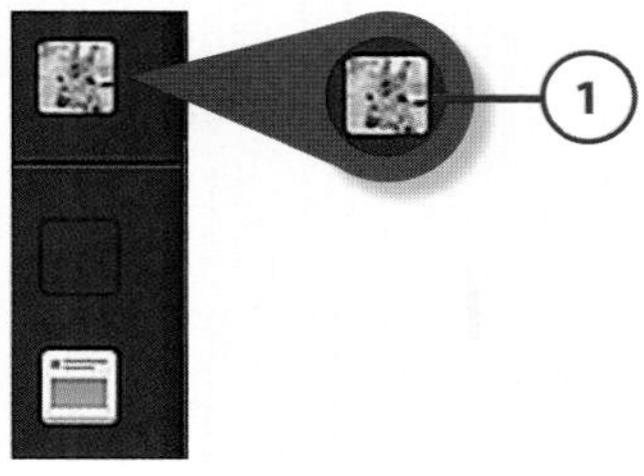

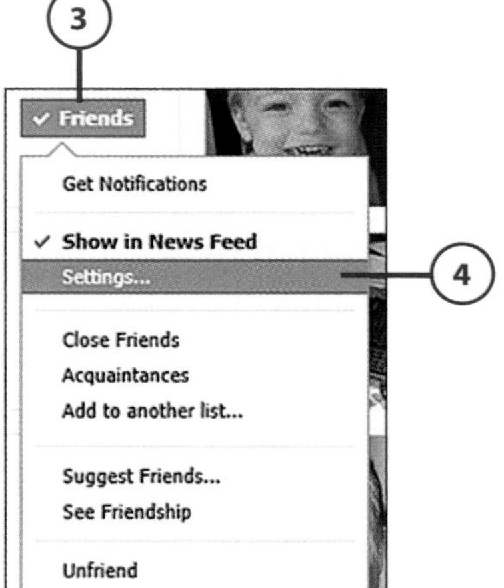

1. Click your name in the sidebar menu to display your Timeline page.
2. Click Friends beneath your name to display your Friends page.
3. Scroll to the person you want to see less of and mouse over the Friends button to display the pop-up menu.
4. Select Settings; this changes the pop-up menu to display additional options.

5. Click Only Important.
6. If you want to not see certain types of updates (photos, games, and so forth), uncheck those options.

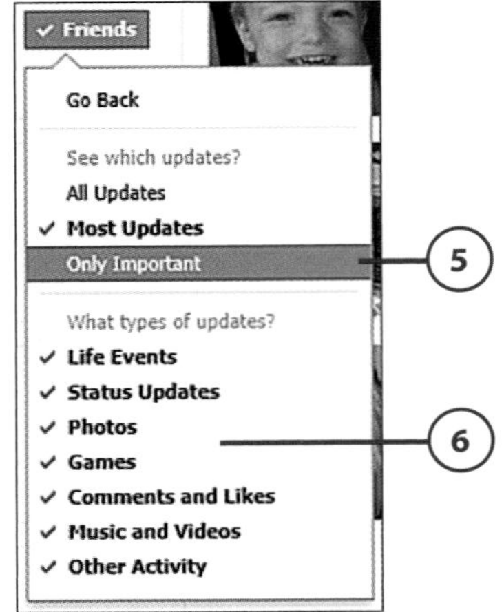

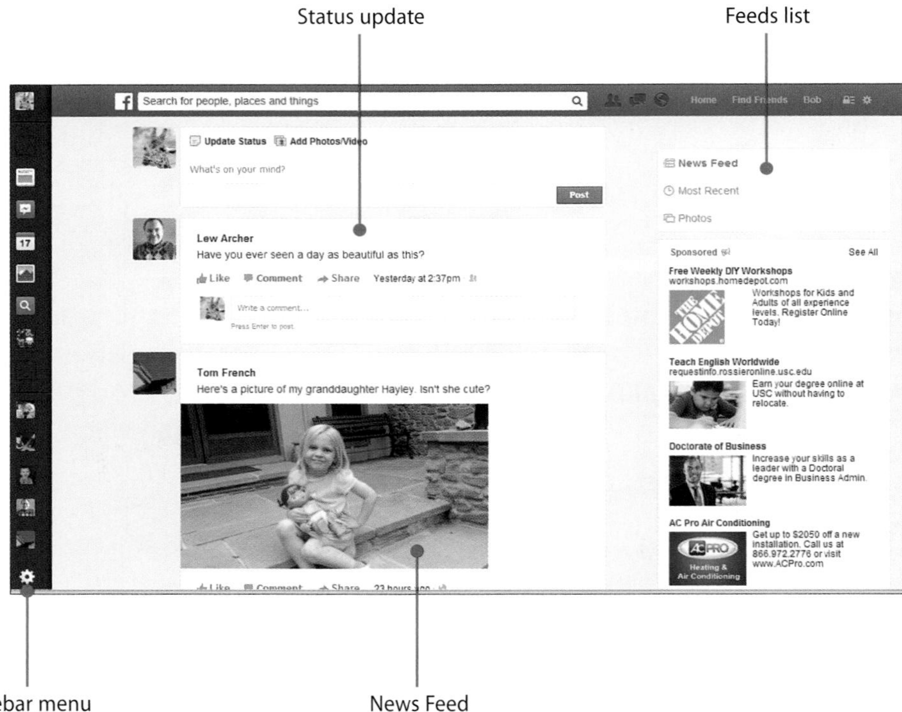
Status update
Feeds list
Search for people, places and things
Home
Find Friends
Bob
Update Status
Add Photos/Video
What's on your mind?
Post
Lew Archer
Have you ever seen a day as beautiful as this?
Like
Comment
Share
Yesterday at 2:37pm
Write a comment...
Press Enter to post.
Tom French
Here's a picture of my granddaughter Hayley. Isn't she cute?
News Feed
Most Recent
Photos
Sponsored
See All
Free Weekly DIY Workshops
workshops.homedepot.com
Workshops for Kids and Adults of all experience levels. Register Online Today!
Teach English Worldwide
requestinfo.rossieronline.usc.edu
Earn your degree online at USC without having to relocate.
Doctorate of Business
Increase your skills as a leader with a Doctoral degree in Business Admin.
AC Pro Air Conditioning
Get up to $2050 off a new installation. Call us at 866.972.2776 or visit www.ACPro.com
Sidebar menu
News Feed

In this chapter you discover how to read and respond to your friends' status updates in your Facebook News Feed.

- → Viewing Updates in the News Feed
- → Viewing Status Updates
- → Responding to Status Updates

Keeping in Touch with Friends and Family

After you've added someone to your Facebook friends list, you'll be kept up to date on what that person is doing and thinking. Everything that person posts to Facebook—text updates, photos, videos, you name it—automatically appears in your News Feed.

Viewing Updates in the News Feed

Facebook's News Feed is where you keep abreast of what all your friends are up to. When a person posts a status update to Facebook, it appears in your personal News Feed.

Display the News Feed

You can easily get to the News Feed from anywhere on the Facebook site, using the ever-present sidebar menu.

1. From the sidebar menu, click the News Feed icon.
2. The News Feed displays in the center of the page with the most relevant posts at the top. Scroll down to view additional posts.

Display Different Feeds

You're not limited to a single News Feed. Facebook lets you display several different feeds in addition to the normal News Feed.

1. Click News Feed to display the default News Feed with the most relevant posts shown first.
2. Click All Friends to display only posts from your friends, not from any companies or celebrities you've liked.
3. Click Following to display posts from celebrities and companies you've liked on Facebook.
4. Click Groups to display posts made in Facebook groups you've joined.
5. Click Photos to display the latest pictures posted by your friends and by pages you've liked.

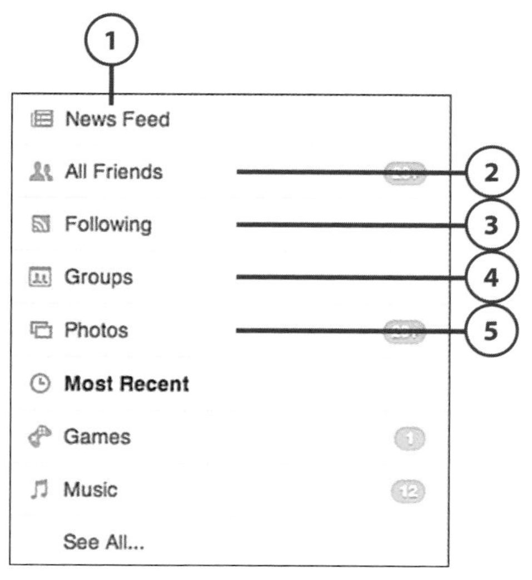

6. Click Most Recent to display the most recent posts first.
7. Click Games to display notices from and about Facebook games you've played.
8. Click Music to display the latest music listened to by your friends, as well as posts from musical artists you've liked.
9. Click See All to display additional feeds.

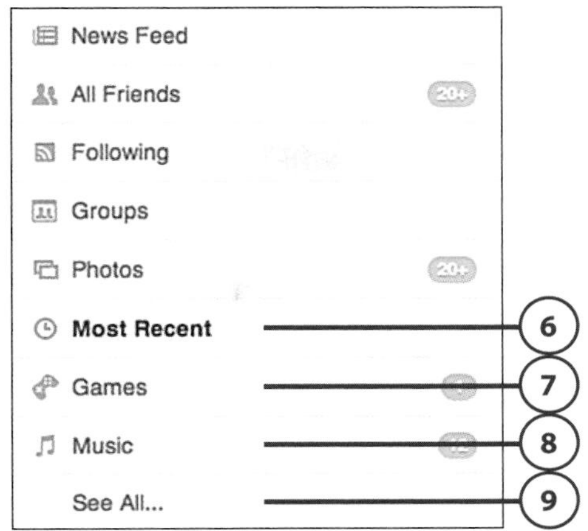

More Feeds

If all these feeds aren't displayed in the Feeds List, click the down arrow to view more.

>>>Go Further

TOP STORIES

By default, Facebook sorts the posts in your News Feed by importance—what it calls Top Stories first. Facebook tries to determine what posts are most important to you, and puts them first in the feed.

The problem is, Facebook's idea of what's important might be different from what you think is important. Facebook's Top Stories sorting might actually bury posts from friends you really want to read.

The solution to Facebook's arbitrary Top Stories sorting is to select the Most Recent feed. This sorts the updates in your feed in chronological order, putting the most recent posts at the top—period.

Viewing Status Updates

The News Feed consists of status updates made by your friends and by company and celebrity pages you've liked on Facebook. (It also includes advertisements, which is a whole other thing.)

View a Status Update

Each status update in your News Feed consists of several distinct components.

1. The poster's profile picture appears on the left side of the post.

Other Users

If a post has been shared by other users, those users' profile pictures also appear on the left side of the post.

2. The poster's name appears at the top of the post. To view more information about this person, mouse over his or her name; to view the poster's Timeline page, click the person's name.
3. The text of the status update appears under the poster's name.
4. When the item was posted is displayed to the right of the Share icon.

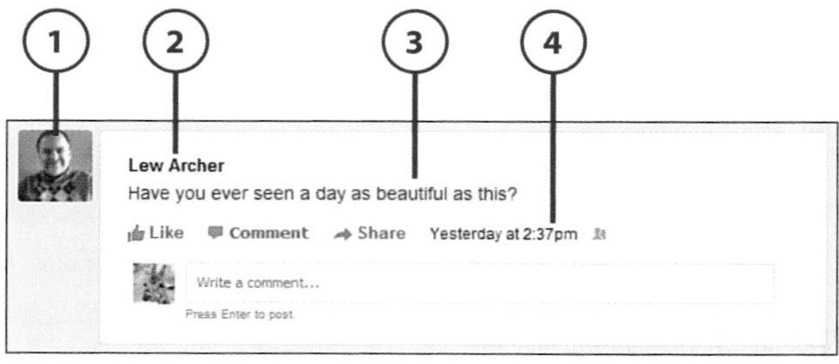

View Links to Web Pages

Many status updates include links to interesting web pages. You can click a link to view the web page posted by your friend.

1. The title of the linked-to web page appears under the normal status update text. Click the title to display the linked-to web page in a new tab of your web browser.
2. Many links include images from the linked-to page, as well as a short description of the page's content.

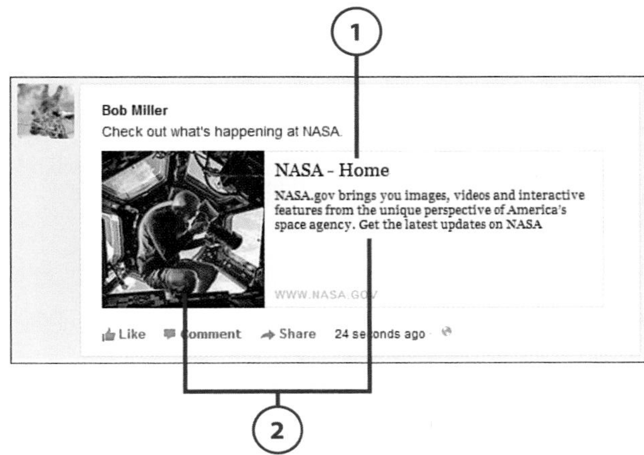

View Photos

It's common for Facebook users to post photos they've taken with their iPhones or digital cameras. These photos appear as part of the status update.

1. The photo appears in the body of the status update. (If more than one photo is posted, scroll to the right to view the additional pictures.)
2. To view a larger version of any picture, click the photo in the post. This displays the photo within its own *lightbox*—a special window superimposed over the News Feed.

3. To close the photo lightbox, click the X in the upper-right corner.

View Videos

Many Facebook users post their own home movies so their friends can view them. Other people like to share videos they find on YouTube and other video sharing sites.

1. A thumbnail image from the video appears in the body of the status update, with a "play" arrow superimposed on top of the image. To play the video, click the image.
2. Many videos play at a larger size within a special video lightbox. To close the video, click the X in the top-right corner.

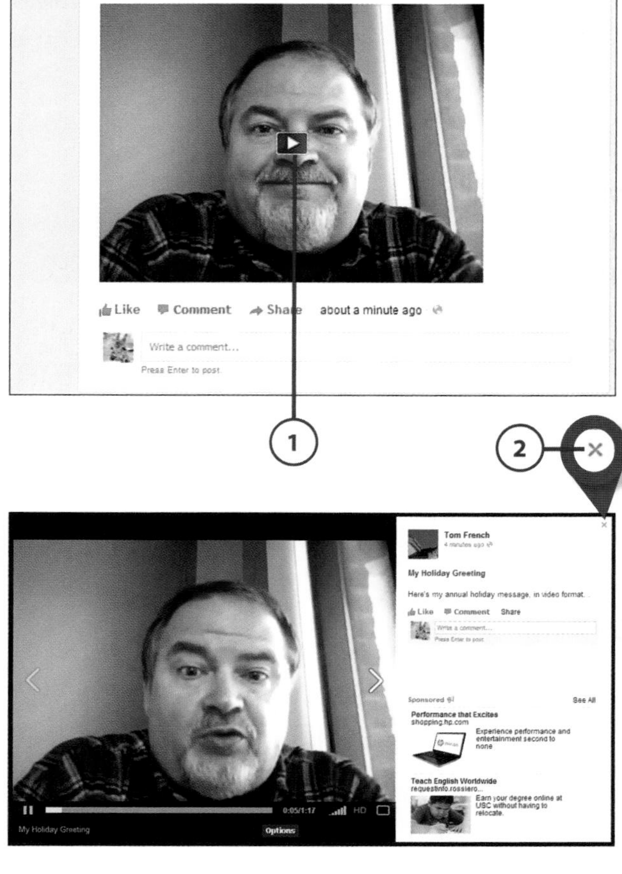

(3) Some videos, such as those from YouTube, play back within the News Feed; click the video thumbnail to begin playback. To pause playback, mouse over the video to display the playback controls and then click the Pause button.

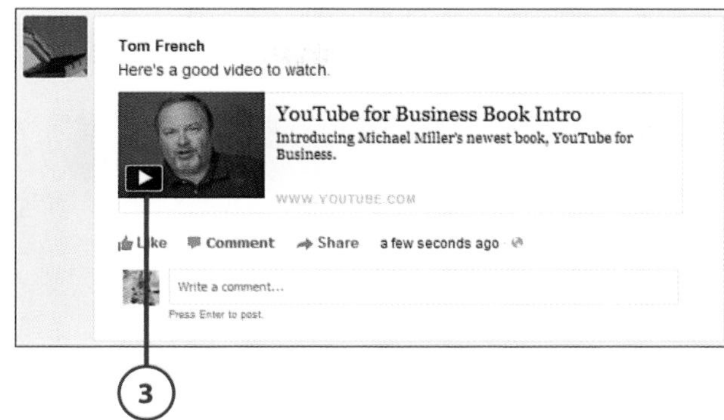

Responding to Status Updates

Facebook is a social network, which means you can interact socially with the status updates your friends make. You can tell your friend you "like" a given post, you can comment on a post, and you can even share a post with other friends.

Like an Update

When you "like" a friend's status update, you give it a virtual "thumbs up." It's like voting on a post; when you view a status update, you see the number of "likes" that post has received.

(1) Click Like underneath the status update.

(2) Other people who have liked this status update are listed under the post.

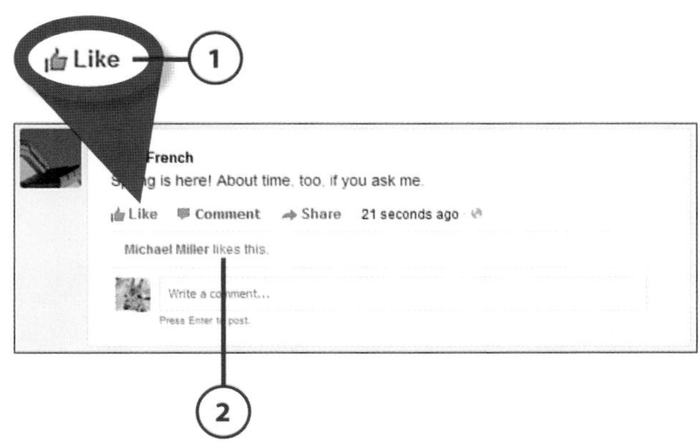

Dislike and Unlike

There is no corresponding "dislike" you can voice for posts you don't really like. However, when you like a post the Like link changes to an Unlike link. If you later change your mind about a post, just click the Unlike link and your "like" goes away.

Comment on an Update

Sometimes you want to comment on a given post, to share your thoughts about the post with your friend. You do this by leaving a public comment, which can then be seen by others viewing the original post.

1. Click Comment underneath the post.
2. Type your comment into the Write a Comment box and press Enter.
3. Comments made by other users appear underneath the original post.

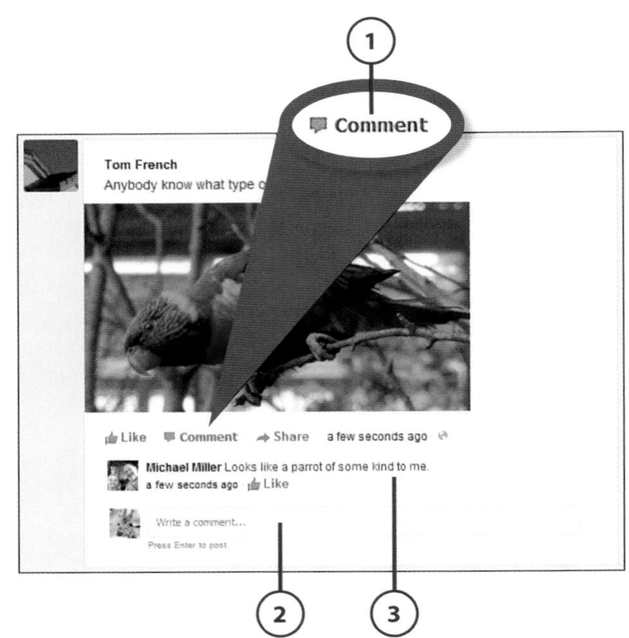

Share an Update

Occasionally you'll find a status update that is interesting or intriguing enough you want to share it with all of your friends. You do this via Facebook's Share feature.

1. Click Share underneath the original post to display the Share This Status dialog box.
2. Click the Share button and select On Your Own Timeline to share it with your entire friends list.
3. Enter any comments you might have on this post into the Write Something box.
4. Click the Share Status button to post the original status update and your newly added comments to your friends.

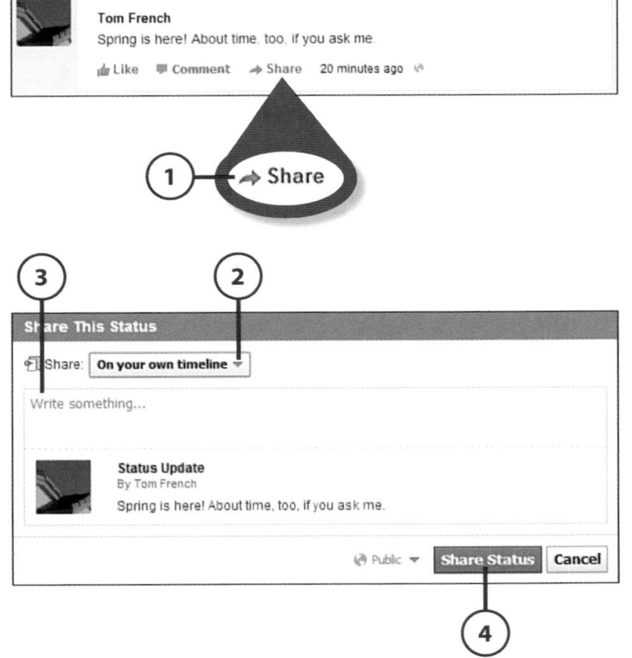

>>>Go Further

SHARE PRIVATELY

If you'd rather share a post privately with selected friends, click the Share button and select In a Private Message. When the dialog box changes, enter the friends names into the To section, write a short message, and then click the Share Status button.

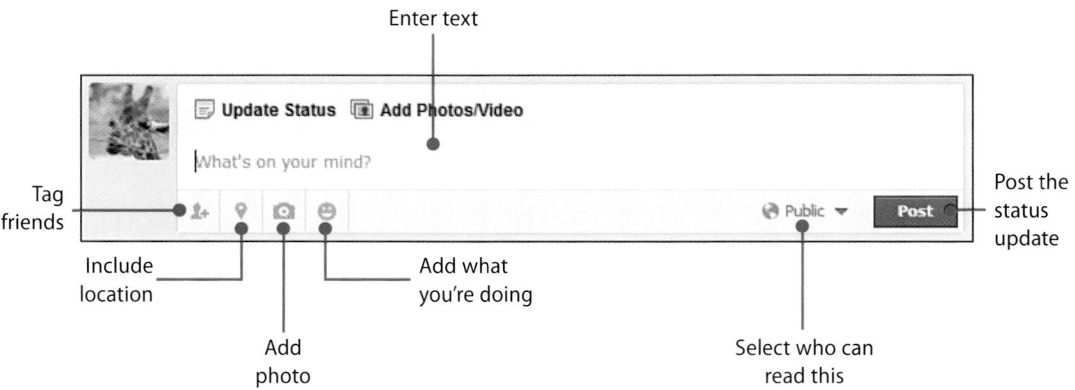
Enter text
Update Status
Add Photos/Video
What's on your mind?
Tag friends
Public
Post
Post the status update
Include location
Add what you're doing
Add photo
Select who can read this

In this chapter you find out how to post Facebook status updates for others to read.

→ Updating Your Status
→ Sharing Content from Other Websites

Updating Friends and Family on Your Activities

To let your family and friends know what you've been up to, you need to post what Facebook calls a *status update*. Every status update you make is broadcast to everyone on your friends list, displayed in the News Feed on their home pages. It's how they know what you've been doing and thinking about.

Updating Your Status

A status update is, at its most basic, a brief text message. It can be as short as a word or two, or it can be several paragraphs long; that's up to you. (Facebook lets you post updates with more than 60,000 characters, which should be more than long enough for most of us.)

Although a basic status update is all text, you can also attach various multimedia elements to your status updates, including digital photographs, videos, and links to other web pages. You can also "tag" other Facebook users and groups in your updates, so that their names appear as clickable links (to their Timeline pages, of course).

Tags

A tag is a way to mention other Facebook users in your status updates and photos. When a person is tagged in a post, that post appears in that person's Facebook feed, so he knows you're talking about him. In addition, readers can click a tagged name to display that person's Timeline page.

Post a Basic Status Update

Facebook makes it easy to post a status update. You have to be signed in to your Facebook account; then it's a simple matter of opening your home page and creating the post.

1. Click the News Feed icon in the sidebar menu to return to your home page.
2. Go to the Publisher box (labeled What's On Your Mind?) at the top of the page and click Update Status. (It's probably selected by default.)
3. Type your message into the What's On Your Mind? box. As you do this, the box expands slightly.
4. Click the Post button when you're done.

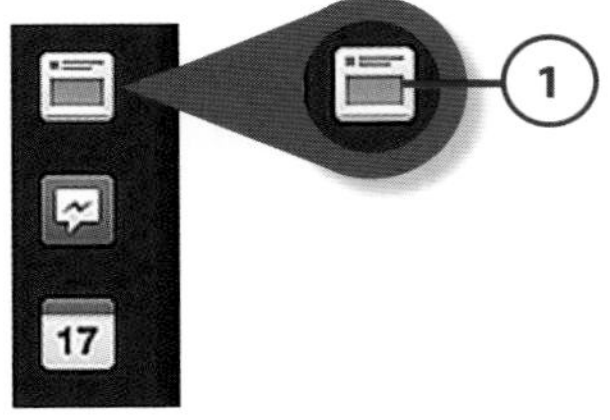

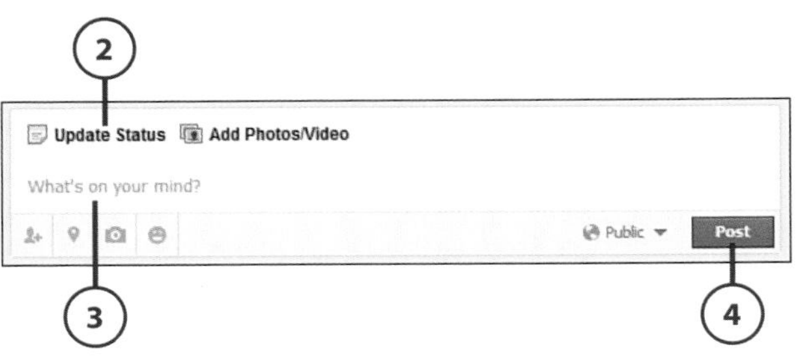

Other Ways to Update

You can also post status updates from the Publisher box located on your Facebook Timeline page, or via text message from your cell phone.

>>>Go Further

HASHTAGS

Facebook has recently added the capability to include *hashtags* in your status updates. A hashtag is like a keyword, a word or phrase that describes the content of your post—and that readers can click to see similar posts with the same hashtag.

A hashtag starts with the hash (#) character, followed by the word or words that describe the content. For example, if your post is about your vacation, you might include the hashtag **#vacation**. Hashtags with more than one word cannot include spaces, so if you're writing about your vacation to Disney World, use the hashtag **#disneyworld**.

Note that hashtags are not case sensitive, so it doesn't matter whether or not you use any capital letters. As far as Facebook is concerned, **#snowbirds** is the same as **#Snowbirds** and **#SNOWBIRDS**.

You might want to include hashtags in a status update if you want that post to show up in other people's searches. The best approach is to add any hashtags to the end of a post, so they don't interrupt the reading of the main text.

When you see a hashtag in a friend's status update, click it to display a list of other posts that include the same hashtag. In this way, hashtags help you search for content on the Facebook site; it's like using a keyword in a Google search.

Post a Link to a Web Page

You can include links to other web pages in your status updates. Not only does Facebook add a link to the specified page, it also lets you include a thumbnail image from that page with the status update.

1. Start a new post as normal.
2. Enter the URL (web address) for the page you want to link to as part of your update.
3. Facebook should recognize the link and display a Link panel. Click the left and right arrows to select a thumbnail image from the web page to accompany the link.
4. Check the No Thumbnail box if you don't want to display an image from the page.
5. Click the Post button when done.

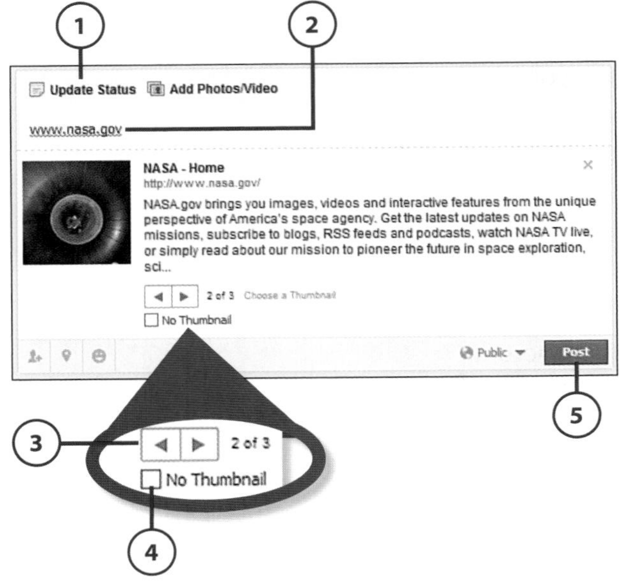

Delete the URL

If you don't want to display the web page's URL in the body of your status update, you can delete the address after the Link panel appears. The link and accompanying image still display under your status update even after you delete the web page URL from your text.

Post a Photograph or Video

Facebook enables you to embed digital photographs and videos in your posts. It's the Facebook equivalent of attaching a file to an email message.

1. Go to the Publisher box and click Add Photos/Video; this presents two new options for your new status update.
2. Click Upload Photos/Video to display the Open dialog box.
3. Navigate to and select the photo or video file(s) you want to upload. You can upload a single video file or multiple photo files; to select more than one file, hold down the Ctrl key while you click each filename.
4. Click the Open button.
5. You're returned to the Publisher box with your photo(s) added. If you like, enter a short text message describing the photo(s) or video.
6. Click the Post button.

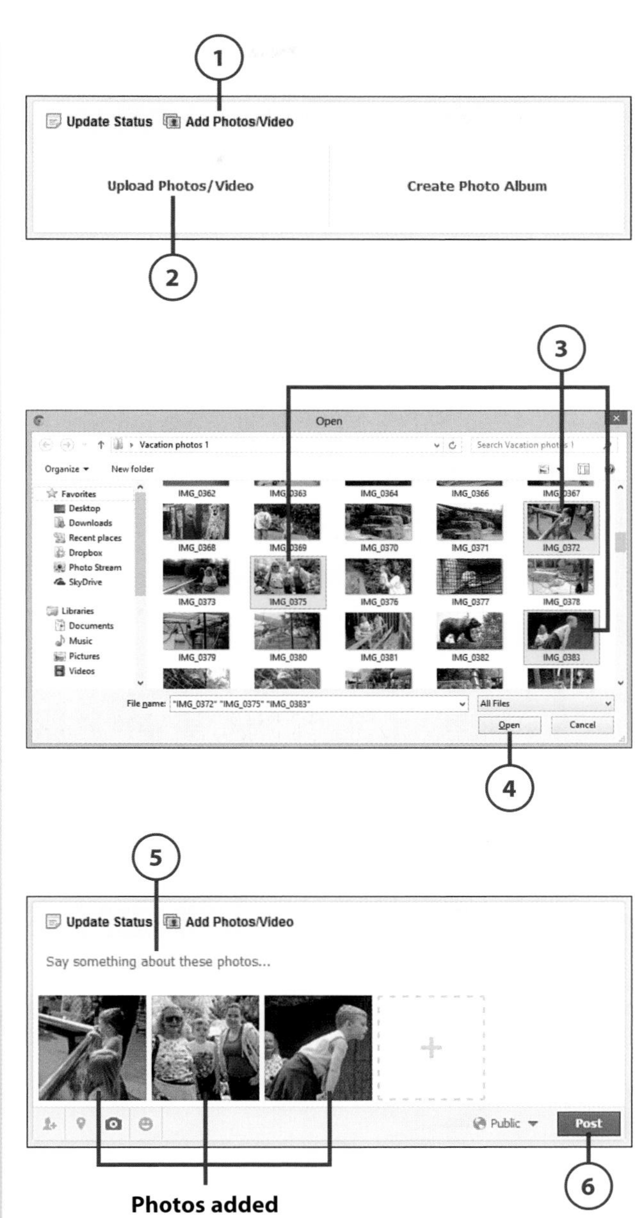

Photos added to status update

Create a Photo Album

By default, photos you upload as status updates are added to your Wall Photos album on Facebook. If you'd rather create a new photo album for an uploaded photo, select Create Photo Album instead of Upload Photo/Video and follow the onscreen instructions from there.

Add Your Location to a Post

Facebook enables you to identify your current location in any post you make. This lets your friends know where you are at any given time.

1. Enter the text of your status update into the Publisher box as normal.
2. Click the Where Are You? button beneath the Publisher box.
3. If Facebook can tell your location automatically, it displays a list of options. Otherwise, start entering your location manually; as you type, Facebook displays a list of suggested locations, along with a map of the current selection.
4. Click the correct location from the resulting list.
5. Click the Post button.

Map of selected location

It's Not All Good

Don't Publicize Your Location

You might not want to identify your location on every post you make. If you post while you're away from home, you're letting potential burglars know that your house is empty. You're also telling potential stalkers where they can find you. For these reasons, use caution when posting your location in your status updates.

Tag a Friend in a Post

Sometimes you might want to mention one of your friends in a status update, or include a friend who was with you when the post was made. You can do this by "tagging" friends in your status updates; the resulting post includes a link to the tagged person or persons.

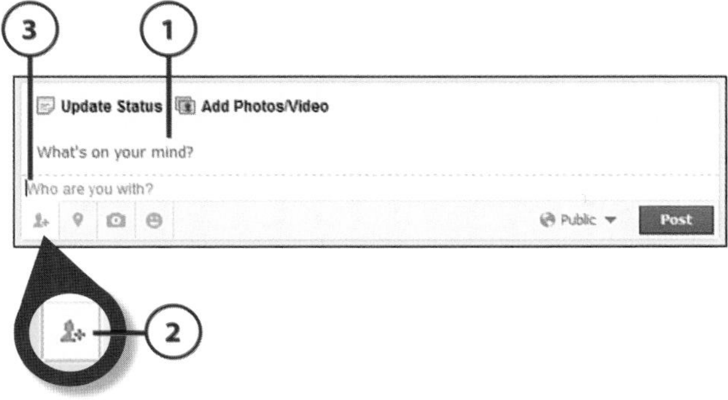

1. Enter the text of your status update into the Publisher box as normal.
2. Click the Who Are You With? button beneath the Publisher box.
3. Enter the name of the person you want to tag. As you type, Facebook displays a drop-down list with matching names.
4. Select the friend from the list.
5. Click the Post button.

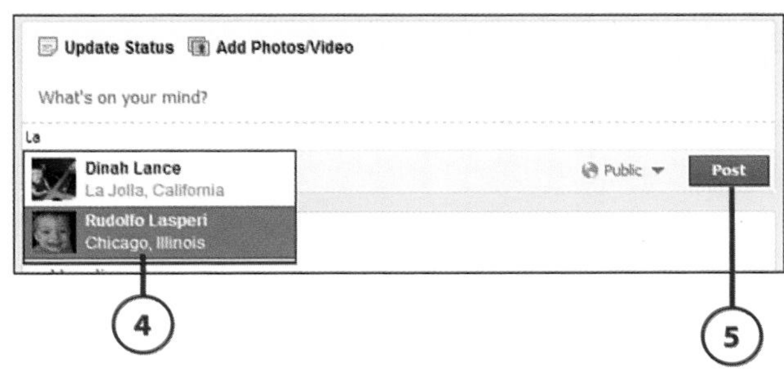

Tagged Friends

Clicking a tagged person's name in a status update displays the Facebook Timeline page for that person.

Tell Friends What You're Doing

Given the huge number of posts in which people write about what they're doing at the moment, Facebook has added a What Are You Doing? option to its status updates. This provides a very quick way to tell your friends what you're doing.

1. Enter the text of your status update into the Publisher box as normal. (Or, if you're just posting what you're doing, leave the Publisher box empty.)
2. Click the What Are You Doing? button beneath the Publisher box.
3. Click within the What Are You Doing? box to display a list of actions —Feeling, Watching, Reading, Listening To, Drinking, Eating, and Playing.
4. Click the action that best describes what you're doing to display a list of options specific to that action.
5. Select the appropriate option if what you're doing is listed.
6. If what you're doing is not listed, type it into the What Are You box above the drop-down menu and then press Enter.

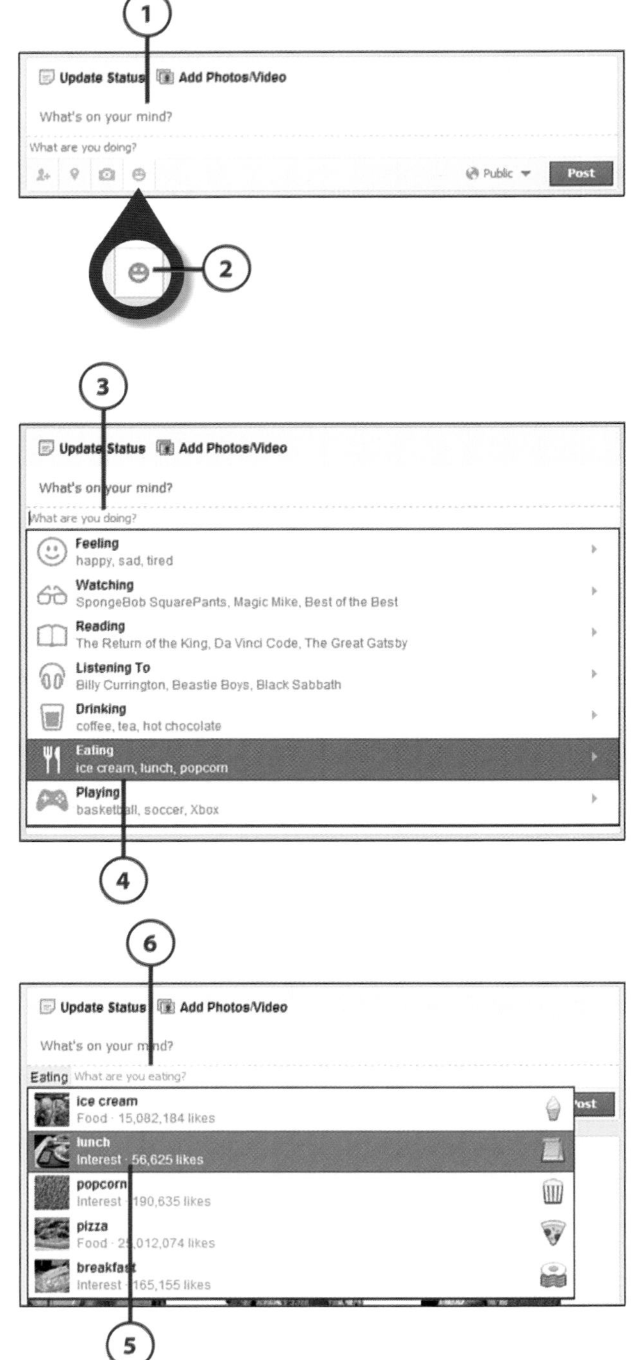

7. Finish the rest of your status update as usual and then click the Post button.

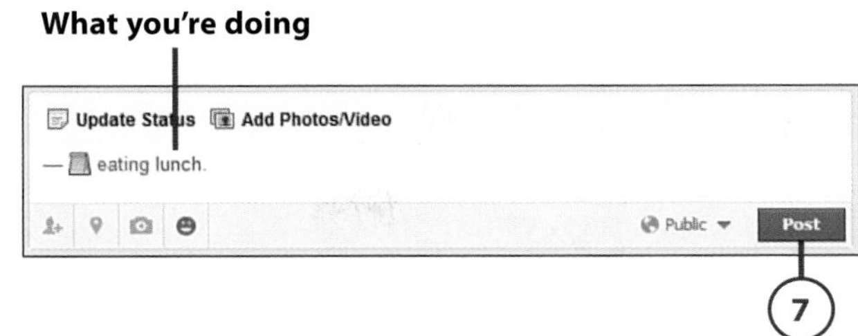

Determine Who Can—or Can't—See a Status Update

By default, everyone on Facebook can read every post you make. If you'd rather send a given post to a more select group of people, you can change the privacy settings on for any individual post. This enables only selected people to see that post; other people on your friends list won't see it at all.

1. Enter the text of your status update into the Publisher box as normal.
2. Click the Privacy button (the second button from the right beneath the post) to display a list of privacy options.
3. Click Public to let everyone on Facebook see the post.
4. Select Friends to make a post visible only to people on your friends list.
5. Click the name of a specific friends list to make a post visible only to the friends on that list.
6. Click Custom to display the Custom Privacy dialog box to select specific individuals who can or can't view this post.

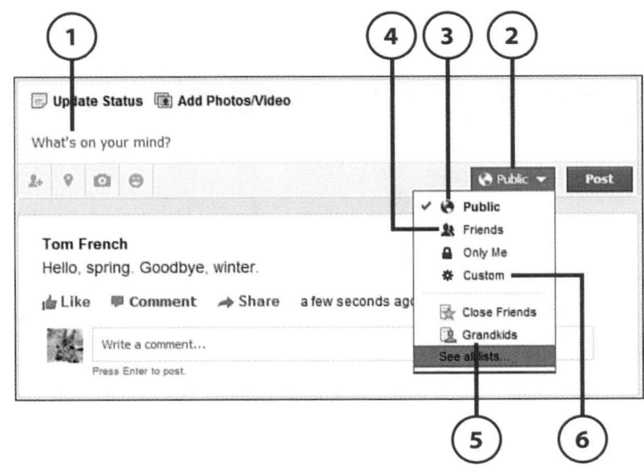

7. Go to the Share This With section and make a selection from the These People or Lists list to make this post visible to specific friends, friends lists, or networks.
8. Check the Friends of Those Tagged option to make this post visible to friends of anyone tagged in the post.
9. Go to the Don't Share This With section and enter names into the These People or Lists box to *hide* this post from specific friends or friends lists.
10. Click the Save Changes button.
11. Click the Post button to send this status update to those people you've selected.

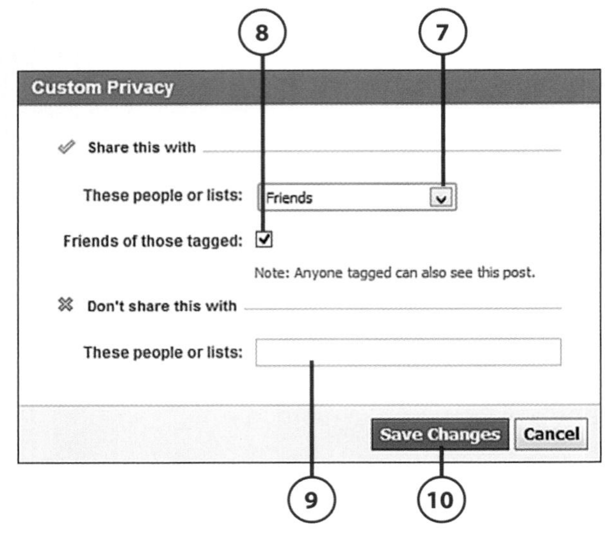

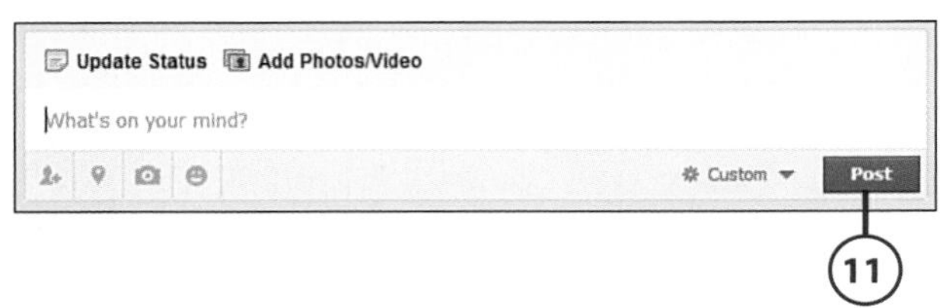

Configure Privacy for All Your Posts

Although you can configure the privacy option for each post you make individually, you can also set universal privacy settings that affect all your status updates. Learn more in Chapter 18, "Keeping Private Things Private."

>>>Go Further

POSTING ETIQUETTE

Writing a Facebook status update is a bit like sending a text message on your cell phone. As such, status updates do not have to—and often don't—conform to proper grammar, spelling, and sentence structure. It's common to abbreviate longer words, use familiar acronyms, substitute single letters and numbers for whole words, and refrain from all punctuation. You see this especially among younger users, but even us seniors can sometimes cheat on the grammar thing.

Then there's the issue of how often you should update your Facebook status. Unfortunately, there are no hard and fast rules as to posting frequency. Some people post once a week, others post daily, others post several times a day. In general, you should post when you have something interesting to share—and not because you feel obligated to make a post.

Sharing Content from Other Websites

Facebook is all about sharing things with your friends. Naturally, you can share your thoughts and activities via status updates; you can also upload and share your personal photos and videos.

But Facebook is also connected to many other sites on the Web. This enables you to share content you find elsewhere with your Facebook friends. It's all about posting content from other websites to your Facebook Timeline—and your friends' News Feeds.

News Sharing

Facebook sharing buttons are especially common on news-type sites, which makes it easy to share the articles you find there.

Post Content from Another Site

Many websites would like you to share their content with your friends on Facebook. When you're browsing another site and find something interesting to share, look for a Facebook button. This button is sometimes included in a special "sharing" section of the page; it's often labeled Facebook, Facebook Share, Facebook Like, or Facebook Recommend.

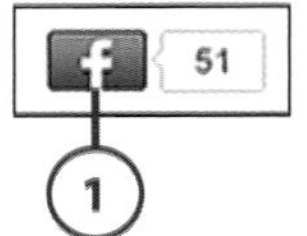

1. Click the Facebook button on the other website.
2. If you're currently signed into your Facebook account, you probably won't need to log in again. However, if you're prompted to sign into your Facebook account at this point, enter your email address and password and then click the Log In button.
3. What you see next depends on the site. In some instances, the link to the page is posted automatically without any comments from you. In other instances, you have the option of including a personal comment with the link; enter your comment and then click the Share, Share Link, or Post button, depending on what you see.

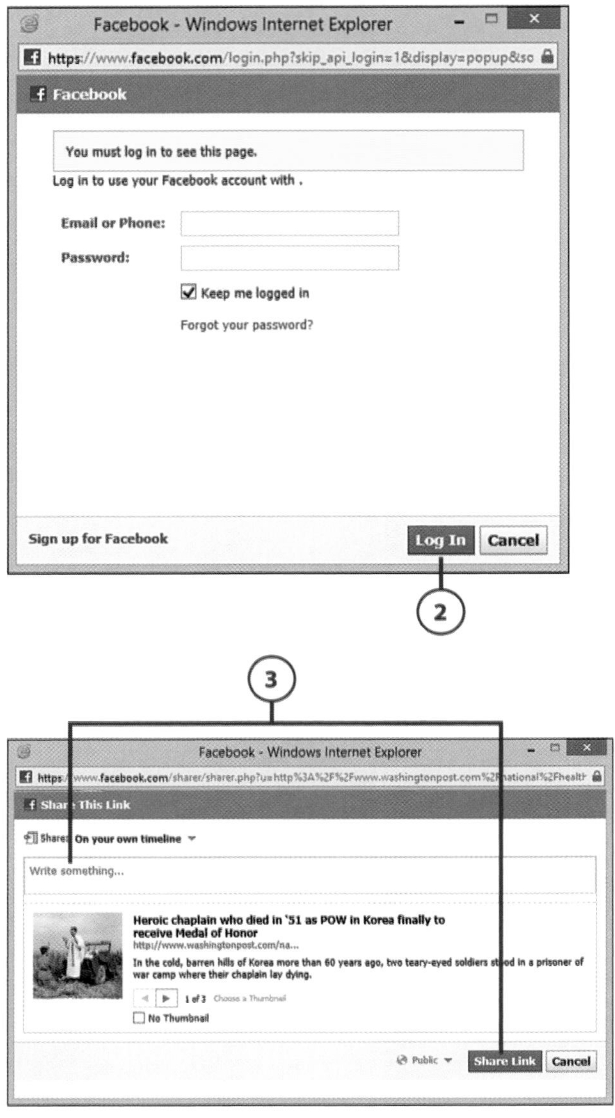

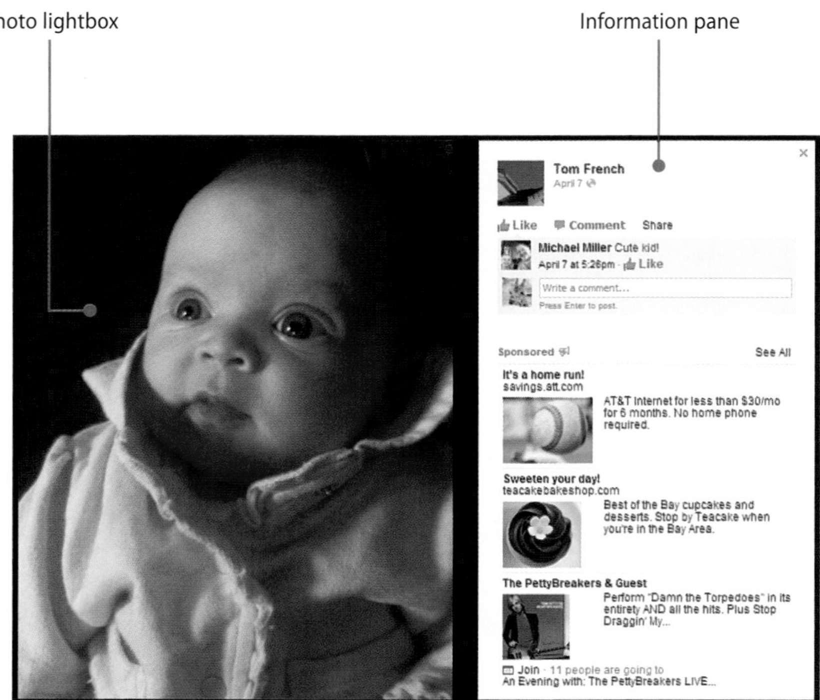
Photo lightbox
Information pane
Tom French
April 7
Like
Comment
Share
Michael Miller Cute kid!
April 7 at 5:26pm · Like
Write a comment...
Press Enter to post.
Sponsored
See All
It's a home run!
savings.att.com
AT&T Internet for less than $30/mo for 6 months. No home phone required.
Sweeten your day!
teacakebakeshop.com
Best of the Bay cupcakes and desserts. Stop by Teacake when you're in the Bay Area.
The PettyBreakers & Guest
Perform "Damn the Torpedoes" in its entirety AND all the hits. Plus Stop Draggin' My...
Join · 11 people are going to
An Evening with: The PettyBreakers LIVE...

In this chapter you find out how to view photos uploaded by your friends to Facebook and how to upload your own photos for your friends to see.

- → Viewing Friends' Photos
- → Sharing Your Photos with Friends
- → Editing Your Photos and Albums

Viewing and Sharing Family Photos

Sharing pictures is a great way to catch up your friends and family on what you've been up to. Everybody loves looking at pictures—whether they're vacation photos or photos of your cute grandkids.

Before everybody got on the Internet, if you wanted to share photos you had to make prints and mail them out to everyone, or invite everybody over to your house for an old-fashioned slide show. Today, however, you can share your photos online—via Facebook.

It should come as no surprise that Facebook is the largest photo-sharing site on the Internet. It's easy to upload photos to a Facebook photo album and then share them with all your Facebook friends. It's equally easy to view your friends' photos on Facebook—and download and print those you'd like to keep for posterity.

Viewing Friends' Photos

Some people on Facebook post photos as part of their regular status updates. These photos appear in your News Feed, as part of the stream of your friends' status updates.

Other Facebook users post photos to special photo albums they've created in the Facebook accounts. This is a more serious and organized way to share a large number of photos online. You can view these photo albums from the user's Timeline page.

View Facebook's Photos Feed

When a friend posts a photo as part of a status update, that photo appears in your News Feed. If you want to view only those updates with photos attached, you can display Facebook's special Photos feed instead.

1. Display the News Feed page and then click Photos in the feed list to display the Photos feed.
2. All photos appear within the bodies of the accompanying status updates. To view a larger version of any picture, click the photo in the post. This displays the photo within its own *lightbox*—a special window superimposed over the News Feed.
3. To close the photo viewer, click the X in the upper-right corner.

View a Friend's Photo Albums

More serious photographers—and those people with lots of photos to share—organize their Facebook photos into separate photo albums. These are virtual versions of those traditional photo albums you've kept in the past. You can then navigate through a friend's photo albums to find and view the photos you like.

1. Click your friend's name or profile picture anywhere on Facebook to open his Timeline page.
2. Click Photos under the person's name to display your friend's Photos page.
3. Click Photos of *Friend* to view all photos of your friend.
4. Click Photos to view all photos posted by your friend.
5. Click Albums to view photos as posted in their photo albums.
6. Click to open the selected album.

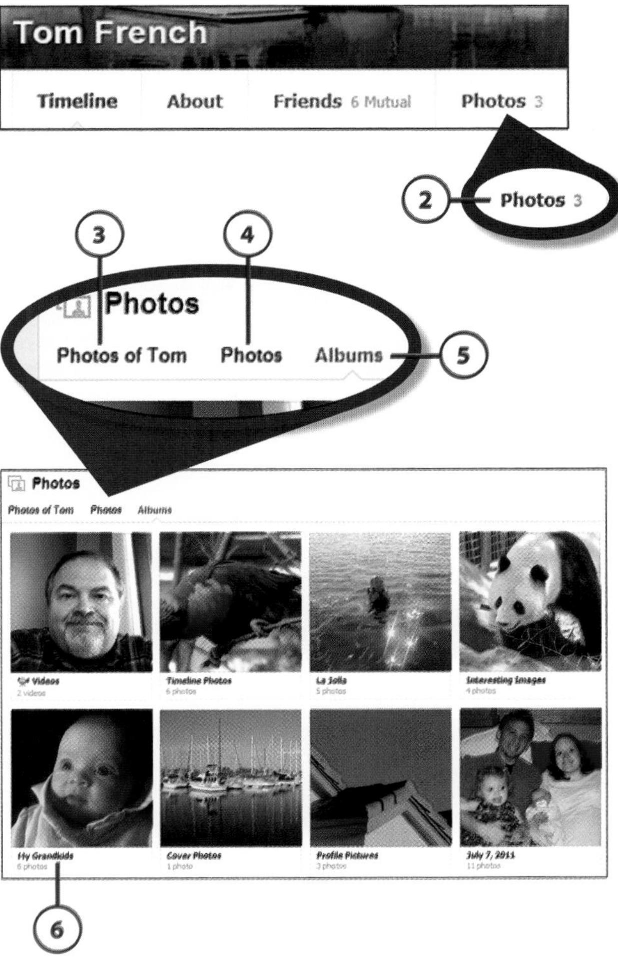

7. Click the thumbnail of the picture you want to view. Facebook displays the selected picture in a lightbox superimposed on top of the previous page.
8. Mouse over the current picture to display the navigational arrows; click the right arrow to go to the next picture or click the left arrow to go to the previous picture.
9. To close the photo viewer, click the X at the top right of the lightbox.

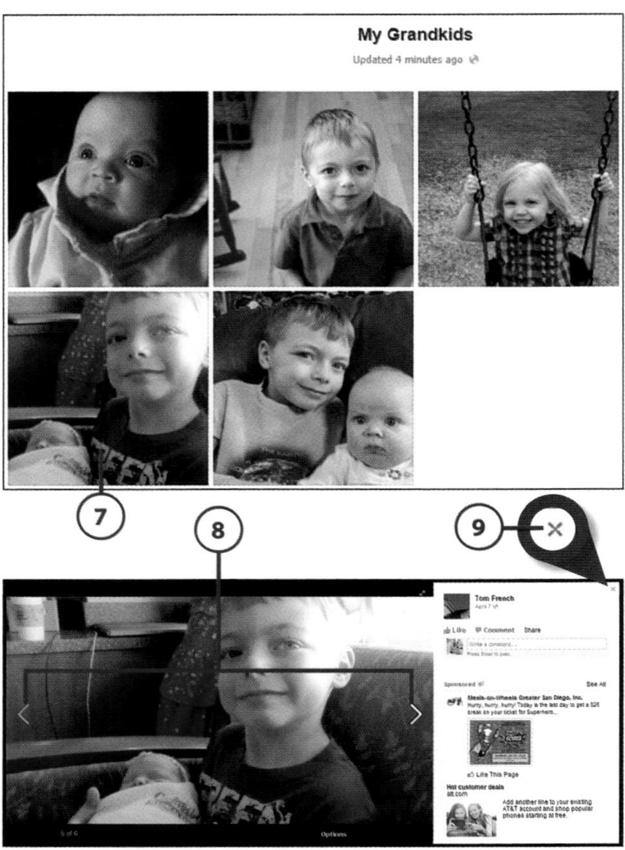

Comment On and Like a Photo

If you'd like to say something about a given photo, enter your comments on the photo page. When others view this photo they will also see your comment.

1. Display the photo and click Comment to the right of the photo viewer.
2. Enter your comments into the Write a Comment box and then press Enter when done.
3. Click Like to "like" a photo without entering any comments about it.

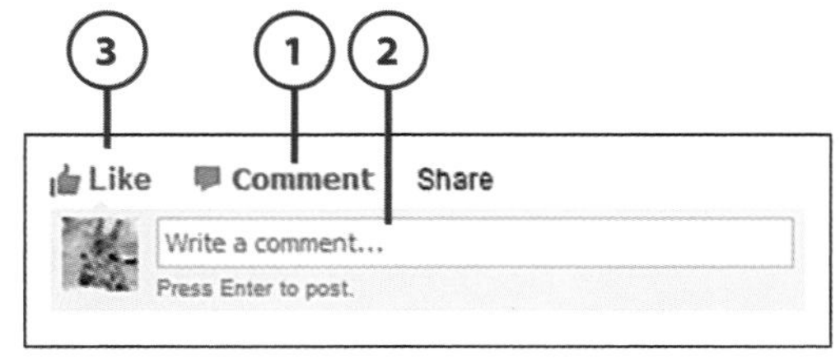

Share a Photo

If you really like a given photo, you can share that photo on your own Timeline—with your own description.

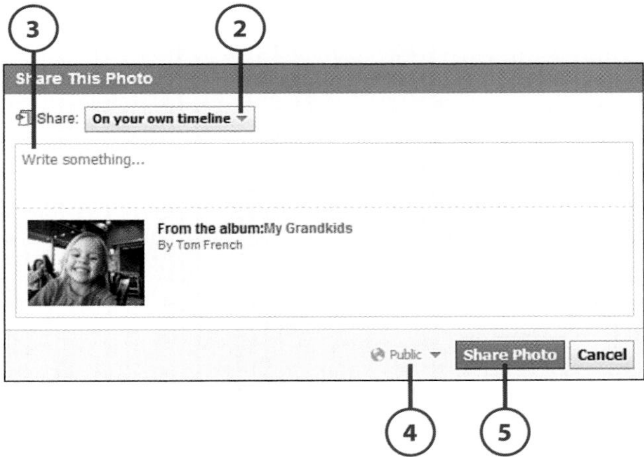

1. Display the photo and click the Share link; this displays the Share This Photo dialog box.
2. Click the Share button and select On Your Own Timeline. (This should be selected by default.)
3. Enter a description of the photo into the Write Something box.
4. Click the Privacy button and select who can view this photo: Public, Friends, Only Me, or Custom.
5. Click the Share Photo button to post this picture to your timeline.

>>>Go Further

SHARING PRIVATELY

You can also share a photo privately with another user or group of users. When the Share This Photo dialog box appears, click the Share button (which is set to On Your Own Timeline by default) and select to share On a Friend's Timeline, In a Group, On Your Page, or In a Private Message. Select this last option to share the photo with a specific individual.

Tag Yourself in a Friend's Photo

If you find yourself in a photo that a friend has taken and uploaded to Facebook, you can "tag" yourself in that photo. When you're tagged in a photo, that photo appears in your Facebook timeline and on your Facebook photo albums page, in the Photos and Videos of You section.

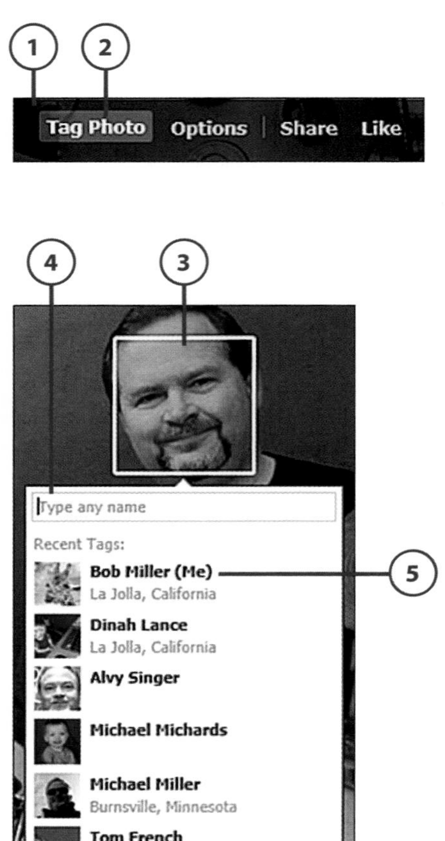

1. Display the photo and mouse over the photo to display the menu at the bottom of the photo.
2. Click Tag Photo.
3. Click your face in the photo. A box appears around your face, with a text box beneath.
4. Enter your name into the text box. A list of matching names appears beneath.
5. Click your name in the list.
6. Your name is now tagged to your face in this photo. Click Done Tagging to finish.

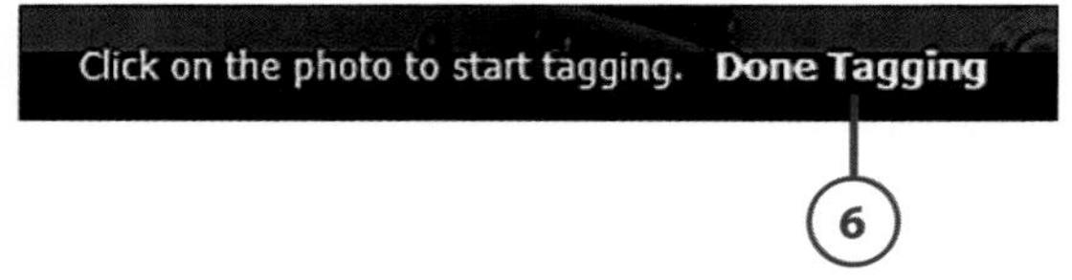

Remove Your Name from a Photo—or Remove the Photo

You might not want to be tagged in a given picture. Perhaps the photo shows you doing something you shouldn't be doing. Maybe the photo is just a bad picture you don't particularly like. Or maybe you just don't like your name or face being "out there" on the Internet without your permission. In any instance, Facebook enables you to remove your name from any photo tagged by a friend; you can even request that a given photo be completely removed from the Facebook site.

1. Display the photo and mouse over the photo to display the menu at the bottom of the photo.
2. Click Options, Report to display the What Would You Like to Happen dialog box.
3. Check I Want to Untag Myself to remove your name from this photo, but leave the photo on Facebook.
4. Check I Want This Photo Removed from Facebook to completely delete the photo from the Facebook site and then click the Remove Tag button.
5. If you chose to remove the photo, check why you want it removed—I Don't Like This Photo of Me, I Think It Shouldn't Be on Facebook, or It's Spam.
6. Click the Continue button and then follow the resulting instructions to complete the process. (The options available depend on why you'd like to remove the picture.)

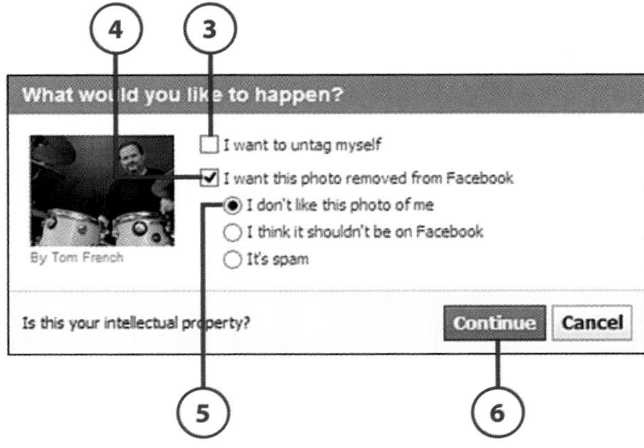

Download a Photo

If you find a friend's photo that you really like, you can download it to your own computer, for your own use.

1. Display the photo and mouse over the photo to display the menu at the bottom of the photo.
2. Click Options, Download.
3. Click Save if you're prompted to open or save the file.
4. If you see the Save As dialog box, select where you want to save the file.
5. Click the Save button.

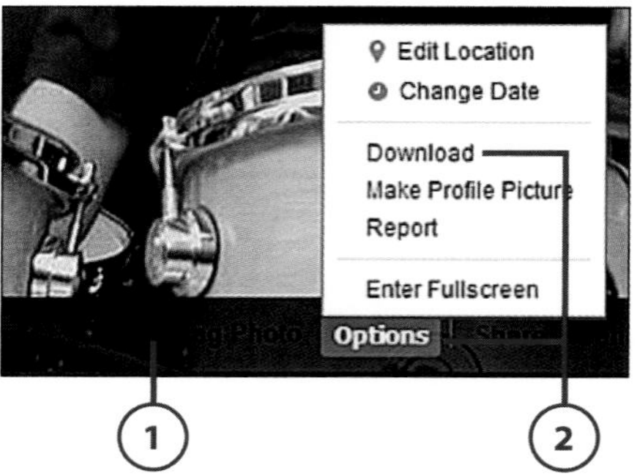

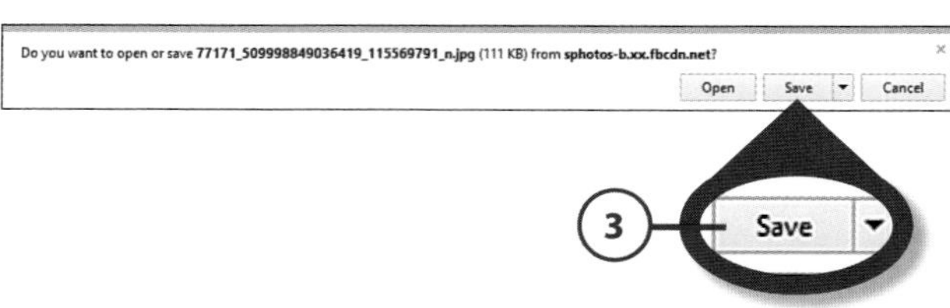

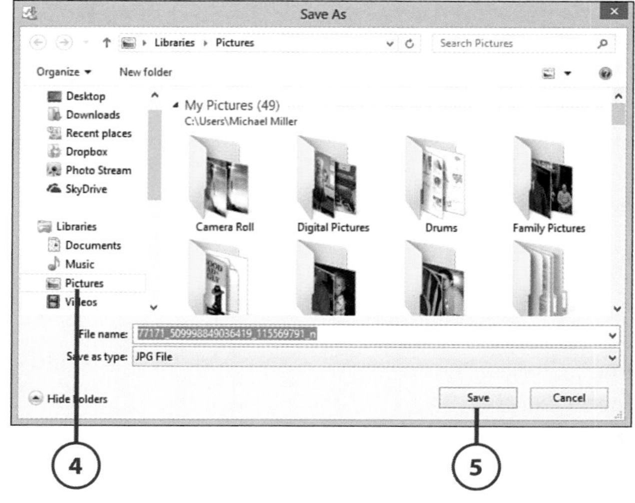

Print a Photo

Facebook does not have a "print" button for the photos on its site. You can, however, print a photo directly from its Facebook page, using the print feature in your web browser.

1. Display and then right-click the photo to display a pop-up menu of options.
2. Select Print Picture.
3. When the Print dialog box appears, select the printer you want to use.
4. Select how many copies you want to print.
5. Click the Print button.

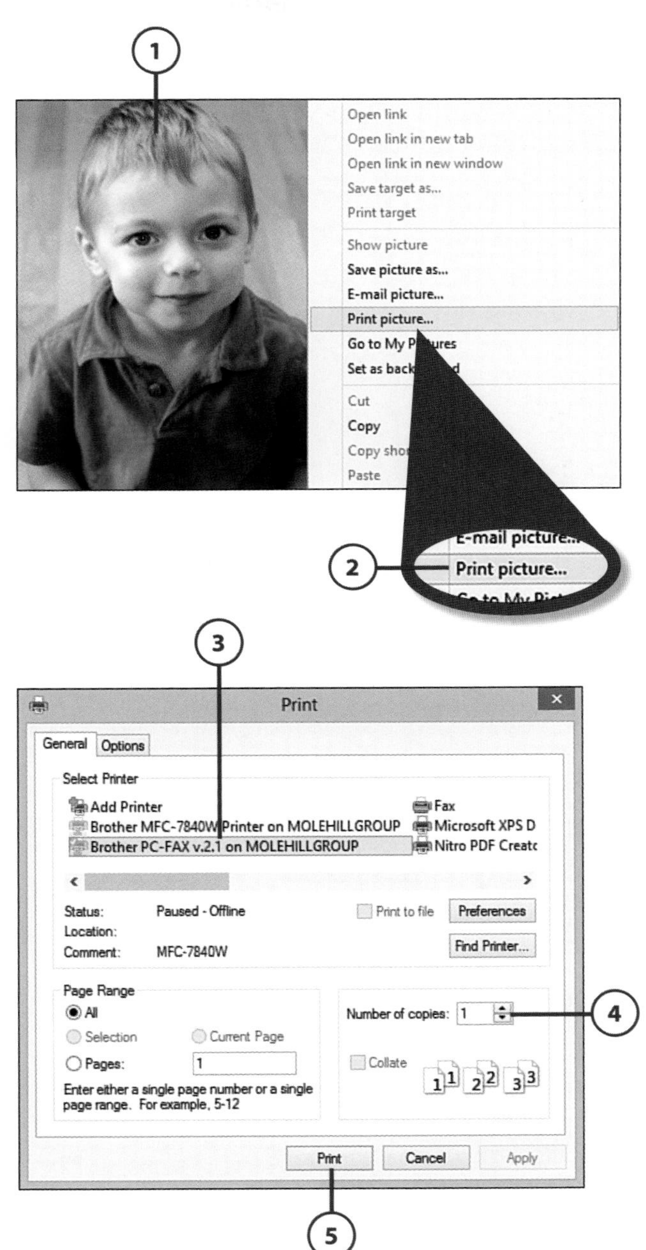

Different Browsers

Your print options might be different depending on the web browser you're using. For example, Internet Explorer 9 offers the Print Picture option from the pop-up menu as described here. If you're using the Google Chrome browser, you need to select Open Image in New Tab from the pop-up menu and then select the Print option from the Customize and Control (gear) menu.

Sharing Your Photos with Friends

It seems like just about everybody these days has a digital camera, or a camera built into his smartphone. That means we're taking a lot more pictures than ever before—and those pictures can be shared with friends and family on Facebook.

The first thing you need to do is transfer your photos from your camera or phone to your computer. Then it's relatively easy to upload and share your own pictures on the Facebook site. You can upload new photos to an existing photo album or create a new album for newly uploaded photos.

>>>Go Further

POSTING PHOTOS FROM YOUR PHONE

If you use your cell phone to take photos, it's even easier to post those photos to Facebook. You don't have to transfer your phone photos to your PC first (although you can); Facebook lets you upload photos directly from your smartphone, using Facebook's mobile app.

If you use an iPhone, Facebook uploading is built into the phone's operating system. Just open the iPhone's Photos app and then open the photo you want to upload. Tap the Share icon at the lower left of the screen and then tap the Facebook icon. When prompted, enter some text to go along with the photo, add location information if you like, and select the privacy level for this post. When you're ready, tap the Post button and the selected photo is posted to your Facebook feed.

This mobile photo posting is explained in more detail in Chapter 20, "Using Facebook on Your iPhone or iPad." It's an easy way to share your photos as you take them.

Upload Photos to a New Photo Album

If you have a lot of photos to share on Facebook, the best approach is to create a series of virtual photo albums. This enables you to organize your photos by topic or date. For example, you might create an album for Summer Vacation 2013, Christmas 2000, Grandkids, or Retirement Party. Organizing your photos into albums also makes it easier for your friends to find specific photos.

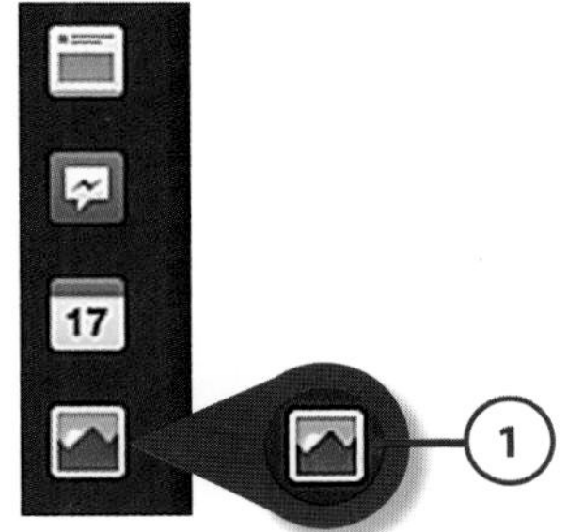

1. Click Photos in the sidebar menu to display your Photos page.
2. Click the Create Album button to display the Select File(s) to Upload dialog box.
3. Select the photos you want to upload.
4. Click the Open button to see the Untitled Album page.

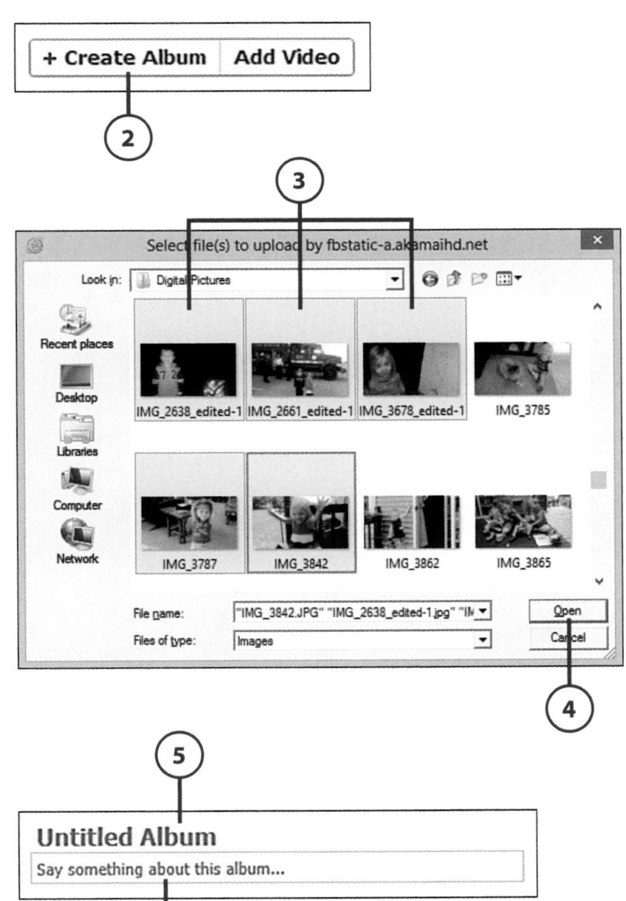

Selecting Multiple Photos

You can upload more than one photo at a time. Hold down the Ctrl key while clicking files to select multiple files.

5. Click Untitled Album and enter the desired album title.
6. Click Say Something About This Album and enter an album description.

Optional Information

All the information you can add to a photo album is entirely optional; you can add as much or as little as you like. You don't even have to add a title—if you don't, Facebook uses the title Untitled Album.

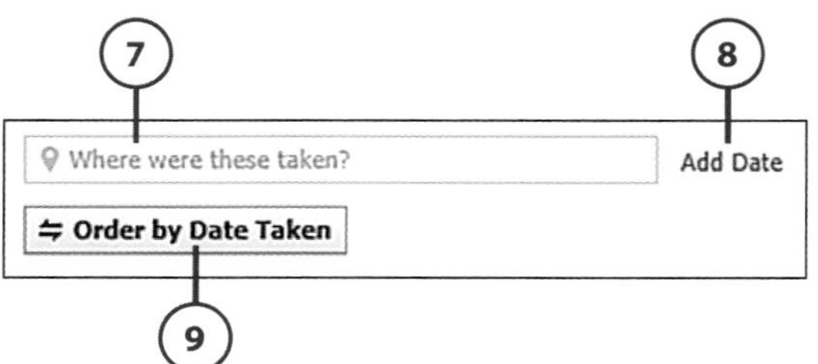

7. Enter a location in the Where Were These Photos Taken? box to enter a geographic location for all the photos in this album. (You can later change the location for any specific photo, as noted in Step 12.)
8. Click Add Date and select a date from the pop-up box to add a date to all the photos in this album.
9. Click the Order by Date Taken button to display these photos in order of when they were taken.

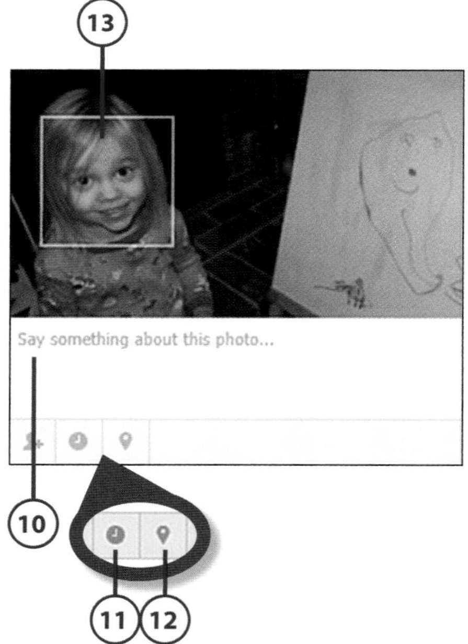

10. Enter a description in the Say Something About This Photo box to enter information about a specific picture.
11. Click a photo's Date button and then select the year, month, and date to enter the date the photo was taken.
12. If you want to enter a location for a specific photo that's different from the location you set for the entire album, click that photo's Location button and then enter a location into the Where Was This? box to enter the place a photo was taken.
13. Click a person's face and enter his or her name when prompted to tag a person who appears in a given photo.

Photo Tagging

You identify people in your photos by *tagging* them. That is, you click a person in the photo and then assign a friend's name to that part of the photo. You can then find photos where a given person appears by searching for that person's tag.

14. Check the High Quality box at the bottom of the screen to upload these photos at a quality suitable for printing. Leave this box unchecked if the photos will only be viewed onscreen.

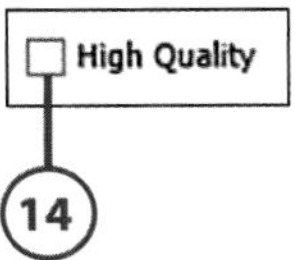

High-Quality Photos

For best possible picture for anyone downloading or printing your photos, check the High Quality option to upload and store your photos at their original resolution. Note, however, that it takes longer to upload high-quality photos than those in standard quality.

15. Click the Privacy button and make a selection—Public, Friends, Only Me, or Custom—to determine who can view the photos in this album.
16. Click the Post Photos button.

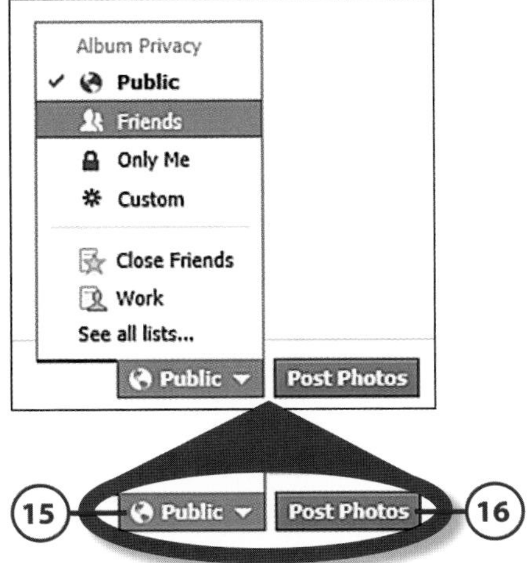

>>>Go Further

PHOTO REQUIREMENTS

You can post just about any kind of photo to your Facebook account. Facebook accepts photos in all popular file types, including JPG, PNG, GIF, TIFF, and BMP. Your picture files have to be no larger than 15MB in size and can't contain any adult or offensive content. You're also limited to uploading your own photos—that is, you can't copy and then upload photos from another person's website. Assuming your photos meet all these requirements, you're ready to upload.

Upload Photos to an Existing Photo Album

After you've created a photo album, you can easily upload more photos to that album.

1. Click Photos in the sidebar menu to display your Photos page.
2. Click Albums to display your existing photo albums
3. Click the album you want to add new photos to.

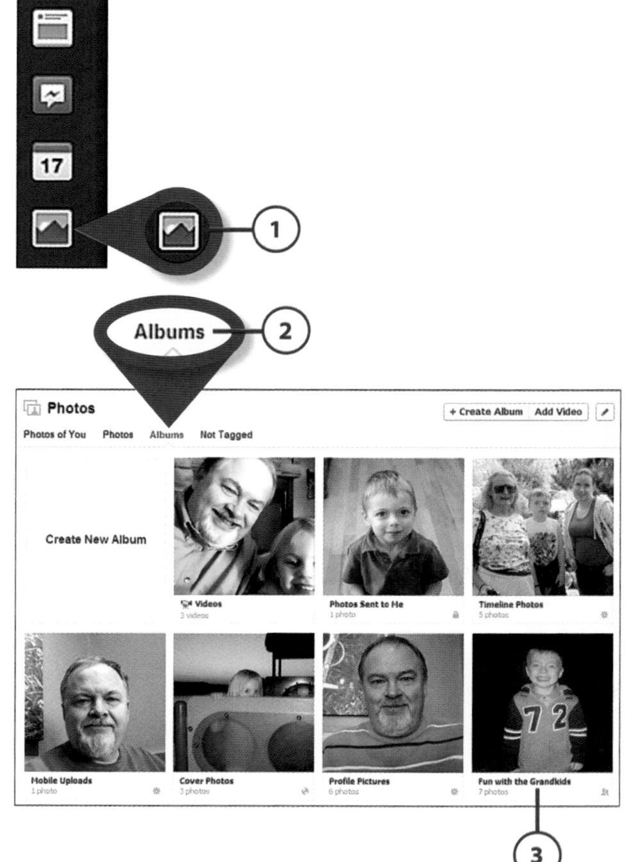

4. When the album page opens, click the Add Photos button to display the Select File(s) to Upload dialog box.
5. Navigate to and select the photos to upload.
6. Click the Open button.
7. The photos you selected are added to the album page. Enter a description in the Say Something About This Photo box to add information about a specific picture.
8. Click a photo's Tag button and then click a person's face and enter his or her name to tag a person who appears in a photo.
9. Click that photo's Date button, and then select the year, month, and date to enter the date the photo was taken.
10. Click that photo's Location button and then enter a location into the Where Was This? box to enter the place the photo was taken.
11. Check the High Quality option to upload photos in the highest possible resolution.
12. Click the Post Photos button.

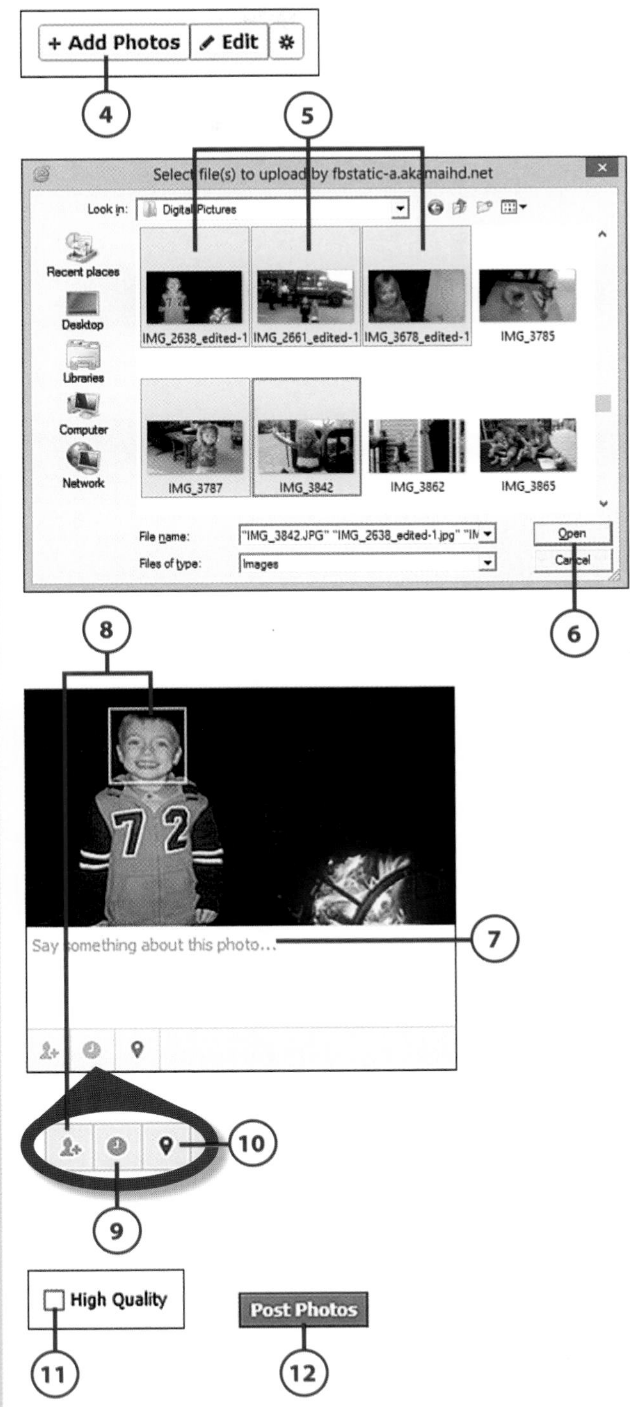

Editing Your Photos and Albums

After you've created a new photo album and filled it with photos, you don't have to be done. You can, at any time, edit or delete individual photos and complete albums.

Edit a Photo's Description

You can, at any time, edit the description of a given photo.

1. Open the photo page for the picture you want to edit, then click the Edit button to open the description panel.
2. Enter your description of the photo into the Add a Description box, or edit the existing description.
3. Enter the names of the people you were with into the Who Were You With? box.
4. Enter where the photo was taken into the Where Was This Photo Taken? box to add location information for the photo.
5. Use the year/month/date controls to change the date associated with this photo.
6. Click the Privacy button and make a new selection to change the privacy settings for this photo.
7. Click the Done Editing button when done.

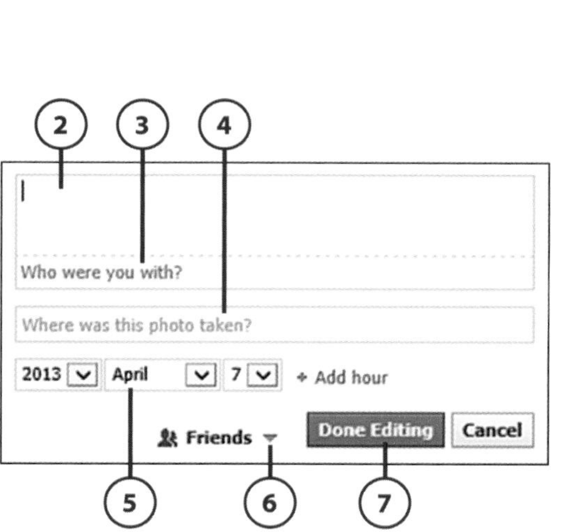

Edit a Photo Album

You can also edit the title, description, and other details of a Facebook photo album. You can change the location and date of the included photos, as well as revise the privacy level.

1. Open the photo album you want to edit and click the Edit button.
2. To change the album title, click the current title and make the appropriate edits.
3. To change the album description, click the current description (under the album title) and make the appropriate edits.
4. To change where these photos were taken, click the current location and enter a new location. (If no location was previously specified, enter a location into the Where Were These Taken? box.)

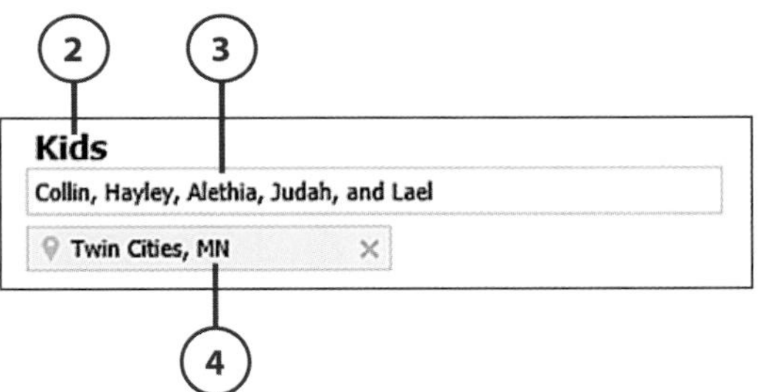

5. To change the date these photos were taken, click the Edit Date button and select a new date from the pop-up box.
6. To change the privacy level of the album, click the Privacy button and make a new selection.
7. Click the Done button when finished.

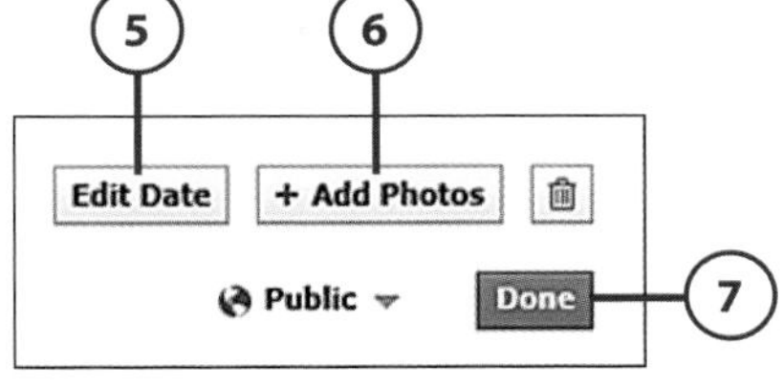

Tag Friends in a Photo

You can, at any time, "tag" friends who appear in the photos you upload. You don't need their permission to do so, either. This makes it easy for your friends to view themselves and other friends in your photos.

Multiple Tags

You can tag multiple people in each photo. For example, if you have a photo of you and a good friend, you can tag both yourself and your friend in the photo. This photo appears in your own photo albums, of course, but it also shows up on your friend's Photos page, in the Photos and Videos of section.

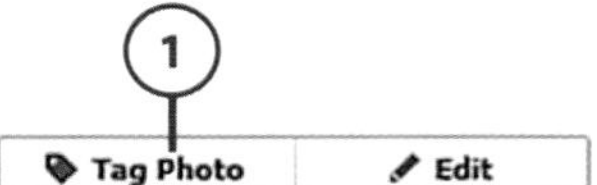

1. Display the photo you want to tag and then click the Tag Photo button to the right of the photo.
2. Click the face of the person you want to tag. Facebook displays a box around the selected person, along with a list of suggested friends.
3. If the person's name is in this list, click it.
4. If the person's name isn't on the list, begin typing the name of the person into the text box and then select the person's name from the resulting list.
5. Click the Done Tagging button.

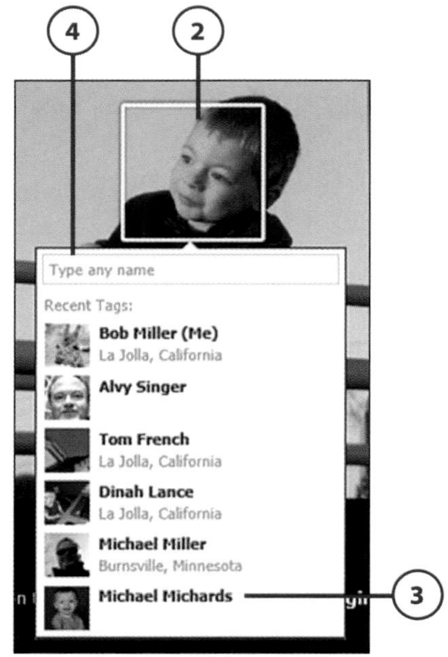

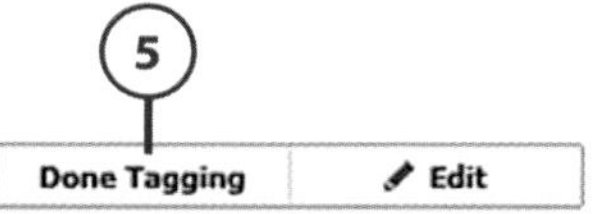

Face Recognition

Facebook employs face-recognition technology that attempts to automatically figure out which friends are in your pictures; if Facebook recognizes a face, it suggests a friend's name for tagging. The goal is to make tagging pictures easier, so that more people do it.

Delete a Photo

If you later discover that you've uploaded a photo you don't want to share, Facebook enables you to delete individual photos within an album.

1. Display the photo you want to delete and then mouse over the photo to display the Options menu.
2. Click Options to display the pop-up menu.
3. Click Delete This Photo
4. Click Confirm in the Delete Photo dialog box.

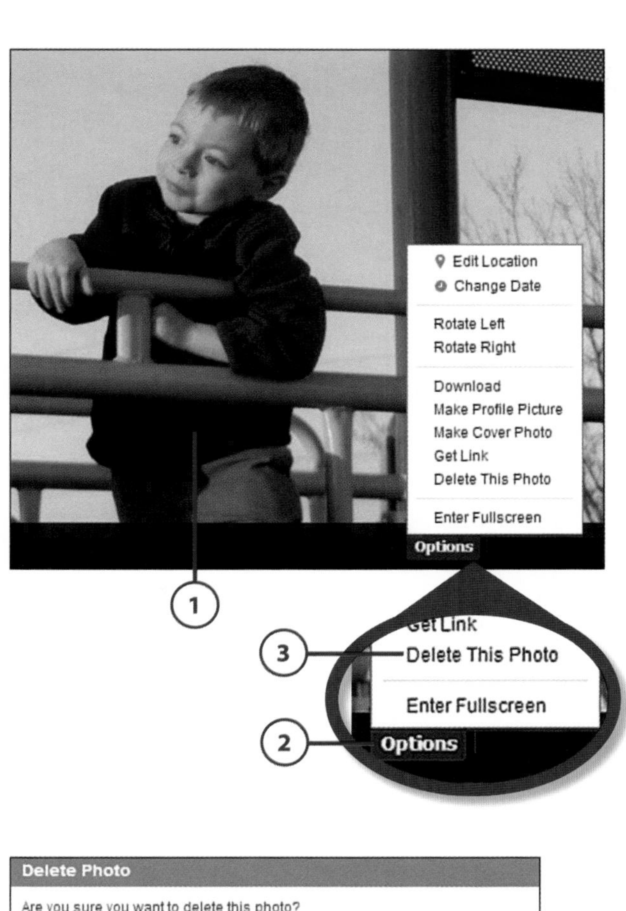

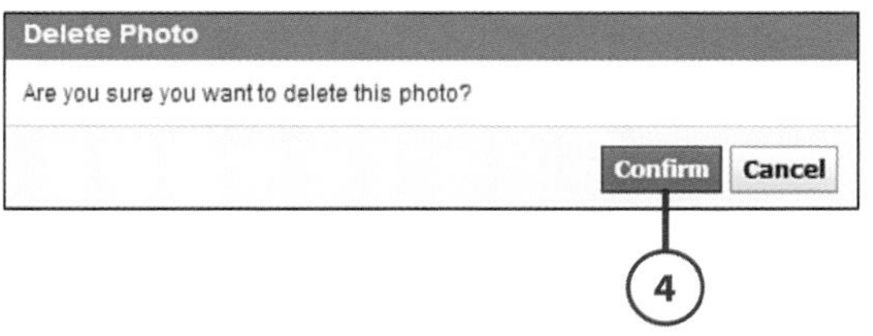

Its Not All Good

Deletion Is Final

When you delete a photo on Facebook, there's no way of undeleting that photo. You can, however, re-upload the photo to the album from scratch.

When you delete a photo album, not only is the deletion final, but you also delete all the photos within that album. Make sure you really want to delete a photo or album before you proceed.

Delete a Photo Album

You're not limited to deleting single photos. You can also delete complete photo albums—and all the photos within.

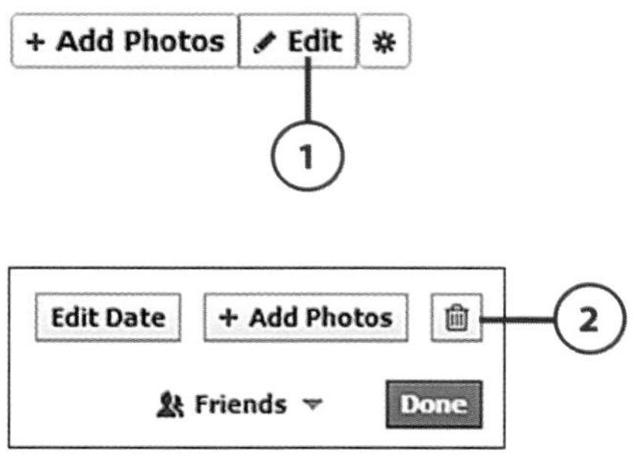

1. Open the album you want to delete and click the Edit button.
2. Click the Delete Album (trash can) button.
3. Click the Delete Album button in the Delete album dialog box.

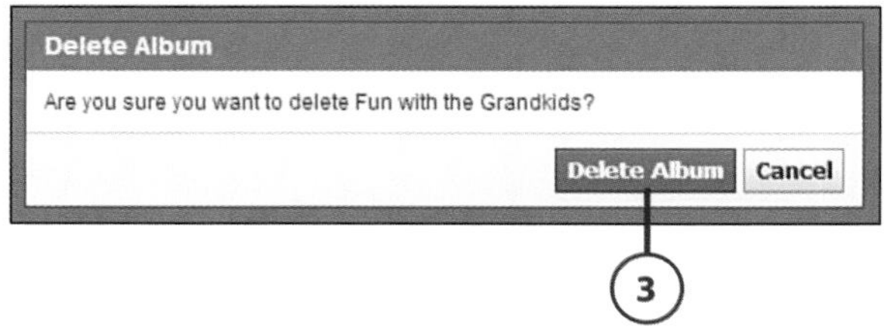

Video player
Video description
Playback controls
Michael Miller
Singing and Dancing in the Front Yard
Hayley and Collin do like to show off a little... — with Amy Elliott and Sherry 'French Elliott' Miller
Like
Comment
Share
Write a comment...
Press Enter to post
Sponsored
See All
Online Leadership Masters
gonzagaonline.com
Advance your career with an online Masters in Leadership from top ranked Gonzaga University. Rated best value. Flexible schedules.
Save on mobile data!
savings.att.com
Use your home network. Internet from AT&T includes 150 GB of data. $14.95/mo for 12 mos.
0:54/1:19
HD
Singing and Dancing in the Front Yard
Options

In this chapter you find out how to share your favorite home movies and videos with your Facebook friends.

→ Viewing Videos from Friends
→ Sharing Your Own Videos on Facebook
→ Sharing YouTube Videos on Facebook

Viewing and Sharing Home Movies

Just as many seniors use Facebook to view and share family photos, Facebook is also a convenient way to view and share home movies and other videos. You can upload any videos you've taken with your camcorder, digital camera, or smartphone, and your friends and family members can view them from the comfort of their computer screens.

And you can view your friends' videos, as well; playback is just a click away. It's a far sight easier than setting up the old 8mm projector and screen in your living room, or even trading VHS tapes!

Viewing Videos from Friends

If one of your friends or family members has a home movie they'd like you to watch, Facebook is the place to share it. You can upload to Facebook just about any type of video, where you (and other friends) can watch it on your computer. In fact, if you access Facebook from your smartphone, you can even watch these home movies in the palm of your hand.

View an Uploaded Video

When one of your friends uploads a video to Facebook, it shows up in your News Feed as a thumbnail image with a playback arrow on top. Playing a video is as easy as clicking that image.

1. Navigate to the status update that contains the video and then click the video thumbnail to play the video.
2. Playback begins in a video player similar to Facebook's photo lightbox. Mouse over the video player to display the playback controls at the bottom.
3. Click the Pause button to pause playback; the button changes to a Play button. Click the Play button to resume playback.
4. Click and drag the volume control to raise or lower the playback volume.
5. Click and drag the time slider move to another point in the video.
6. For those videos that were recorded and uploaded in high definition (HD), click the HD button to view the video in high def.
7. Click the Fullscreen button to display the video on your full computer screen. Click Esc on your computer keyboard to return to normal playback mode.

View Time

The elapsed and total time of the video is displayed to the right of the time slider in the playback controls.

Comment On and Like a Friend's Video

Just as you can comment on a friend's status update, you can also comment on any video he uploads. All comments are displayed beneath the video in the news feed.

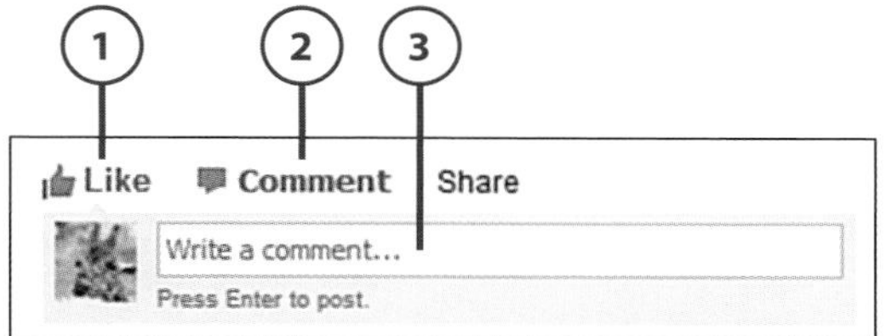

1. Click the Like link to the right of the video player to like the video.
2. Click the Comment link to the right of the video player to comment on the video. This expands the Comment box.
3. Type your comments into the Comment box; press Enter when done.

View All of a Friend's Videos

All the videos a friend has uploaded are displayed in a Videos album on the friend's Photos page. You can play back any video from here.

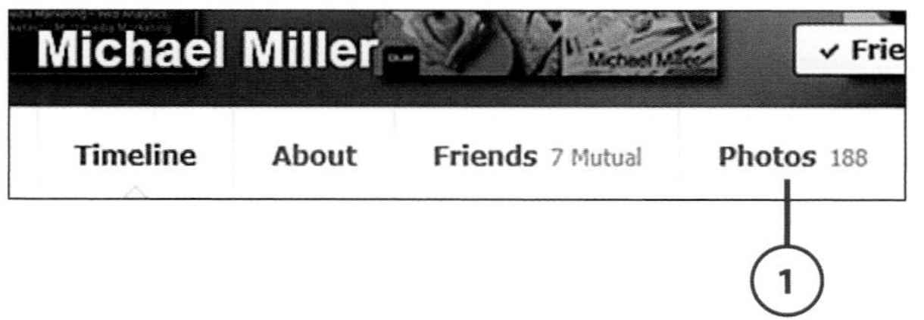

1. Go to your friend's Timeline page and click the Photos button underneath the cover image to display your friend's Photos page.

2. Click Albums to display your friends' photo albums.
3. Click the Videos album to display all this person's videos.

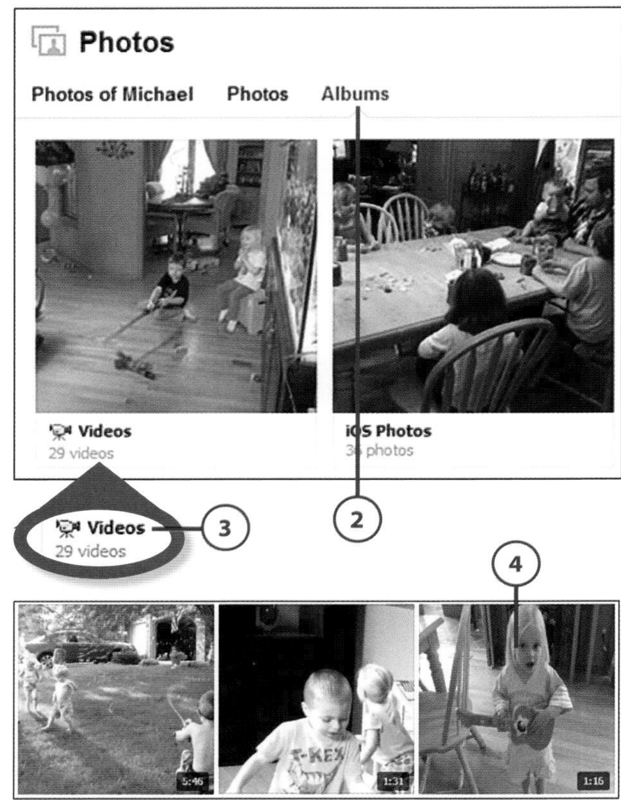

Upload Order

The videos in the Videos album are organized by date uploaded. Newest uploads are displayed first.

4. Click a video thumbnail to play that video.
5. Playback begins in a video player similar to Facebook's photo lightbox. To display playback controls, mouse over the video.
6. Click the Pause button to pause playback; the button changes to a Play button. Click the Play button to resume playback.
7. Click and drag the volume control to raise or lower the playback volume.
8. Click and drag the time slider move to another point in the video.
9. For those videos that were recorded and uploaded in high definition (HD), click the HD button to view the video in high def.
10. Click the Fullscreen button to display the video on your full computer screen. Press Esc on your computer keyboard to return to the video playback page.

Close the Video Player

To close the video player, click the X in the upper-right corner above the description.

Sharing Your Own Videos on Facebook

If you shoot your own home videos, you can share them with friends and family by uploading them to Facebook. Facebook lets you upload videos already stored as digital files or create new videos in real time from your computer's webcam.

>>>Go Further

VIDEO EDITING AND UPLOADS

When uploading videos to Facebook, the video files must be no more than 20 minutes long and no more than 1024MB in size. Facebook accepts videos in all major video file formats, including high-definition videos.

You might want to edit your videos before you upload them, to cut out dead spots and string together multiple clips. You can do this on your computer, using a video-editing software program. The most popular programs include Adobe Premiere Elements (www.adobe.com/products/premiereel/, $99.99), Pinnacle Studio HD (www.pinnaclesys.com, $49.99), and Sony Vegas Movie Studio HD (www.sonycreativesoftware.com/moviestudiohd/, $49.95). All produce files that you can upload to your Facebook account.

Upload a Video File

Facebook lets you upload just about any type of video and share it as a status update, which means all your friends should see it as part of their News Feeds. Your uploaded videos also end up in the Videos album on your Photos page, accessible from your Timeline for all your friends to view.

1. Click Photos in the sidebar menu to open your Photos page.

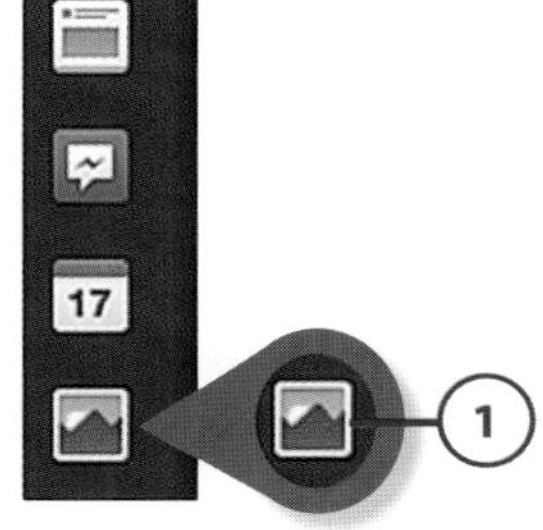

2. Click the Add Video button to display the Upload Video dialog box.
3. Click the Browse or Open button to display the Choose File to Upload or Open dialog box.
4. Navigate to and select the video file you want to upload.
5. Click the Open button to return to the Upload Video dialog box.
6. Enter a title for this video into the Title box.
7. Enter a short description of the video into the Description box.
8. Enter a location in the Where box to specify where the video was taken.
9. Click the Privacy button and select who can view this video: Public, Friends, or Custom.
10. Click the Save button when done.

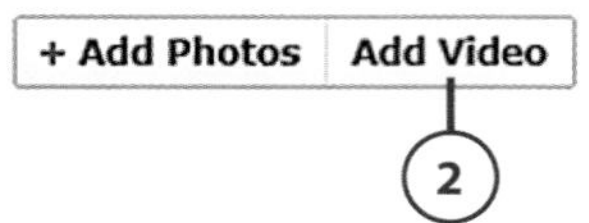

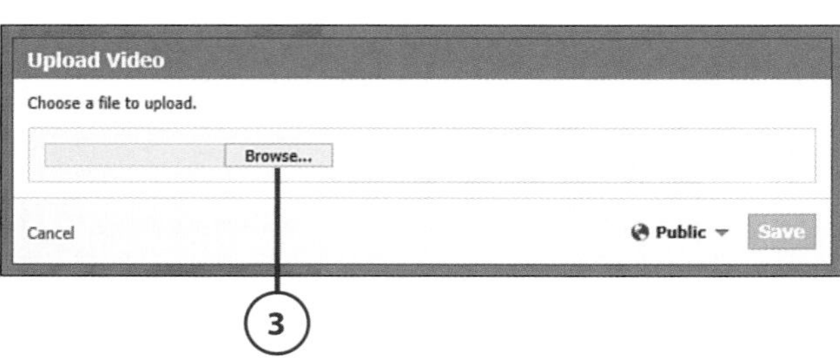

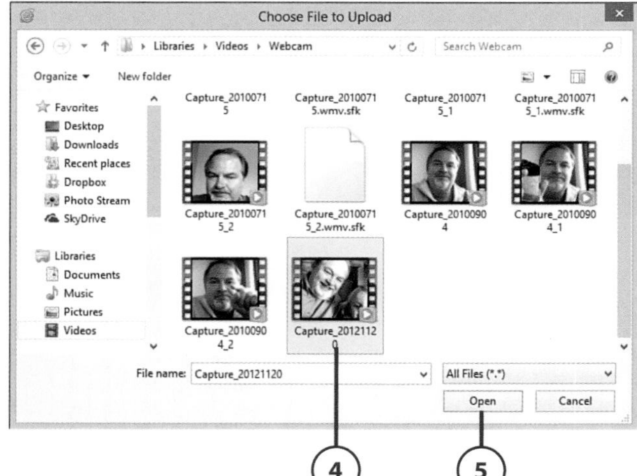

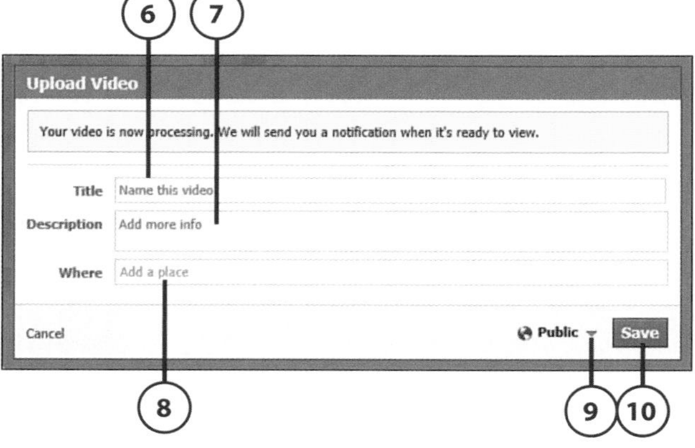

Processing

After a video is uploaded, Facebook must process it into the proper format to distribute on its site. This might take several minutes. You should be informed when the processing is complete; you can then edit the video description if you like, or select a thumbnail image for the video.

Edit Video Information

You can enter or edit information about any video you've uploaded at any time. You can also tag friends appearing in a video, as well as select a thumbnail image for the video.

1. From your Photos page, display all your albums and then click to open the Videos album.
2. Click the video you want to edit.
3. When the video playback page appears, mouse over the video and click Options to display the pop-up menu.
4. Click Edit This Video to display the Edit Video page.

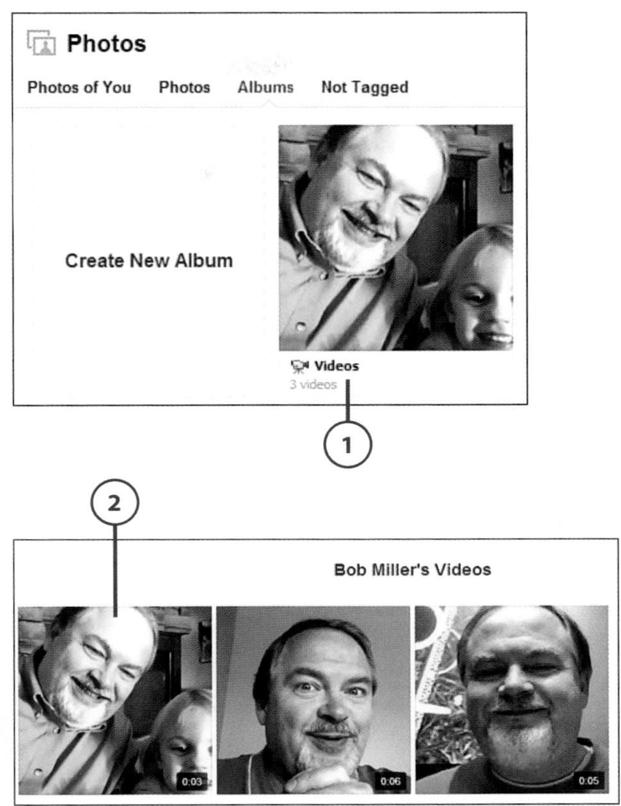

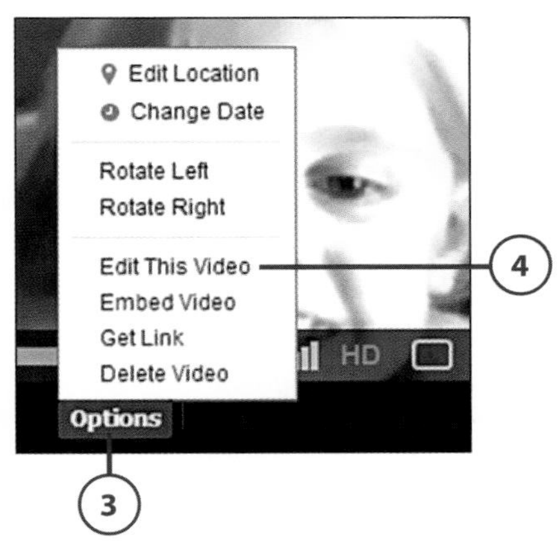

5. To "tag" a person appearing in the video, enter his or her name into the In This Video box.
6. Go to the Title box and make any necessary changes to the video's title.
7. Go to the Where section and enter a location to add location information for the video.
8. To add information about when the video was recorded, go to the When section and click Add Year, then select a year. Click Add Month, then select a month. Click Add Day and select a day.
9. Go to the Description box and make any necessary changes to the video's description.
10. Click the Privacy button and make a new selection to change who can view this video.
11. For longer videos, you can select from several thumbnail images for the video. Click the left and right arrows in the Choose a Thumbnail to select a thumbnail image.
12. Click the Save button when you're done making changes.

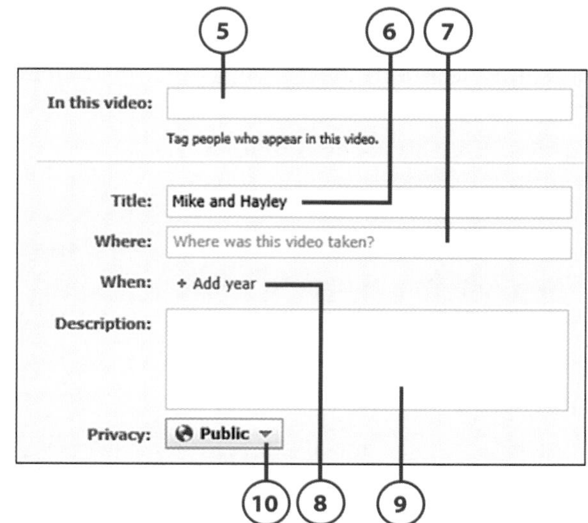

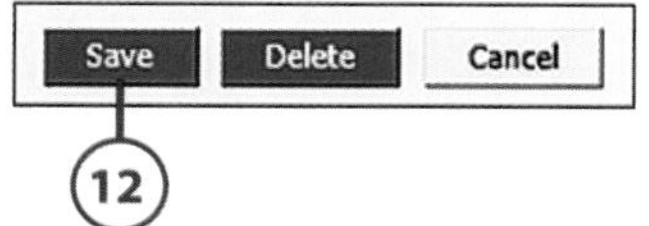

Delete a Video

Ever upload a video you later decided you really don't want anybody else to watch? Fortunately, Facebook enables you to delete any video you've previously updated.

1. From your Photos page, display all your albums and then click to open the Videos album.
2. Click the video you want to delete.
3. When the video playback page appears, mouse over the video and click Options to display the pop-up menu.
4. Click Delete Video.
5. Click the Confirm button in the Delete Video dialog box.

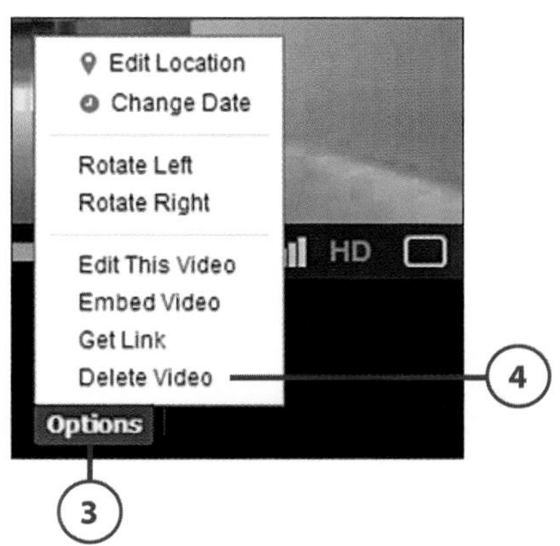

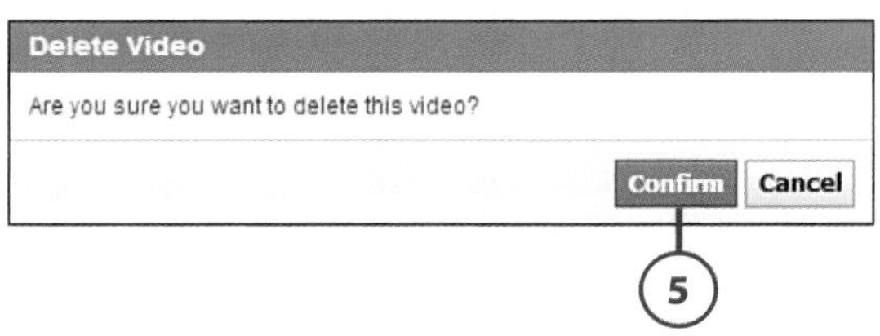

Sharing YouTube Videos on Facebook

YouTube (www.youtube.com) is the world's largest online video community, with hundreds of millions of videos available for viewing. Many Facebook users like to share videos from the YouTube site with their Facebook friends. YouTube makes it easy to do this.

YouTube Account

To share YouTube videos, you first must have either a YouTube or Google account. Both are free.

Share a YouTube Video

You can share videos you've uploaded yourself to YouTube. You can also share any public video uploaded from other YouTube users.

1. Use your web browser to go to YouTube (www.youtube.com) and log in to your YouTube account.
2. Navigate to the video you want to post to Facebook and click Share beneath the video player to expand the Share panel.
3. Click the Facebook button.
4. Enter an accompanying message into the large text box in the Post to Your Wall window.
5. Click the Privacy button to determine who can view this video.
6. Click the Share button. The video is posted as a status update to your Facebook timeline.

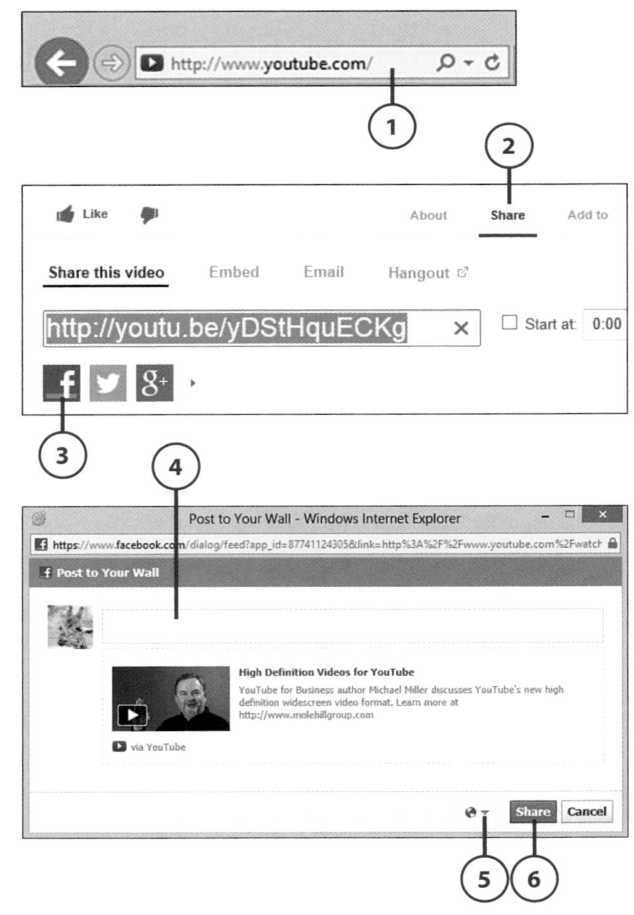

Linking Accounts

The first time you try to share a YouTube video on Facebook, you see the Facebook Login window. Enter your email address and Facebook password, and then click the Login button. (You won't see this window after this first time.)

View a Shared YouTube Video

When one of your friends shares a YouTube video, it appears as a status update in your News Feed. You can view the YouTube video directly within your News Feed.

1. Go to the status update that includes the YouTube video and then click the thumbnail image to begin playback.
2. Mouse over the video to display the playback controls.
3. Click the Pause button to pause playback; click the Play button to resume playback.
4. To view the video on the YouTube site, click the YouTube icon.

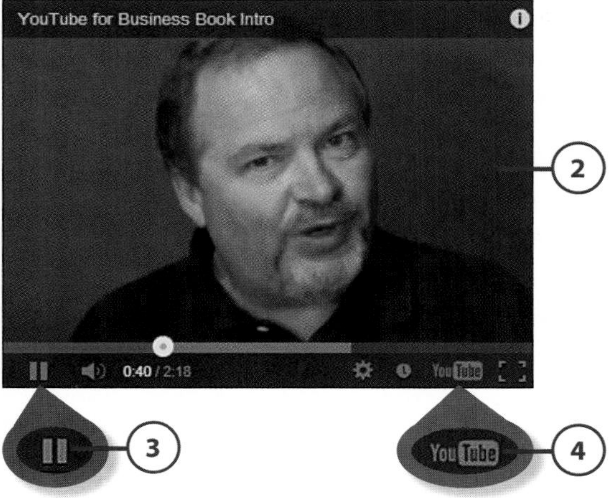

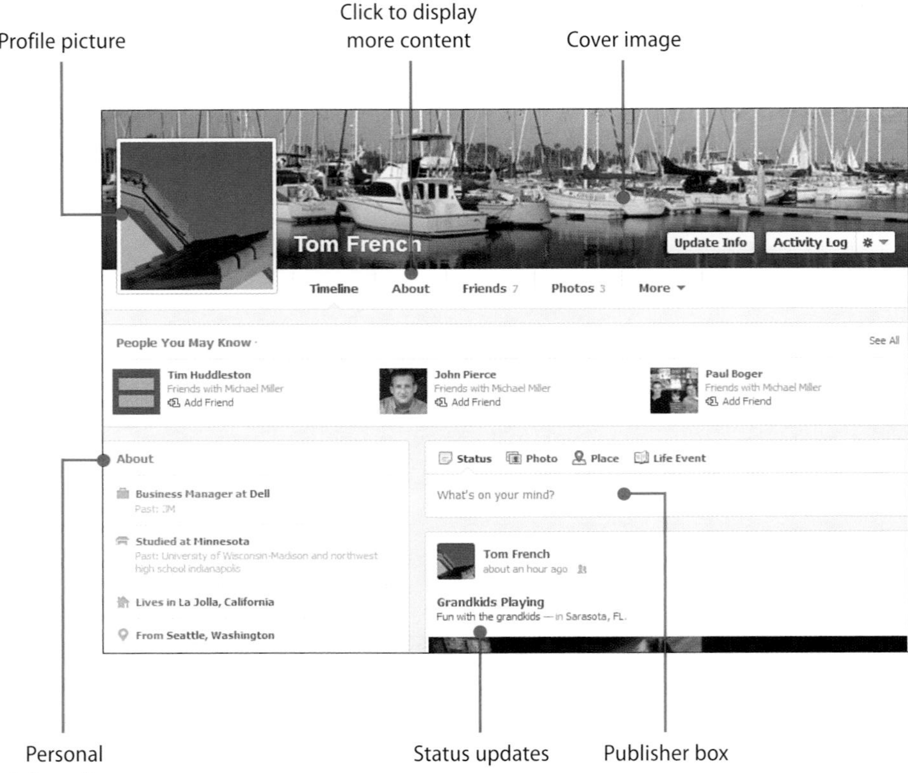

Profile picture
Click to display more content
Cover image
Tom French
Update Info
Activity Log
Timeline
About
Friends 7
Photos 3
More
People You May Know
See All
Tim Huddleston
Friends with Michael Miller
Add Friend
John Pierce
Friends with Michael Miller
Add Friend
Paul Boger
Friends with Michael Miller
Add Friend
About
Business Manager at Dell
Studied at Minnesota
Past: University of Wisconsin-Madison and northwest high school indianapolis
Lives in La Jolla, California
From Seattle, Washington
Status
Photo
Place
Life Event
What's on your mind?
Tom French
about an hour ago
Grandkids Playing
Fun with the grandkids — in Sarasota, FL.
Personal information
Status updates
Publisher box

In this chapter you find out how to personalize your Facebook Timeline page.

- → Changing the Look and Feel of Your Timeline
- → Editing the Contents of Your Timeline

Personalizing Your Timeline

When old friends want to see what you've been up to all these years, they turn to a single Facebook page. Your Timeline page hosts all your personal information and status updates, so that friends and family can learn all about you at a glance. Fortunately, you have some control over what gets displayed on your Timeline—it's your personal page on the Facebook site.

Changing the Look and Feel of Your Timeline

All your personal information, including the status updates you've posted, are displayed on your Facebook Timeline page. Your Timeline is essentially your home base on Facebook, the place where all your Facebook friends can view your information and activity.

You access your own Timeline page by clicking your name on the Facebook toolbar. From there, you can customize (to a degree) how your Timeline looks, and what information it contains.

Change Your Profile Picture

Your Timeline page includes your account's profile picture—and this is the first thing many people change. Your profile picture is an image of your choosing (it can be a picture of you or of anything, really) that appears not only on your Timeline page, but also accompanies every post you make on the Facebook site. (For example, your profile picture appears in your friends' News Feeds, alongside each of your status updates.)

You can easily change the image that appears as your profile picture. Some users change this image frequently; others find a photo they like and stick to it.

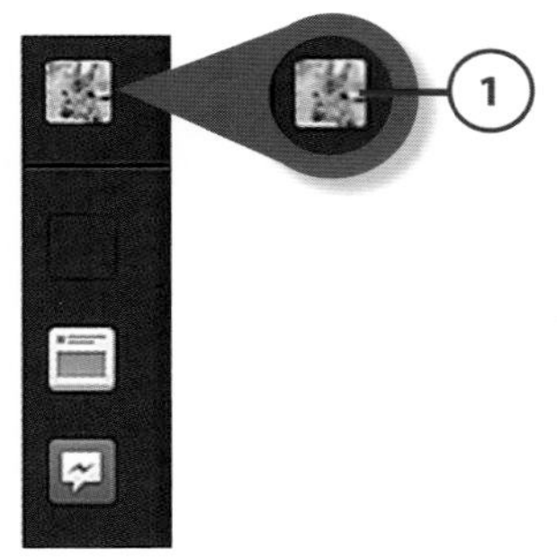

1. Click your picture in the sidebar menu (or your name in the toolbar) to display your Timeline page.
2. Mouse over your profile picture and click Edit Profile Picture to display a menu of options. (If this is the first time adding a profile picture, click the Add Profile Picture button instead.)
3. Select Upload Photo to display the Choose File to Upload or Open dialog box if you're uploading a photo from your computer. (Skip to Step 6 if you instead want to take photo with your webcam.)

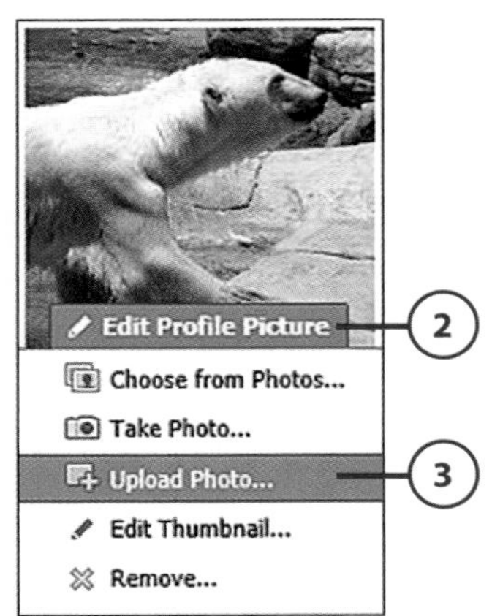

4. Navigate to and select the photo you want to use.
5. Click the Open button.
6. You can also shoot a new profile picture using your computer's webcam. From the Timeline page, mouse over your profile picture, select Edit Profile Picture, and then select Take Photo to display the Take a Profile Picture dialog box.
7. Smile and click the Take button; this initiates a 3-2-1 countdown before the picture is taken.
8. Click the Set as Profile Picture button.

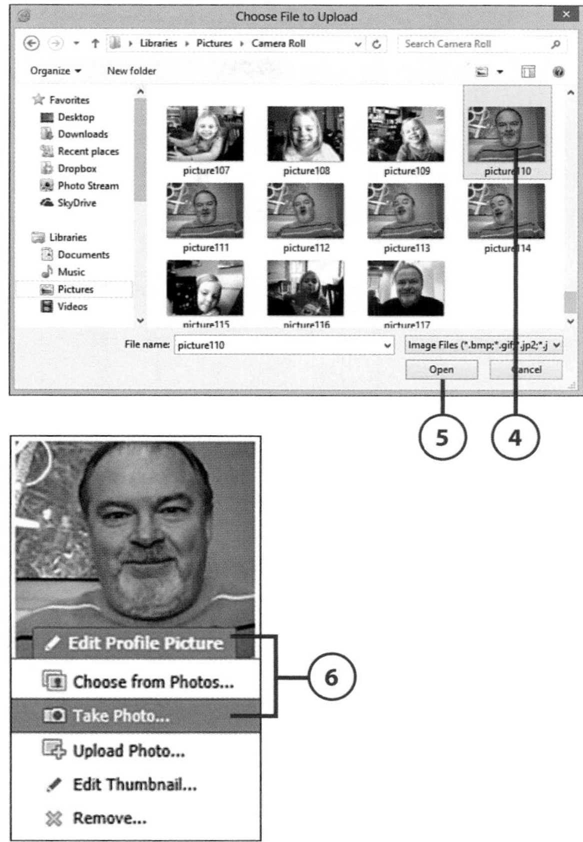

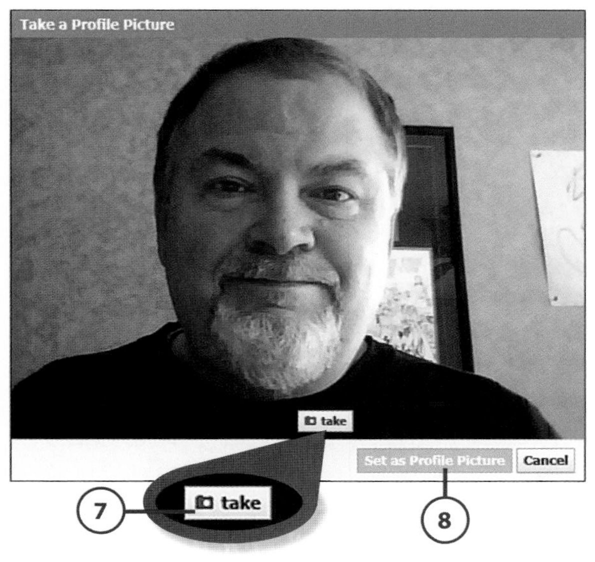

Edit Your Picture Thumbnail

In many instances, the photo you choose for your profile picture isn't framed correctly for use as your thumbnail image. You can, however, recrop the image to better fit the thumbnail dimensions.

1. From your Timeline page, mouse over your profile photo and select Edit Profile Picture to display a menu of options.
2. Click Edit Thumbnail to display the Edit Thumbnail dialog box.
3. Use your mouse to drag the thumbnail image until it looks like you want it to look.
4. If you'd rather resize your picture to fit the thumbnail space (which could add black bars above/below or to the right/left of the picture), check the Scale to Fit box.
5. Click the Save button.

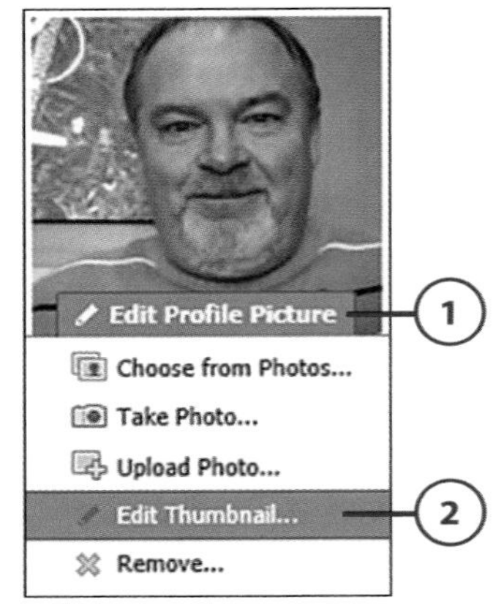

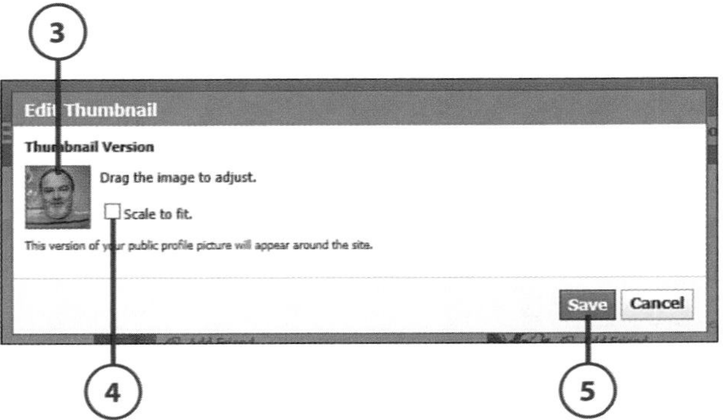

Remove a Picture

To remove your current profile picture without replacing it with a new picture, mouse over your profile picture and select Edit Profile Picture, Remove. This results in a default silhouette image where your profile picture should be.

Add a Cover Image

By default, your profile picture appears against a shaded background at the top of your Timeline page—not very visually interesting. You can, however, select a background image (called a *cover image*) to appear on the top of the page. Many people choose landscapes or other artistic images that provide an interesting but non-obtrusive background to their profile picture; others choose more personal photos as their covers.

Cover Image Specs

Your cover image should be wider than it is tall. The ideal size is 851 pixels wide by 315 pixels tall—although if you upload a smaller image, Facebook stretches it to fill the space.

1. To add your first cover image, go to your Timeline page and click the Add a Cover button. A pop-up menu with several options displays.

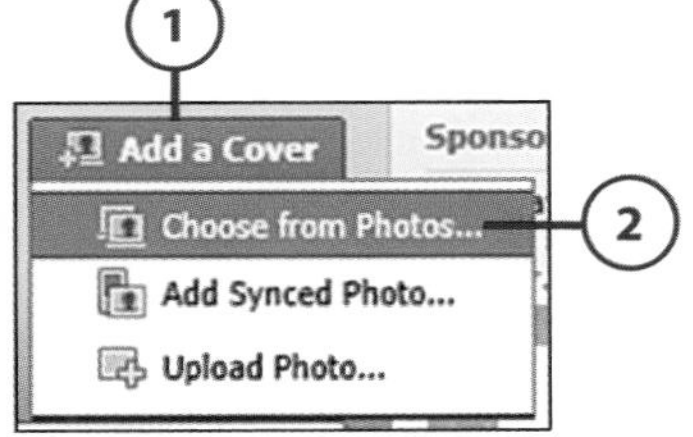

Change an Existing Cover

To change an existing cover image, mouse over the image and click the Change Cover button.

2. To select from a photo already uploaded to Facebook, click Choose from Photos to display the Choose from Your Photos dialog box.

3. Click one of the photos you see, or click View Albums to select a photo from one of your photo albums.
4. To select a photo stored on your computer, click the Add a Cover button and then click the Upload Photo option to display the Choose File to Upload or Open dialog box.
5. Navigate to and select the picture you want to use.
6. Click the Open button.

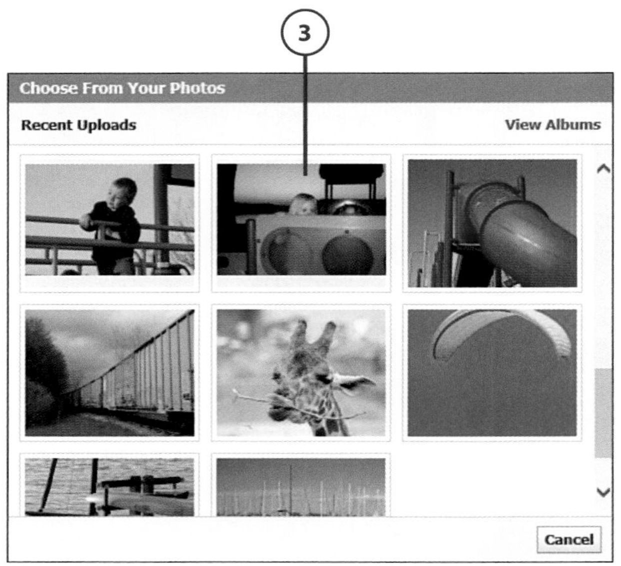

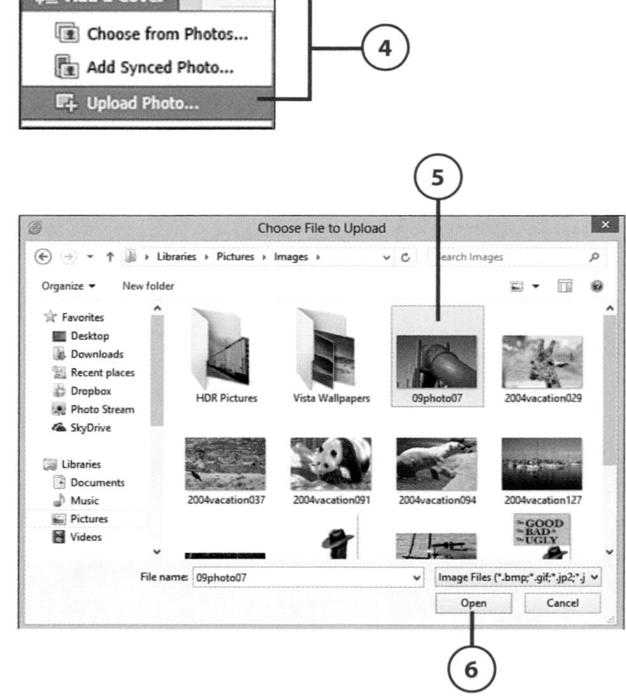

7. You're prompted to reposition the cover image by dragging it around the cover image space. Use your mouse to reposition the image as necessary.
8. Click the Save Changes button.

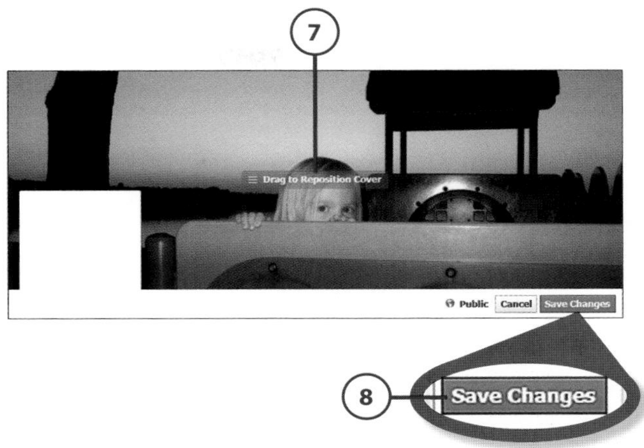

Reposition Your Cover Image

You can at any time reposition the picture used as your cover image. Mouse over your cover image, click Change Cover, and then click Reposition. Use your mouse to position the image as you wish, and then click the Save Changes button.

Editing the Contents of Your Timeline

Beneath the cover image on your Timeline page are buttons that lead to additional information and content, such as your friends list and photos you've uploaded. You can't change these buttons; they are what they are.

Scroll down and you see your Timeline proper, in two-column format. The left column contains personal information about you, in various themed boxes—About, Friends, Photos, Places, and the like. The right column contains all the status updates and other Facebook activities in which you've participated, in reverse chronological order. (Newest first, in other words.)

You can edit most of the personal information displayed on your Timeline page, to either add new events or hide information you'd rather not leave public. You can also choose to hide unwanted status updates, or highlight those updates that are more important to you.

Hide and Delete Status Updates

The main section of your Timeline displays all the status updates you've made on Facebook, from the first day you signed up to just now. You don't have to display every single status update, however; if there's an embarrassing update out there, you can choose to either hide it from view or completely delete it.

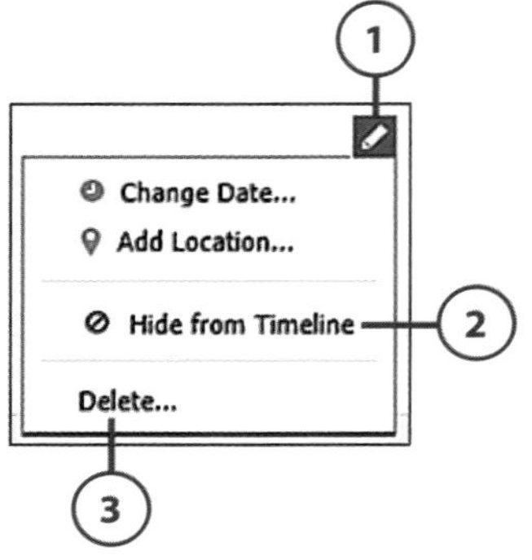

1. Go to your Timeline page, mouse over the status update, and then click the Edit or Remove button to display a menu of options.
2. Click Hide from Timeline to hide this update but not permanently delete it. (Hidden posts can be unhidden in the future.)
3. Click Delete to permanently delete this update from Facebook. (Deleted posts cannot be undeleted.)

Not Everything Can Be Deleted

Not all status updates can be deleted. If the Delete option doesn't appear, you should opt to hide the update instead.

Highlight Your Favorite Status Updates

You can draw attention to your favorite or most important status updates by highlighting them on your Timeline. A highlighted post appears with a blue banner at the top-right corner.

1. Go to your Timeline page and mouse over the status update you want to highlight.
2. Click the Highlight (star) icon.

Unhighlight a Post

If you change your mind about what's important, you can "un-highlight" a previously highlighted post. Just return to the post on your Timeline and click the Remove from Highlights banner.

View and Edit Your Facebook Activity

Your Timeline page presents all your Facebook activity in a nice, visually attractive fashion. However, if you want a more straightforward view of what you've done online, you can display and edit your Activity Log. This is a chronological list of everything you've done on the Facebook site, from status updates to links to comments you've made on others' posts.

Go Further

CLEAN UP YOUR TIMELINE

Many users find the Activity Log the most efficient way to clean up entries on their Timelines. It's easier to see what's posted (and available to post) from the more condensed Activity Log listing than it is by scrolling through the entire Timeline.

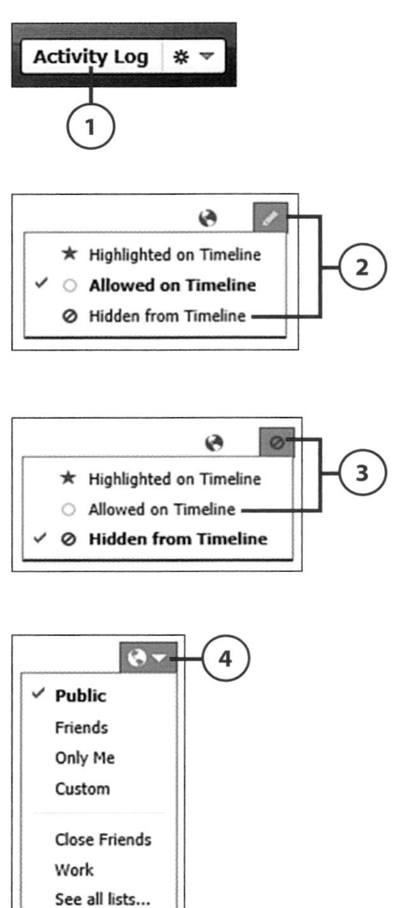

1. From your Timeline page, click the Activity Log button under the cover image. This displays your Facebook Activity Log.
2. Click the Allowed on Timeline (pencil) button for an item and then click Hidden from Timeline to hide that item from your Timeline.
3. Click the Hidden from Timeline button for a hidden item and then click Allowed on Timeline to redisplay a hidden item on your Timeline.
4. To change who can view an item, click the Privacy button and select Public, Friends, Only Me, or Custom.

Update Your Profile Information

Not everyone fully completes their profiles when first joining Facebook. Maybe you forgot to include certain information, or maybe you entered it wrong. In any case, Facebook lets you easily edit or update the personal information in your Facebook profile. You can also select who can view what information.

Go Further

THE MORE FACEBOOK KNOWS...

All the personal information that Facebook requests of you is optional—you don't have to enter it if you don't want to. Know, however, that the more Facebook knows about you, the better it can suggest appropriate activities and match you with potential friends. For example, Facebook makes more and more relevant friend suggestions when you add every school you've attended and every employer you've worked for. So enter as much information as you're comfortable with, and let it go at that.

1. Go to your Timeline page and click the Update Info button inside your cover image. This displays your About page, with the Work and Education section open for editing.

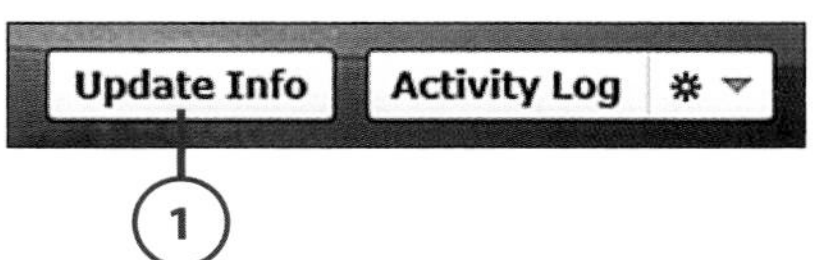

2. Click Edit next to any item you want to change and then edit the information as necessary.
3. Click the Privacy button next to that item and then select who can view this information—Public, Friends, Only Me, or Custom.

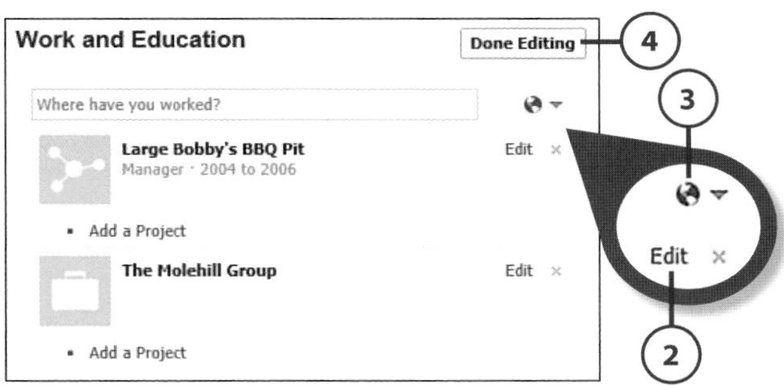

Only Me

Selecting the Only Me option makes that piece of information visible only to yourself. No one else on Facebook, not even your friends, can see it.

4. Click Done Editing to close editing on this section.
5. To edit another section of your profile, click the Edit button for that section and then repeat steps 2 through 4.

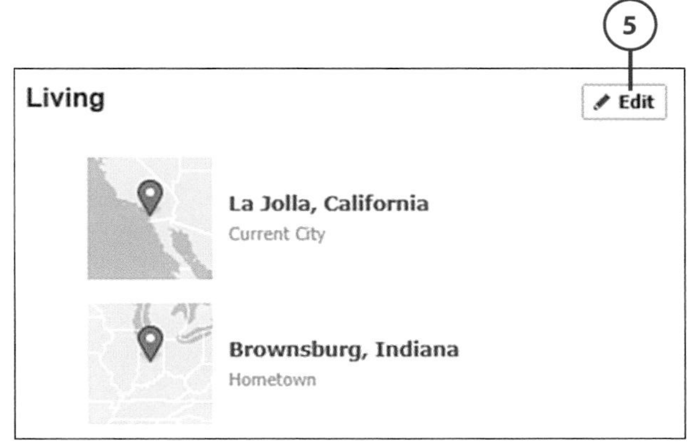

>>>Go Further

WHO KNOWS WHAT?

Not everyone viewing your profile needs to see all your information. For example, you might want everyone to view your birthdate, but not necessarily the year of your birth. You might want only your friends to view your relationship status, or you might not want to share your personal contact information with anyone. You can fine-tune your profile as granularly as you like, in this fashion, to create a clear division between your public and private lives.

Add a Life Event

Facebook's intention with the Timeline is to tell the "story of your life" on a single page. (In fact, Facebook calls the status updates you post "stories.") But Facebook can display only those events it knows about based on what you've entered into your personal profile. You can, however, supplement this information by adding other milestones—what Facebook calls *life events*—to your Timeline.

1. On your Timeline page, go to the Publisher box and click Life Event. This expands the Publisher box to include a list of different types of events.
2. Click the type of event you want to add—Work & Education, Family & Relationships, Home & Living, Health & Wellness, or Travel & Experiences.

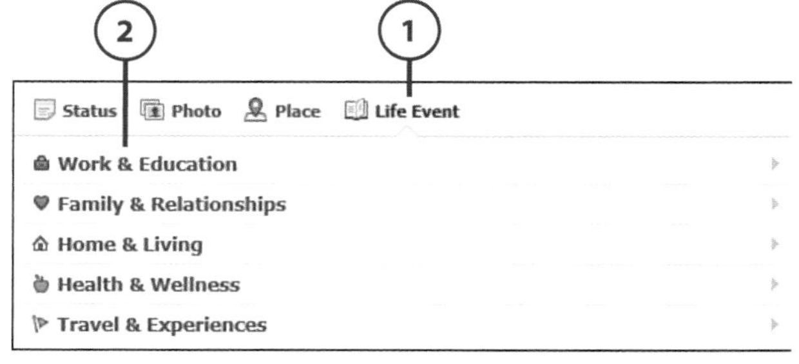

3. Facebook displays options for the type of event you selected. The options available differ by the type of event; select the option that best applies to the event you want to add, or select Other Life Event to add anything not listed here.
4. You now see a panel specific to the type of event you selected. For example, if you opted to enter your retirement, you see the Retirement panel, with fields for When, Profession, Location, and so forth. Enter the appropriate information for this event.
5. In many instances, there is the opportunity to add photos related to the event. Click Upload Photos to choose pictures stored on your computer, or Choose from Photos to select pictures previously uploaded to a Facebook photo album.
6. To determine who can view this event, click the Privacy button and select from the available options—Public, Friends, Only Me, and Custom.
7. Click the Save button. The new event is posted to your Timeline.

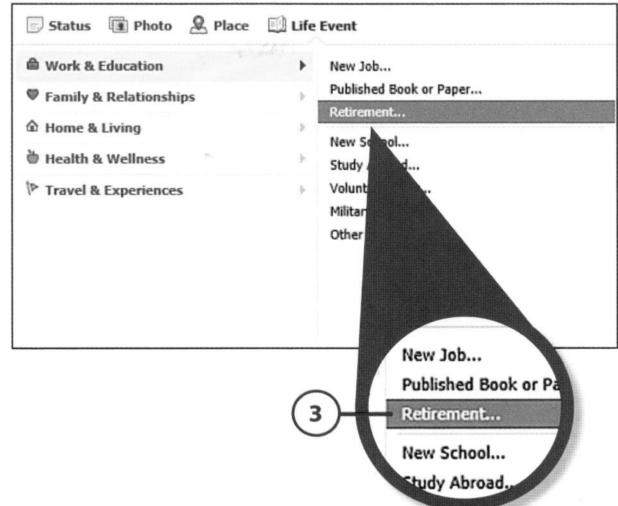

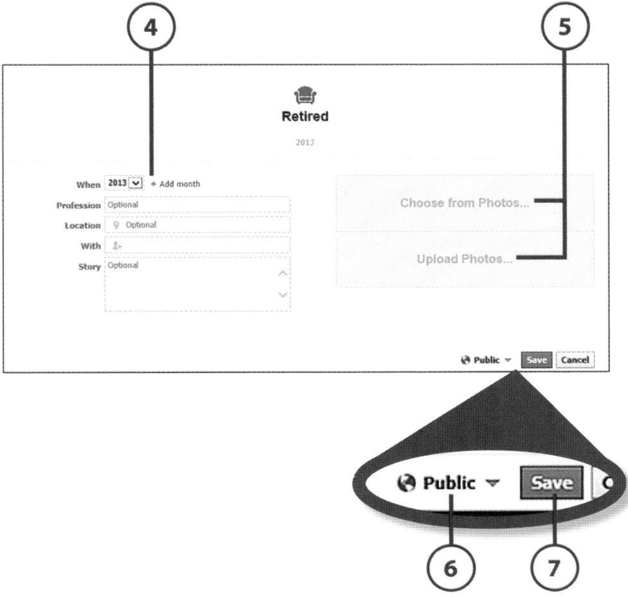

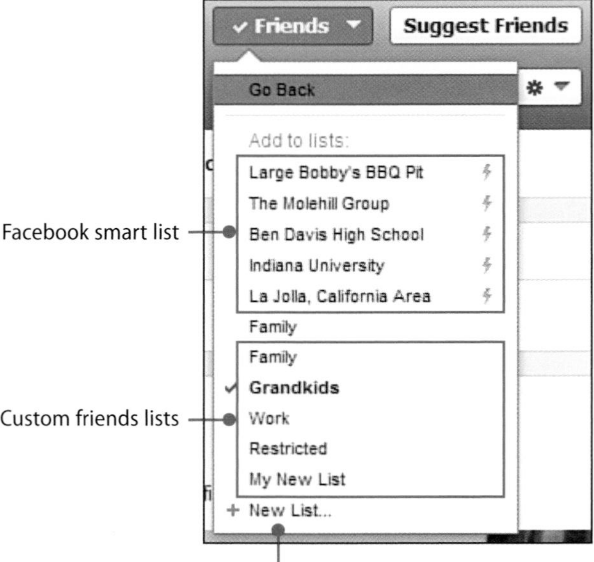

Friends
Suggest Friends
Go Back
Add to lists:
Large Bobby's BBQ Pit
The Molehill Group
Ben Davis High School
Indiana University
La Jolla, California Area
Family
Family
Grandkids
Work
Restricted
My New List
New List...
Facebook smart list
Custom friends lists
Click to create a new friends list

In this chapter you find out how to manage your Facebook friends by creating multiple friends lists.

- → Creating Friends Lists
- → Viewing and Posting to Your Friends Lists

8

Organizing Your Friends into Lists

After you've been on Facebook for any length of time, you'll find that you've made quite a few Facebook friends. Between old friends from your youth, current friends and neighbors, and assorted family members, you might end up with anywhere from a few dozen to a few hundred friends on Facebook.

When you get this many Facebook friends, however, they become difficult to manage. You end up with an overwhelming number of people to track in your News Feed, and probably create posts that are better suited to some friends than others.

The solution is to organize your Facebook friends into custom lists within your main list. A custom friends list lets you send status updates, photos, and other files to selected friends only, instead of to all your friends. It also lets you simplify your News Feed by viewing only posts from specific lists of friends.

Creating Friends Lists

After you make more than a few dozen Facebook friends, it's time to organize those friends into smaller groups—what Facebook calls friends lists. You can then opt to send individual status updates only to members of a selected list, or to view only those status updates posted by members of a list.

For example, you might want to create a list that contains only your immediate family members—kids and grandkids—or you can create a list of more extended family members. You can create a list of those people in your town or neighborhood that you socialize with, or of people you play golf or bridge with. You can create a list of people in your spouse's book club or your grandson's soccer team. You can even create lists for a church group, neighborhood association, or people who attended your last class reunion. What kinds of lists are entirely up to you.

No Approval Necessary

A Facebook list is not something that your friends have to join or even approve; there's no two-way participation. A list is simply a subset of your master friends list, broken out so you can send your updates only to members of that list.

>>>Go Further

SMART LISTS

To help you get started with friends lists, Facebook creates a handful of automatic lists for you, which it calls *smart lists*. The three default smart lists are Close Friends, Acquaintances, and Family.

In addition, Facebook creates smart lists based on your work, school, and local affiliations. For example, if you went to college at Indiana University, you might see an Indiana University list, populated with friends who went to school there. If you worked at Dow Chemical, you might see a Dow Chemical list with your friends who also worked there.

Add Friends to a List

You can add friends to Facebook's built-in smart lists or to lists you've previously created. You can even assign any given friend to multiple lists.

1. Navigate to a friend's Timeline page and click the Friends button.
2. Click Add to Another List.
3. Click the name of the group you want to add this friend to.

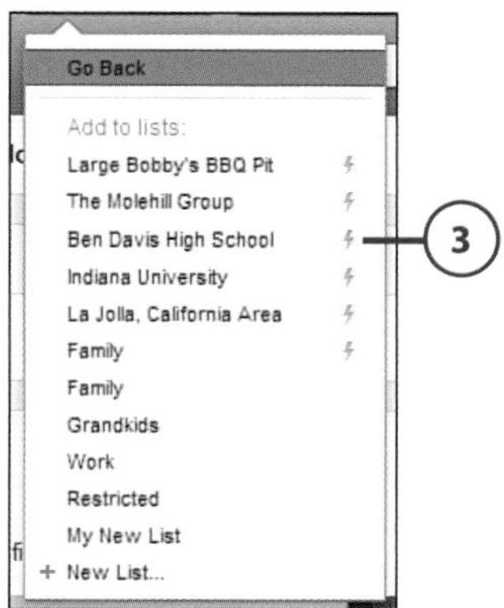

Create a New Friends List

You can create as many tightly focused friends lists as you like. You create a new list by choosing the first friend to add to that list; you can then add other friends to that list.

1. Navigate to a friend's Timeline page and click the Friends button.
2. Click Add to Another List.

3. Click New List.
4. Enter a name for this list into the New List box.

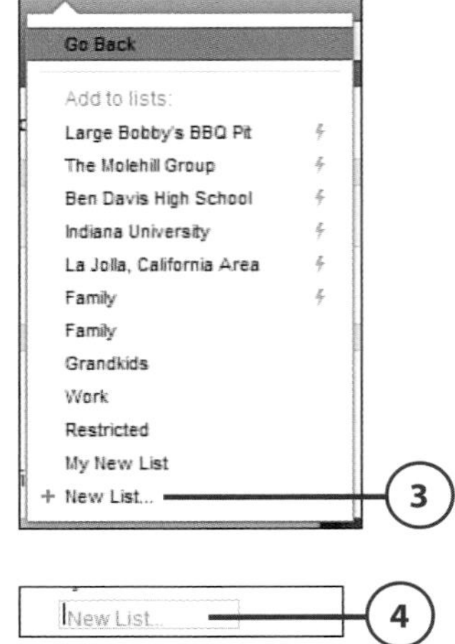

Remove a Friend from a List

What do you do if you accidentally place someone in the wrong list—or later decide you don't want to include an individual in that list? It's easy to remove any given person from a Facebook list.

1. Navigate to a friend's Timeline page and click the Friends button.
2. Click Add to Another List. This displays a list of all your current lists; the lists this person belongs to have check marks next to their names.
3. *Uncheck* the name of the group you want to delete this friend from.

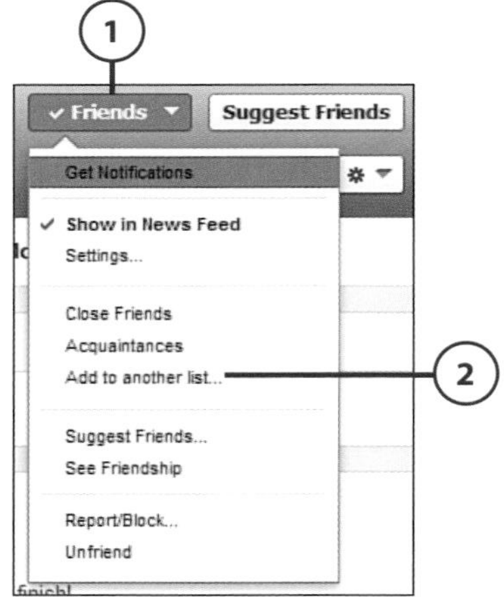

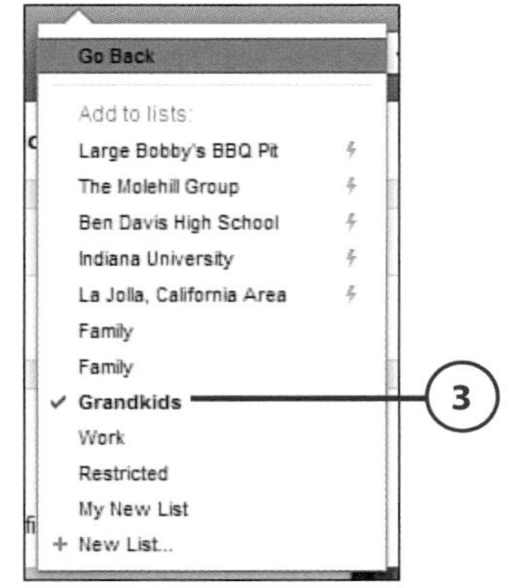

Viewing and Posting to Your Friends Lists

After you've created a customized friends list, you can then post new status updates directly to the people on that list. You can also read posts only from people on that list. Both of these activities are real time-savers and help you target the posts you make to those people most interested in them.

View Posts from a Friends List

One of the benefits of friends lists is making it easy to read only those updates from list members. All your friends lists are displayed in the Friends section of the left sidebar on the Facebook home page.

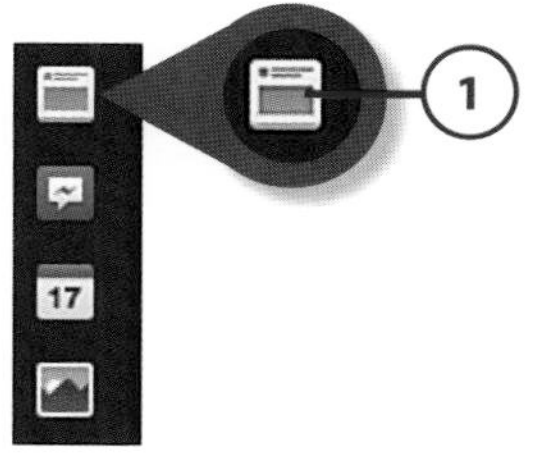

1. Click News Feed in the sidebar menu to display your Home page.
2. Go to the Feeds list and click See All; this expands the Feeds list to display all your friends lists.

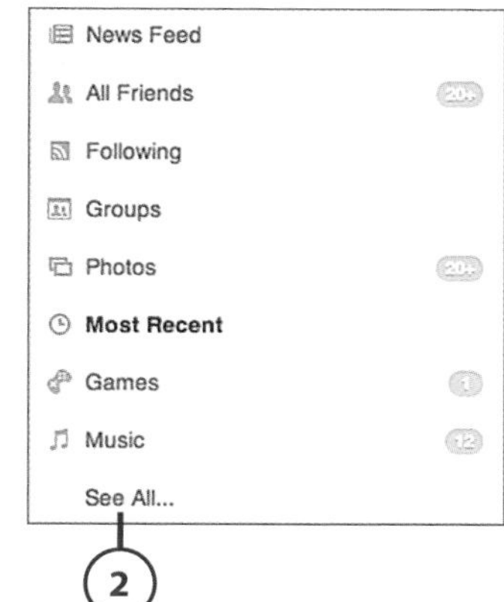

3. Click the list you want to see in your feed.

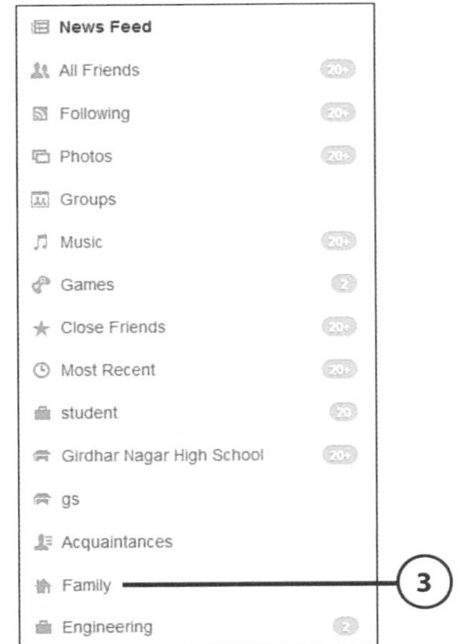

Send a Status Update to a Friends List

When you're creating a new status update, you can opt to post only to members of a given list. This lets you target specific posts to specific groups of people, based on the topic.

1. Go to your Facebook home page and create a status update as you would normally.
2. Click the Privacy button to display the list of options; this should include your most-used custom friends lists.
3. If the friends list you want isn't displayed, click See All Lists to view additional lists.
4. Click the name of the list you want to post to.
5. Click the Post button to send the status update to members of the selected list.

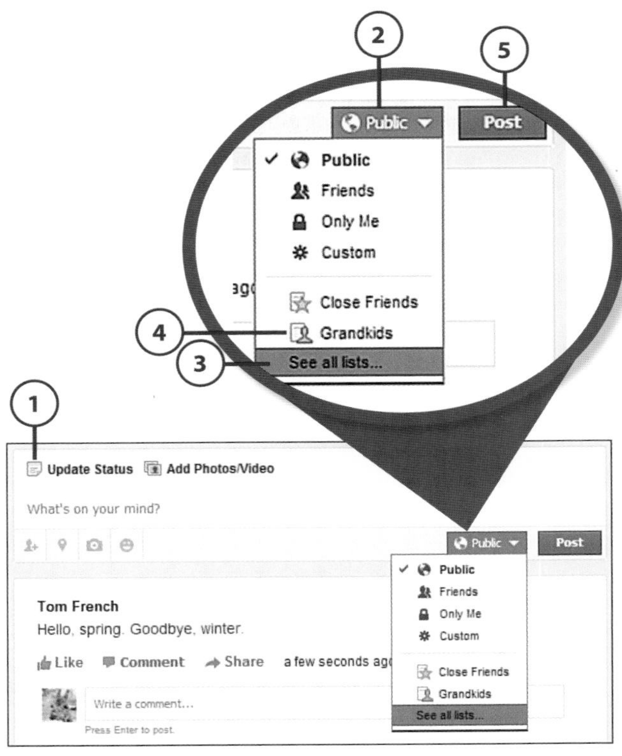

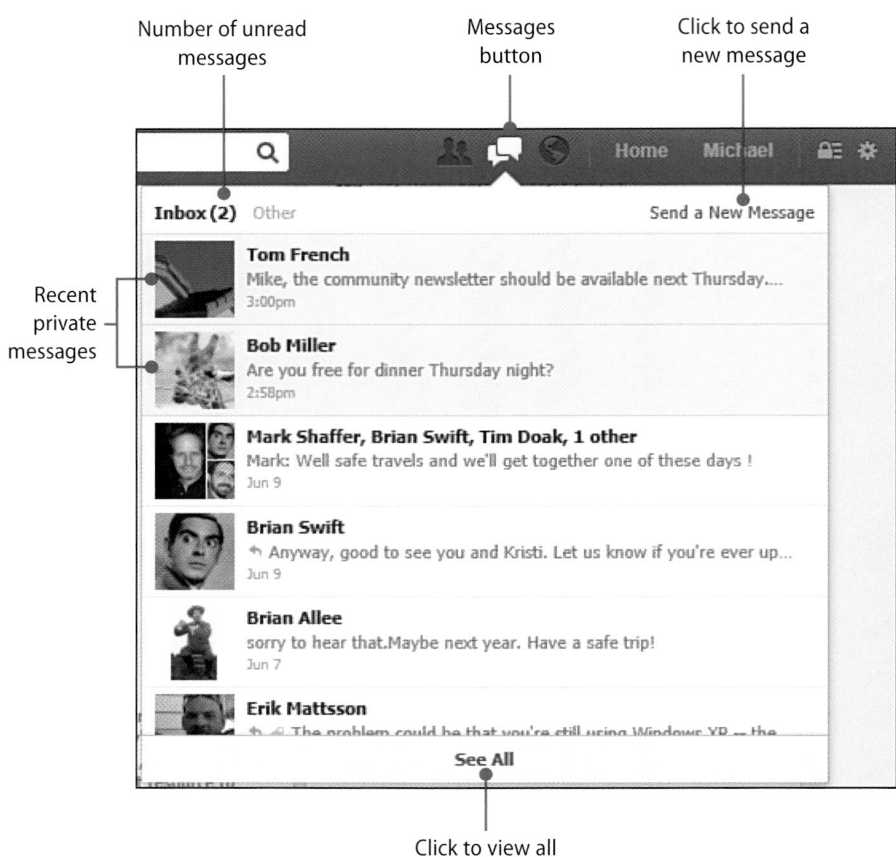
Number of unread messages
Messages button
Click to send a new message
Home
Michael
Inbox (2)
Other
Send a New Message
Recent private messages
Tom French
Mike, the community newsletter should be available next Thursday....
3:00pm
Bob Miller
Are you free for dinner Thursday night?
2:58pm
Mark Shaffer, Brian Swift, Tim Doak, 1 other
Mark: Well safe travels and we'll get together one of these days !
Jun 9
Brian Swift
Anyway, good to see you and Kristi. Let us know if you're ever up...
Jun 9
Brian Allee
sorry to hear that.Maybe next year. Have a safe trip!
Jun 7
Erik Mattsson
See All
Click to view all private messages

In this chapter you find out how to send and receive private messages to and from other Facebook users.

- → Sending Private Messages
- → Viewing Private Messages

9

Exchanging Private Messages

Facebook is a public social network, which means it encourages public interaction between you and your friends. But you might not want all your communication to be public; sometimes you just want to send a private message to someone you know.

That's why, in addition to its public status updates, Facebook includes a private messaging feature for its members. It's kind of like sending an email to a friend or family member—but without having to access your email program or service.

Sending Private Messages

Facebook lets any user send private messages to any other user. These messages do not appear on either person's News Feed or Timeline page; it's the Facebook equivalent of private email.

Send a Private Message

Sending a private message to another Facebook user is as easy as sending an email to that person—even easier, actually. Your master Facebook friends list functions much as a contacts list in an email program; you can add a recipient to a message just by typing a few letters of her name.

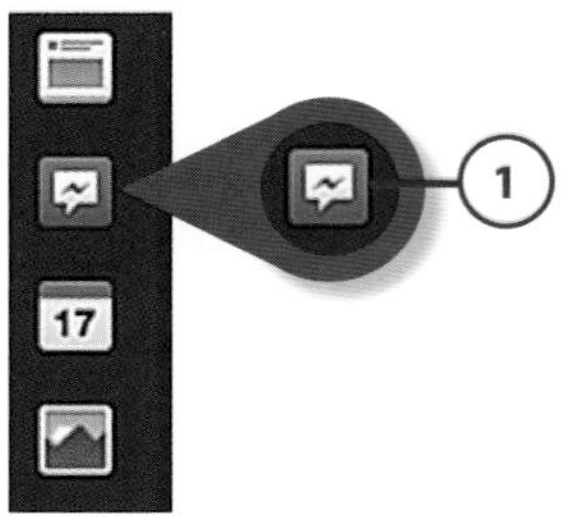

1. Click Messages in the sidebar menu to display the Messages page.

2. Click the New Message button to display the New Message pane.
3. Enter the name of the recipient into the To box.
4. As you type, Facebook displays matching friends; select the desired recipient from the list.

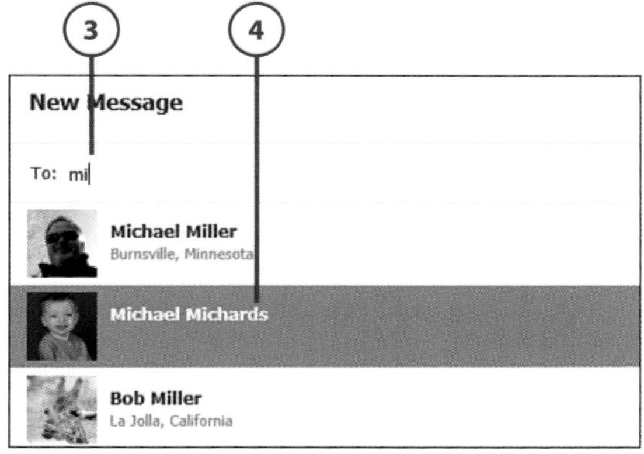

5. Enter your message into the Write a Message box.
6. Press Enter or click the Send button to send the message on its way.

>>>Go Further

FACEBOOK EMAIL

One important feature of Facebook's Messages system is that every Facebook member has his own unique @facebook.com email address, linked to his or her Facebook username and account. For example, if your Facebook username is **johnsmith**, your Facebook email address is **johnsmith@facebook.com**.

This email address comes in handy when you want to communicate with someone who is not a Facebook member. When you send a private message to another Facebook user, it's delivered via Facebook's Messages system. But when you send a message to someone who is not a Facebook user, it's delivered via email, using your Facebook email address. So you don't have to exit to your normal email service to send a message to a non-Facebook user; you can do it all from within Facebook.

Share a Photo via Private Message

Facebook's private messages are quite similar to traditional emails. This includes providing the ability to include photos in your messages. This is a great way to privately share those family photos you've uploaded to Facebook—without making them public for all of Facebook to see.

1. Open a new private message as described in the "Send a Private Message" task.
2. Click Add Photos to open the Choose File to Upload or Open dialog box.
3. Navigate and select the picture you want to attach.
4. Click the Open button.

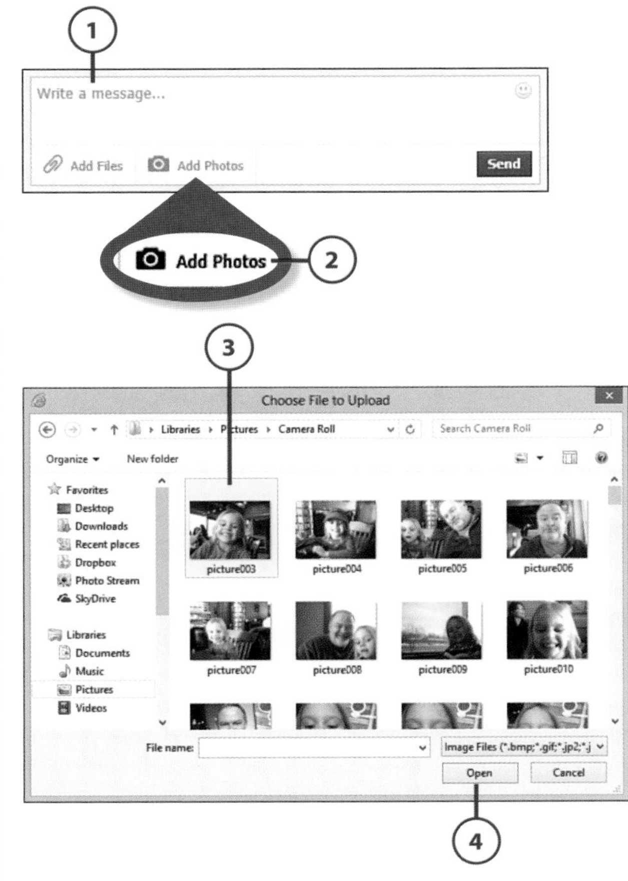

5. Complete your message and click the Send button.

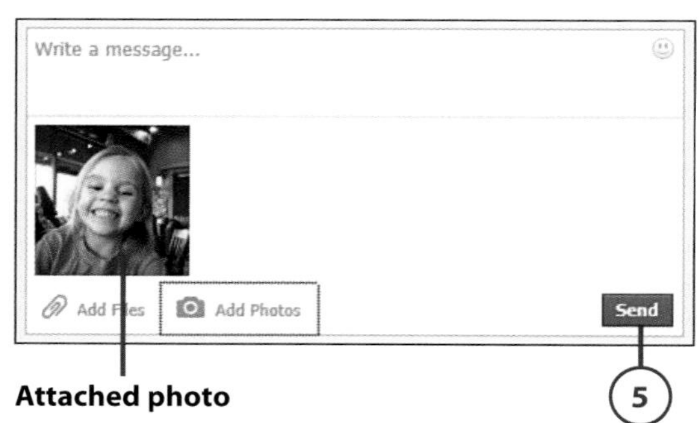

Attached photo

Photos and Videos

You can also send videos via Facebook private message. Follow these same steps, but select a video file instead of an image file.

Attach a File to a Message

You can also use Facebook's private message system to send other types of files to your Facebook friends. For example, you might want to send a Word document file to someone you work with on community projects, or an Excel spreadsheet file to your accountant or financial advisor.

1. Open a new private message as described in the "Send a Private Message" task.
2. Click Add Files to open the Choose File to Upload or Open dialog box.
3. Navigate to and select the file you want to attach.
4. Click the Open button.
5. Complete your message and click the Send button.

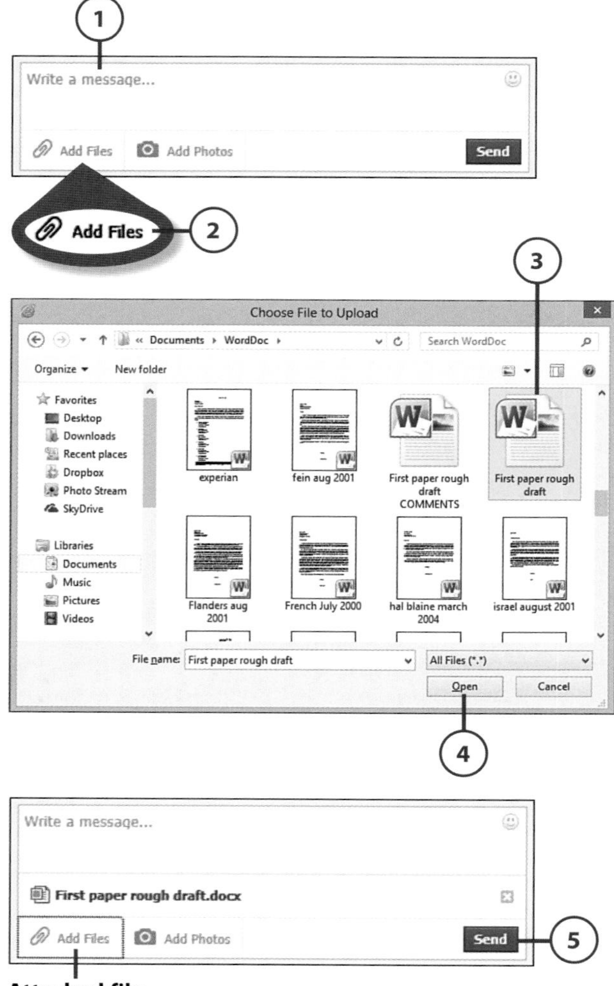

Attached file

Viewing Private Messages

When you receive a new private message from a friend, you see a red number on top of the Messages button on the Facebook toolbar. Click the Messages button to read all your new private messages. Better yet, open the separate Messages page to view all your private messages—new and old.

Read a Message

Facebook's Messages page serves as your inbox for all messages sent to you from across the Facebook site, including private messages, email messages, chat (instant) messages, and even text messages sent via mobile phone. To Facebook, one type of message is just like another; it really doesn't distinguish between the different types of messages.

Message Types

To see what type of message you've received on the Messages page, look for the icon displayed next to each message, beside the time/date indicator. An envelope icon indicates an email message; a word balloon icon indicates a chat or instant message; a phone icon indicates a text message; and no icon means you got a private message from a Facebook friend.

---

1. Click the Messages button in the Facebook toolbar to view your most recent messages.
2. Click any message snippet to view the entire message in a separate page.
3. To view all your messages, click See All to open the Messages page.

4. All your messages and communications you've received are displayed here, newest first. Click a message header to read the message in the center content pane.
5. The content pane displays all messages to and from the same person, in the form of a flowing conversation. The newest messages are at the bottom of the page, so you'll probably need to scroll down to read them.

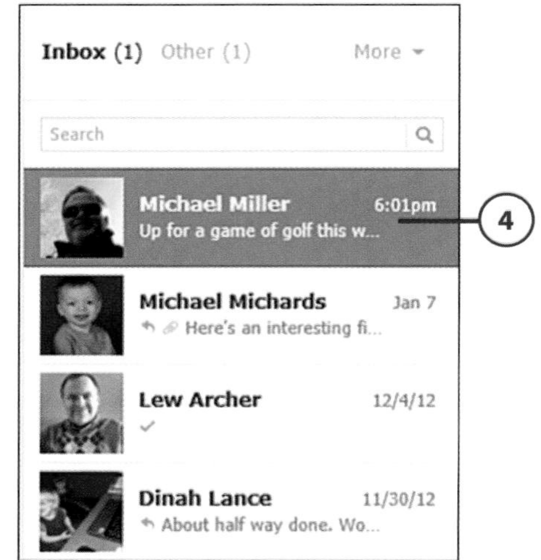

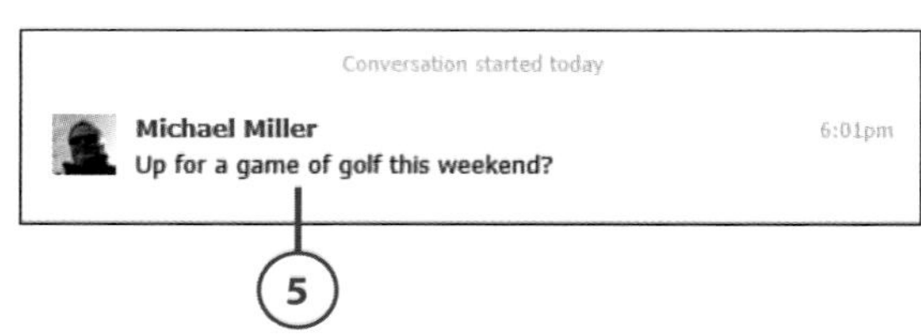

>>>Go Further

OTHER MESSAGES

Not all messages are displayed on the main Messages page. By default, the Inbox displays only messages from other Facebook members, not messages sent via email from outsiders.

To view messages sent from non-Facebook members to your Facebook email address, click Other at the top of the sidebar. This also displays messages invitations from Facebook pages you've liked.

Reply to a Message

Naturally, you can reply to any private message sent to you from another Facebook member. You do this from the message itself on the Messages page.

1. Open the Messages page and click the message you want to reply to.
2. Enter your message into the text box at the bottom of the content pane.
3. Click Reply to send the new message to your Facebook friend.

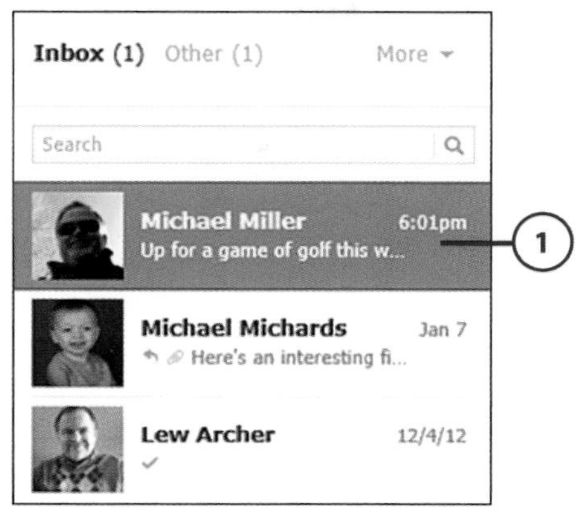

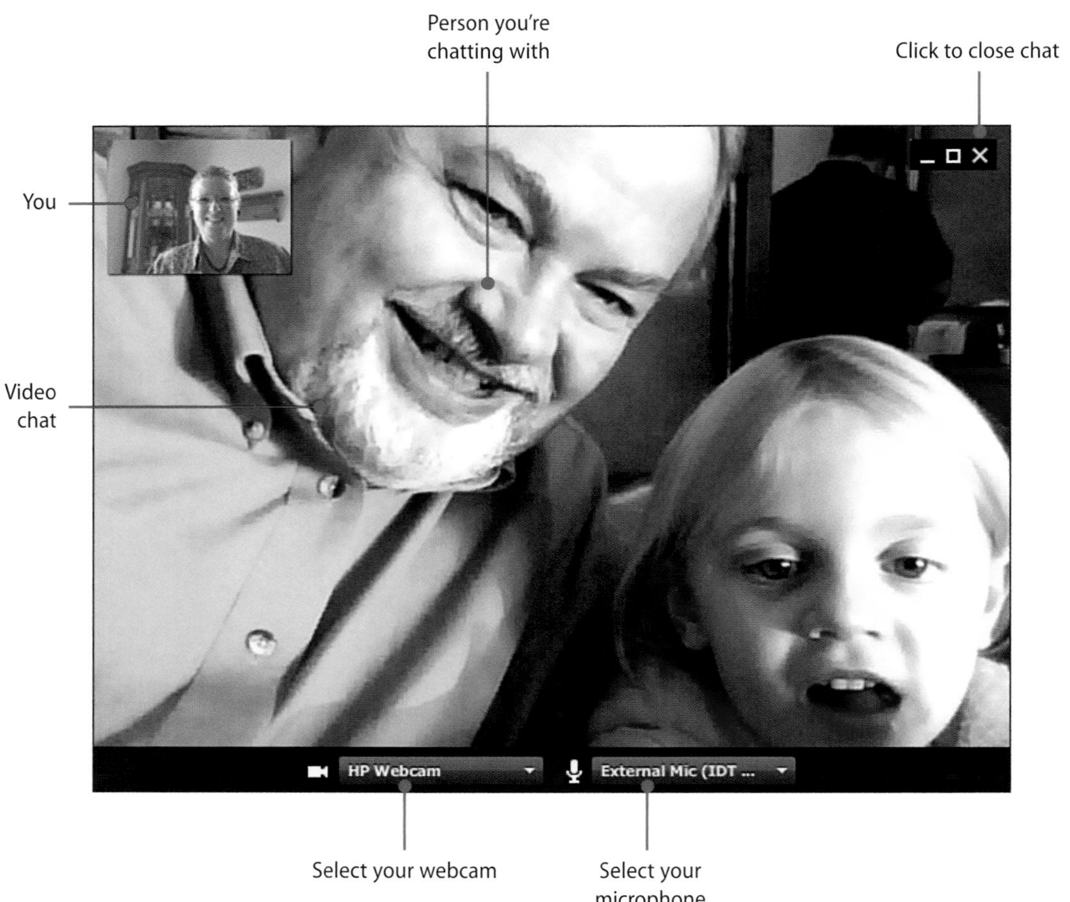
Person you're chatting with
Click to close chat
You
Video chat
HP Webcam
External Mic (IDT ...
Select your webcam
Select your microphone

In this chapter you find out how to conduct one-on-one text and video chats with your Facebook friends.

- → Text Chatting on Facebook
- → Video Chatting on Facebook

10

Chatting with Friends and Family in Real Time

If you have family members who have moved far away from the family home, if you're a snowbird, or if you just like to travel, you know how hard it is to spend long times away from the people you love. Exchanging the occasional email is fine, but it's not quite the same as being there.

Facebook has a solution to this problem—two solutions, actually. First, you can do online text messaging—what Facebook calls chat—with anyone on your Facebook friends list. And if that's not good enough, you can conduct face-to-face video chats with distant friends and family, using your computer screen and webcam. It's just like being there!

Text Chatting on Facebook

What Facebook calls chat is really a form of online instant messaging, which itself is kind of like text messaging, but on your computer instead of your phone. With Facebook chat you can carry on real-time text conversations with other Facebook members using the Facebook website.

Start a Chat Session

You can start a chat session with any of your Facebook friends who are also online and willing to spend a few minutes texting with you. It's a great way to go one-on-one with the people you love.

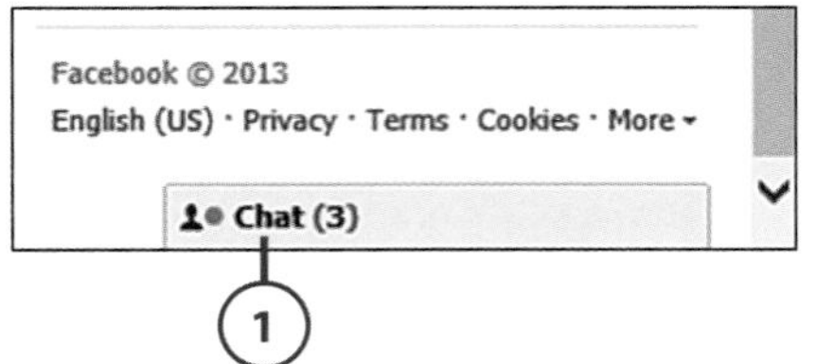

1. Click the Chat gadget at the bottom-right corner of any Facebook page to display the full Chat panel.

Wide Displays

If your web browser is wide enough, Facebook might display the Chat panel as part of the sidebar menu. If so, you'll see the list of online friends at the lower left of the page, underneath the other sidebar menu items.

2. Friends who are online and ready to chat are identified with a round green icon. Click the name of the friend you want to chat with to open an individual Chat panel with the selected friend.
3. Type a text message in the bottom text box and press Enter.
4. Your messages, along with your friend's responses, appear in consecutive order within the Chat panel. Continue typing new messages as you want.
5. To end the chat session and close the Chat panel, click the X at the top right of the panel.

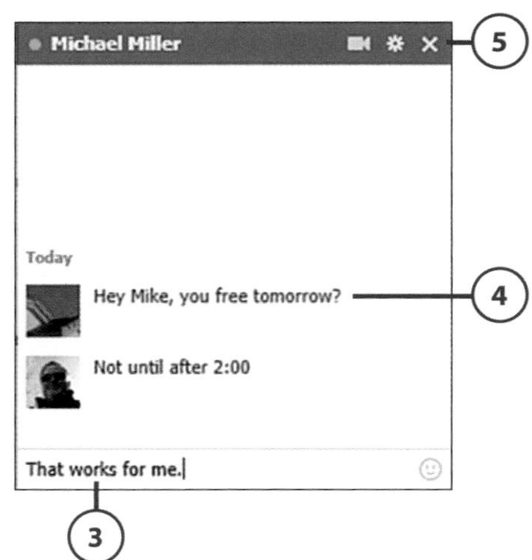

Answer a Chat Request

You can initiate a chat session with a friend, or a friend can invite you to chat. Answering a chat request is as easy as typing on your computer keyboard.

1. When another user invites you to chat, you hear a short sound and see a new Chat panel for that person open on your Facebook page.
2. Start typing to reply to your friend's initial message. Your conversation appears in the body of the Chat panel.
3. To end the chat session, click the X at the top of the Chat panel.

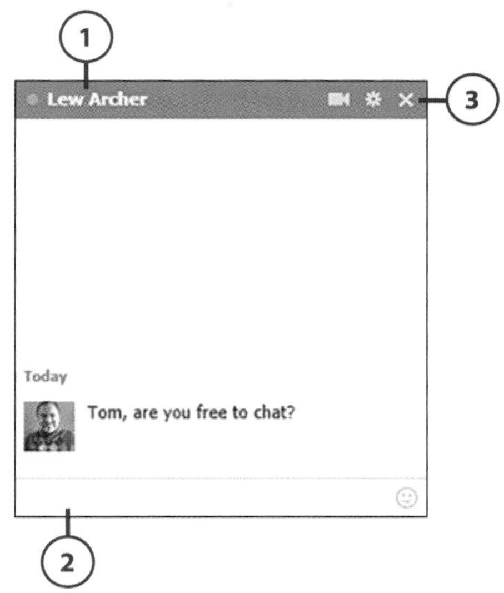

>>>Go Further

DISABLING CHAT

If you'd rather not be available for online chats, you can turn off Facebook chat. Open the Chat panel, click the Options (gear) button, and then click Turn Off Chat. To turn Chat back on, repeat this process and click Turn On Chat instead.

You can also choose to "hide" from certain friends in chat by clicking the Options button and then clicking Advanced. When the Advanced Chat Settings dialog box appears, check Turn On Chat for All Friends Except and then enter the names of those friends you don't want to chat with.

Likewise, you can choose to enable chat only for certain friends. Open the Advanced Chat Settings dialog box, check Turn On Chat for Only Some Friends, and then enter the names of selected friends.

Video Chatting on Facebook

If you have a webcam built into or attached to your computer, you can talk to other Facebook users face-to-face using Facebook's video chat feature. Video chatting is a great way to get up-close and personal with distant family and friends; you can see them and they can see you.

Skype

Facebook's video chat feature is powered by Skype, one of the more popular Internet-based voice and video communication services. In fact, you can connect your Facebook and Skype accounts, so that your Facebook friends appear as Skype contacts.

Start a Video Chat

You can establish a video chat with any of your Facebook friends who have a working webcam on their computers. Naturally, the friend you want to talk to also has to be online at the same time you are, but then you can fire up your webcams and start talking.

Install the Chat Applet

The first time you use Facebook's video chat, you are prompted to download and install the necessary background chat applet on your computer. Follow the onscreen instructions to do so.

1. Go to your friend's Timeline page and click the Call button. (If your friend doesn't have a working webcam, you won't see a Call button.)

2. When your friend answers the call, Facebook displays the video chat window. Your friend appears in the main part of the window; your picture is in a smaller window at the top left. All you have to do is talk.

3. When you're ready to close the chat, hover over the chat window and then click the X at the top-right corner.

Webcams and Microphones

Most webcams (and notebooks with built-in webcams) also have built-in microphones. The camera in the webcam captures your picture, and the microphone in the webcam captures your voice. Just speak into the webcam to talk during a video chat.

Convert a Text Chat into a Video Chat

You can also start a video chat from within a current text chat.

1. Go to your Facebook home page and click the Chat gadget at the bottom-right corner to display the full Chat panel.

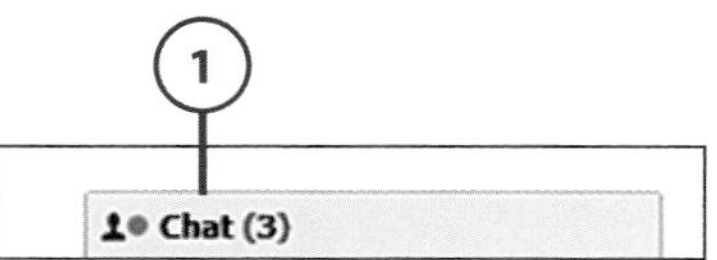

2. Click the name of the friend you want to chat with to open a new individual Chat panel.

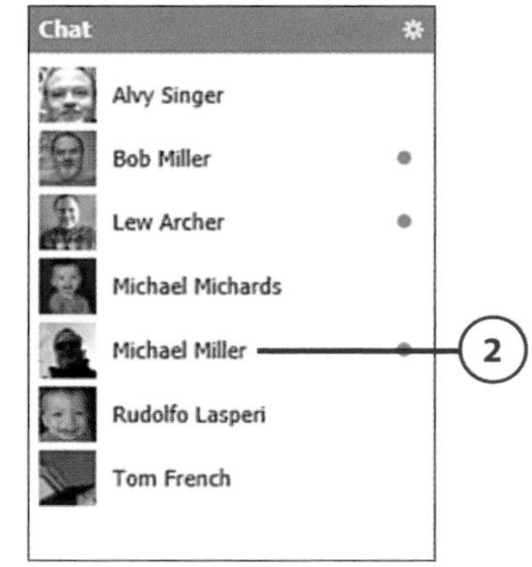

3. Click the video camera icon in the top-right corner of the Chat panel to switch to a video chat; this opens a new video chat window.
4. When you're ready to close the chat, hover over the chat window and then click the X at the top-right corner.

>>>Go Further

VIDEO MESSAGES

If your friend is unavailable to chat, Facebook prompts you to leave a video message for that person. Your friend can then view and respond to that message when she's next online.

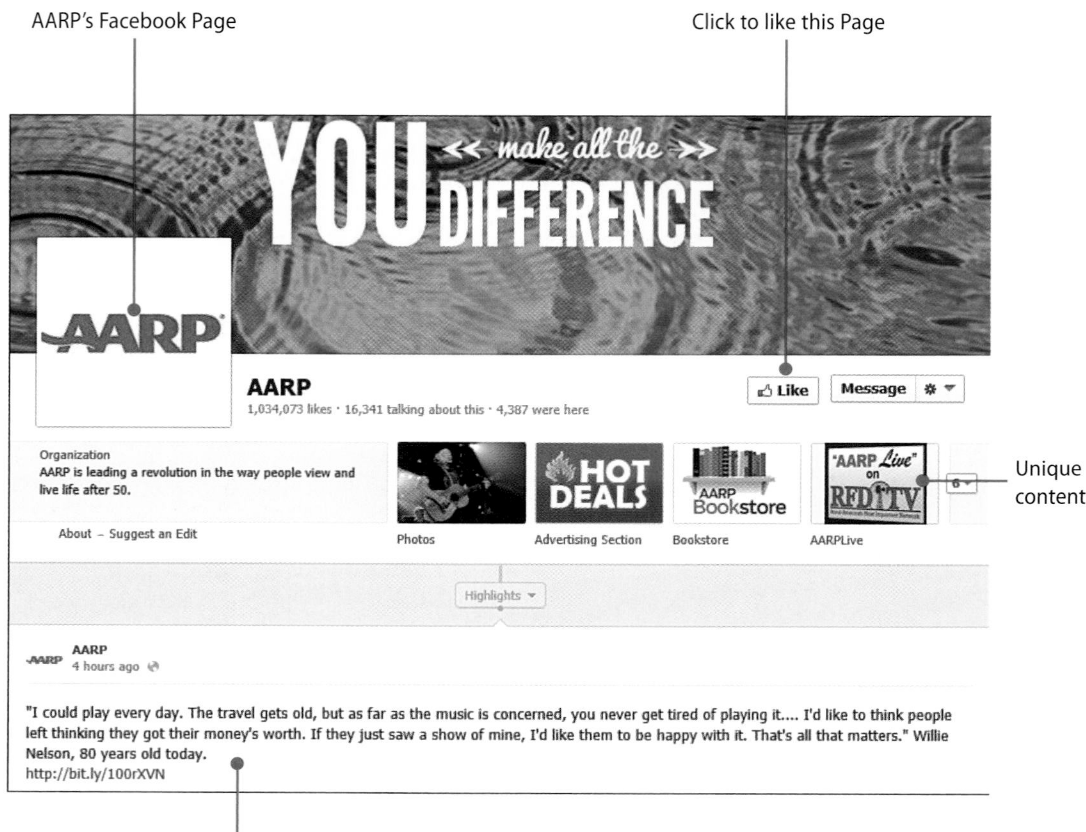
AARP's Facebook Page
Click to like this Page
YOU make all the DIFFERENCE
AARP
AARP
1,034,073 likes · 16,341 talking about this · 4,387 were here
Like
Message
Organization
AARP is leading a revolution in the way people view and live life after 50.
About – Suggest an Edit
HOT DEALS
AARP Bookstore
"AARP Live" on RFD TV
Photos
Advertising Section
Bookstore
AARPLive
Unique content
Highlights
AARP
4 hours ago
"I could play every day. The travel gets old, but as far as the music is concerned, you never get tired of playing it.... I'd like to think people left thinking they got their money's worth. If they just saw a show of mine, I'd like them to be happy with it. That's all that matters." Willie Nelson, 80 years old today.
http://bit.ly/100rXVN
Status updates

In this chapter you find out how to follow companies and celebrities on Facebook.

→ Finding Companies and Celebrities on Facebook
→ Following Companies and Celebrities on Facebook
→ Managing the Pages You Follow

Liking Pages from Companies and Celebrities

Regular people on Facebook have their own Timeline pages. Businesses and celebrities on Facebook, however, have their own special pages that are kind of like Timeline pages but different; they're tailored for the needs of customers and fans. These pages—rather unimaginatively called Facebook Pages—are how you keep abreast of what your favorite brands, products, and celebrities are up to.

Finding Companies and Celebrities on Facebook

Even though businesses, celebrities, and public figures aren't regular users, they still want to use Facebook to connect with their customers and fans. They do this through Facebook Pages—essentially Timeline pages for companies and public figures. If you're a fan of a given company or celebrity, you can "like" that entity's Facebook page—and keep abreast of what that company or individual is up to. It's kind of like joining an online fan club through Facebook.

Search for Companies and Celebrities

Many companies and organizations have Facebook Pages for their brands and the products they sell. For example, you can find and follow Pages for Walmart, Starbucks, McDonalds, and the AARP on Facebook.

Many famous people—entertainers, athletes, news reporters, politicians, and the like—also have Facebook Pages. So if you're a fan of Paul McCartney, Tom Hanks, Jack Nicklaus, or Bill O'Reilly, you can follow any or all of them via the Facebook Pages.

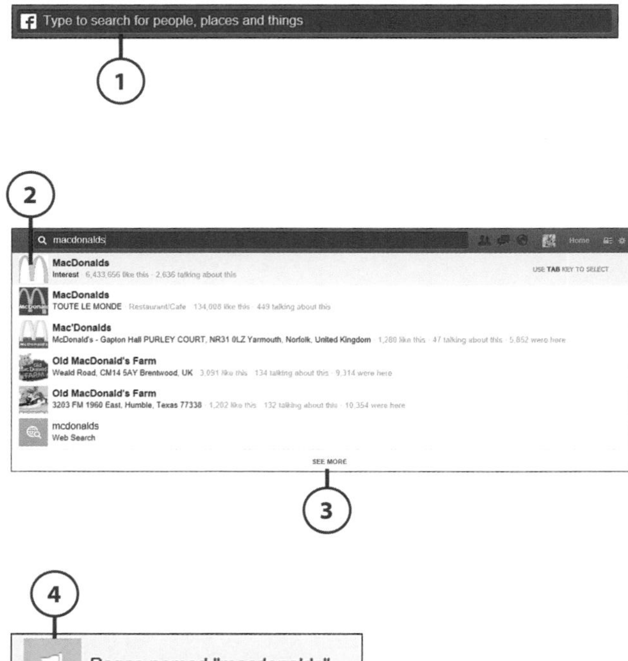

1. Enter one or more keywords that describe the person, company, or organization into the Search box on the Facebook toolbar. As you type, Facebook displays a list of pages and people that match your query.
2. If the Page you want is listed, click it.
3. If the Page you want is not listed, click See More at the bottom of the list.
4. Click the Pages Named entry to display a list of pages that match your query.
5. Click the name of the Page you want to view.

View a Facebook Page

A professional Facebook Page is very similar to a personal Timeline page, right down to the timeline of updates and activities. Pages can feature specialized content, however, which is located at the top of the page, under the cover image. For example, a musician's page might feature an audio player for that performer's songs; other pages might let you view pictures and videos, or even purchase items online.

1. Click About to read more about this person or company.
2. Click Photos to view the Page's official pictures.
3. Click any other content to view that content.
4. Click and type into the Post box to post your own message to this Page.
5. Scroll down to view status updates and other postings.
6. Click Like to like a specific post.
7. Click Comment and then type into the Comment box to leave a comment on a specific post.

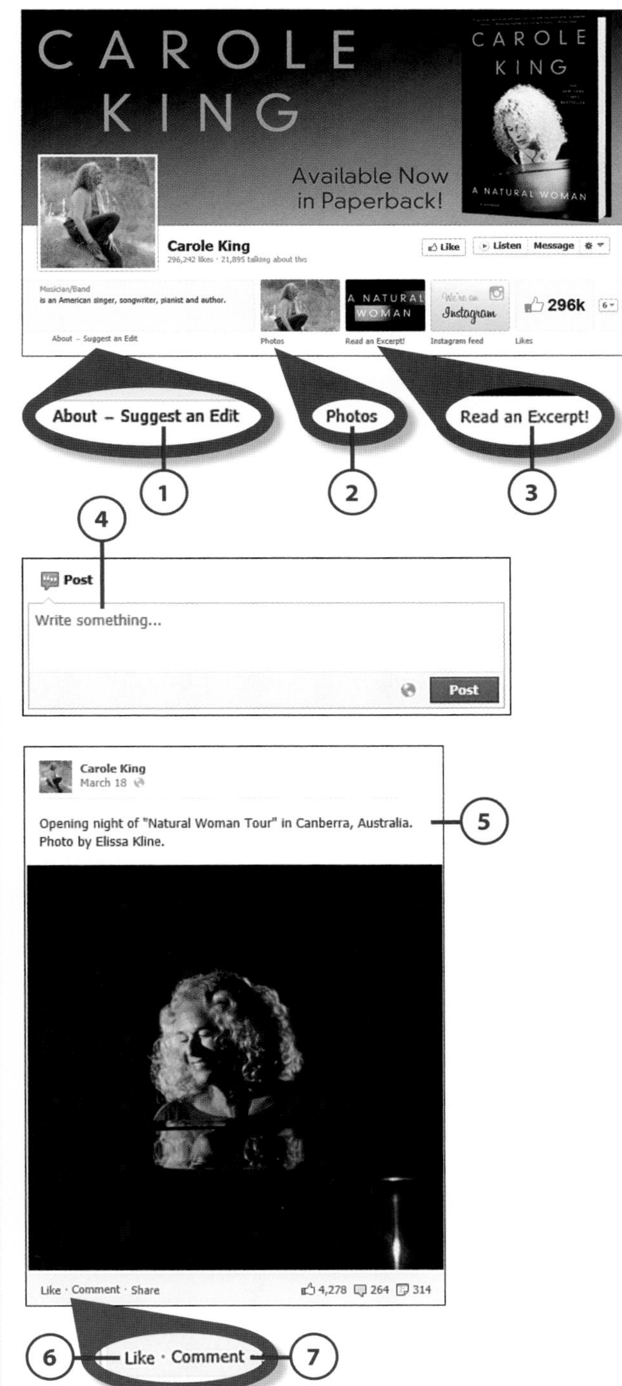

>>>Go Further

WHO GETS A PAGE?

Just about any public person or entity can create a Facebook page. You can create Facebook pages for businesses, brands, and products; for musicians, actors, and other celebrities; for politicians, public servants, and other public figures; and for school classes, public organizations, special events, and social causes.

If you want to create your own Page for your business or community organization, go to www.facebook.com/pages/, click the Create Page button, and follow the onscreen instructions from there. To create a Page you must be an official representative of the group or company behind the page; fans can't create official Pages for the companies and entertainers they follow.

Following Companies and Celebrities on Facebook

Most companies and celebrities with Facebook pages use their Pages to keep their customers or fans informed of news and events. Some companies use their Pages to offer promotions and special offers to customers.

Updates from a given company or celebrity appear on that entity's Facebook Page. You can also view posts from the Pages you've liked in a special Following feed you can display on your Facebook home page.

Like a Facebook Page

A celebrity or company on Facebook can't be your friend; that is, you can't add a professional Page to your Facebook friends list. Instead, you can choose to like that Page so that you can follow all the posts made by that entity. Unlike friending an individual, the Pages you like do not follow all the status updates that you make on a regular basis. You can begin following a Page by using one of the following options.

Liking

Liking is a one-way thing. When you like a Page you follow that Page, but that Page doesn't follow you.

1. From any list of Pages, click the Like button to follow a specific page.
2. From a company or celebrity's Facebook Page, click the Like button to follow that page.

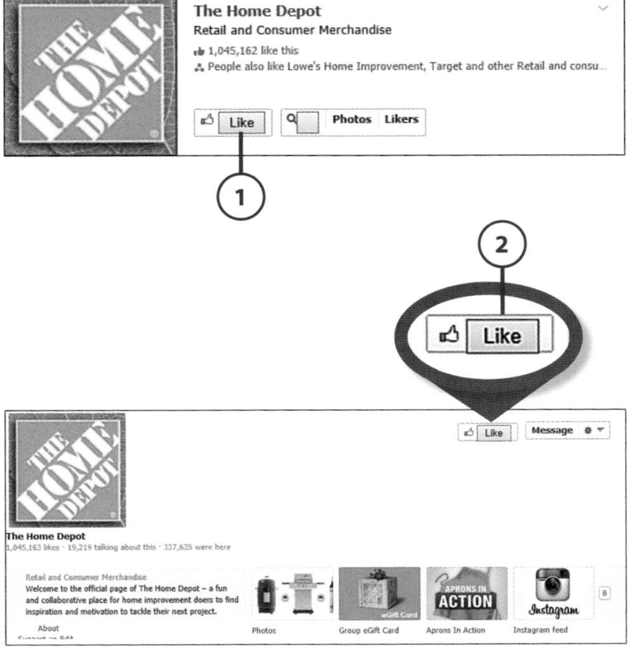

View Posts from Pages You Like

Obviously, you can visit a given Page to view the latest updates and content. You can also view updates from all the Pages you like in Facebook's Following feed. This is kind of like a News Feed for the Pages you've liked, not for the individuals you're friends with.

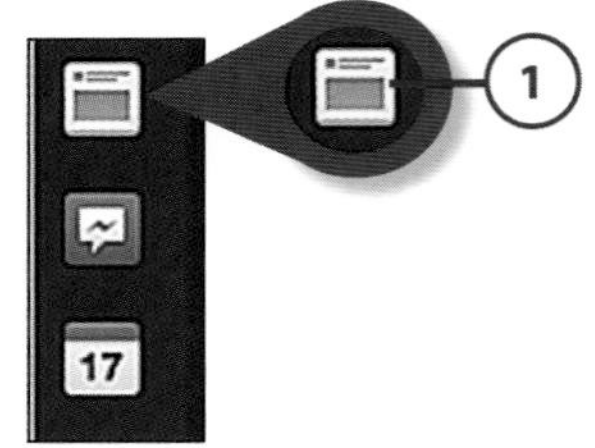

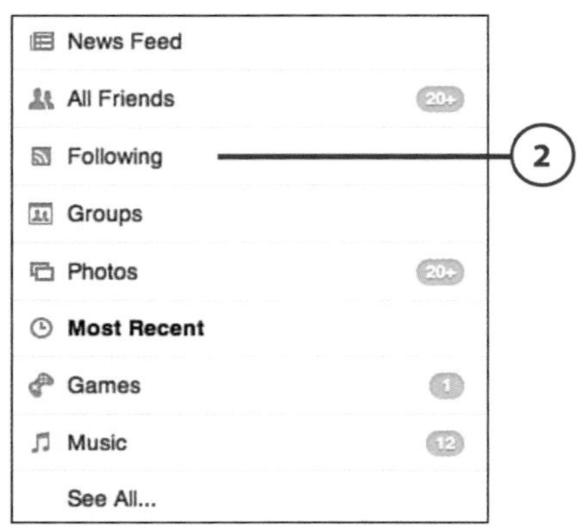

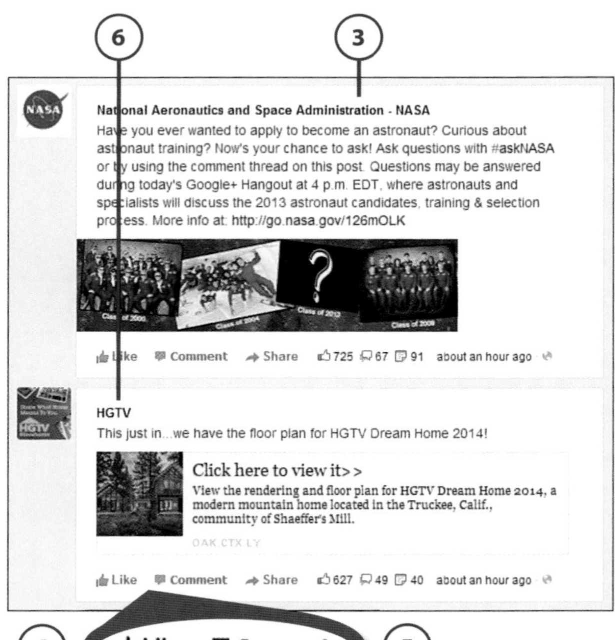

1. Click the News Feed icon in the sidebar menu to display your Facebook home page.
2. Click Following in the Feed list to change the News Feed to the Following feed.
3. Posts from all the Pages you follow are listed here, newest first. Scroll down to view more posts.
4. Click Like to like a status update.
5. Click Comment and type into the Comment box to comment on an update.
6. Click the Page's name to go to that Facebook Page.

Managing the Pages You Follow

Some people only follow a handful of professional Facebook Pages. Others find dozens of Pages to follow. If you're a more prolific follower, you might want to manage your Pages list over time.

View Your Favorite Pages

Not sure of who exactly you're following? Then it's time to display all your favorite Facebook Pages, in the Pages list.

1. Click your picture in the Facebook toolbar to display your Timeline page.
2. Click More under your cover image and select Likes to display those Pages you've liked.
3. Click the type of page you're looking for—Interests, Foods, Activities, and so on.
4. Click any given image to display that specific Page.

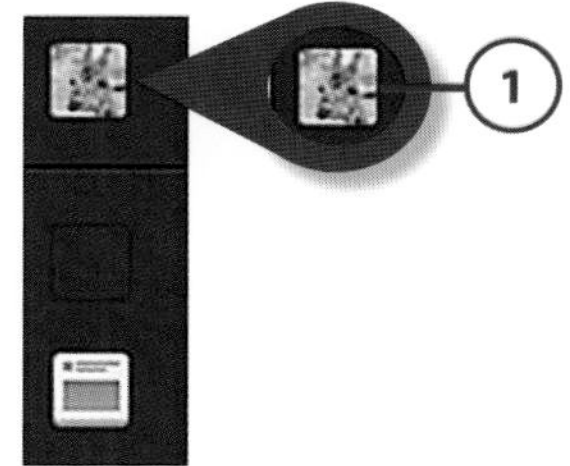

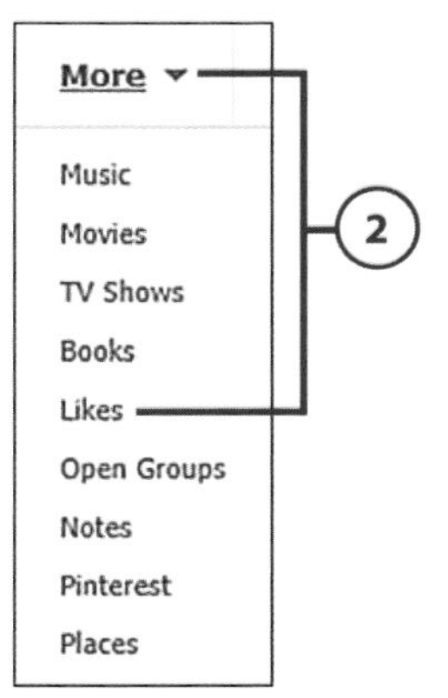

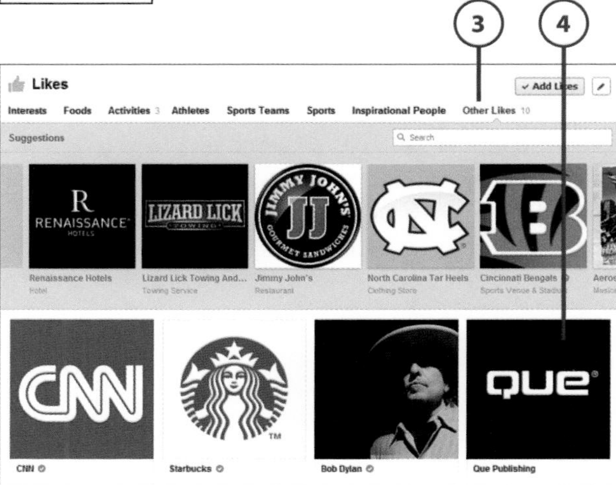

Unlike a Page

Just because you liked a given company or celebrity at one point in time doesn't mean you'll continue to like that entity forever. Your tastes change, after all, or you might find you don't like the posts a given Page is making.

When you find yourself not liking a Page so much, you can "unlike" that Page. Unliking a Page removes it from your Following feed, so you won't receive any more status updates or notifications from it.

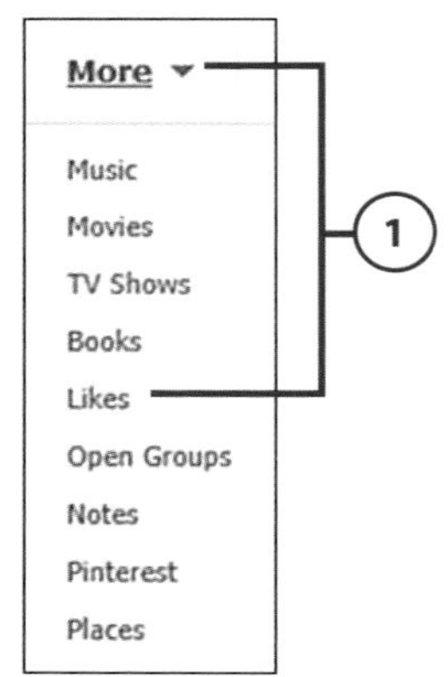

1. From your Timeline page, click More, Likes to display all the Pages you currently like.
2. Mouse over the image for the Page you no longer like and then mouse over the Liked button to display a menu of options.
3. Click Unlike.

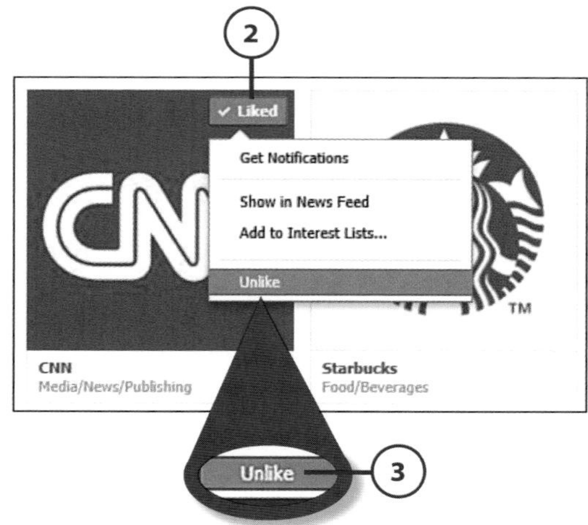

Re-liking

You can always re-like an unliked page in the future. Just repeat the steps in the "Like a Facebook Page" section, earlier in this chapter, to like the page, and you'll be following it again.

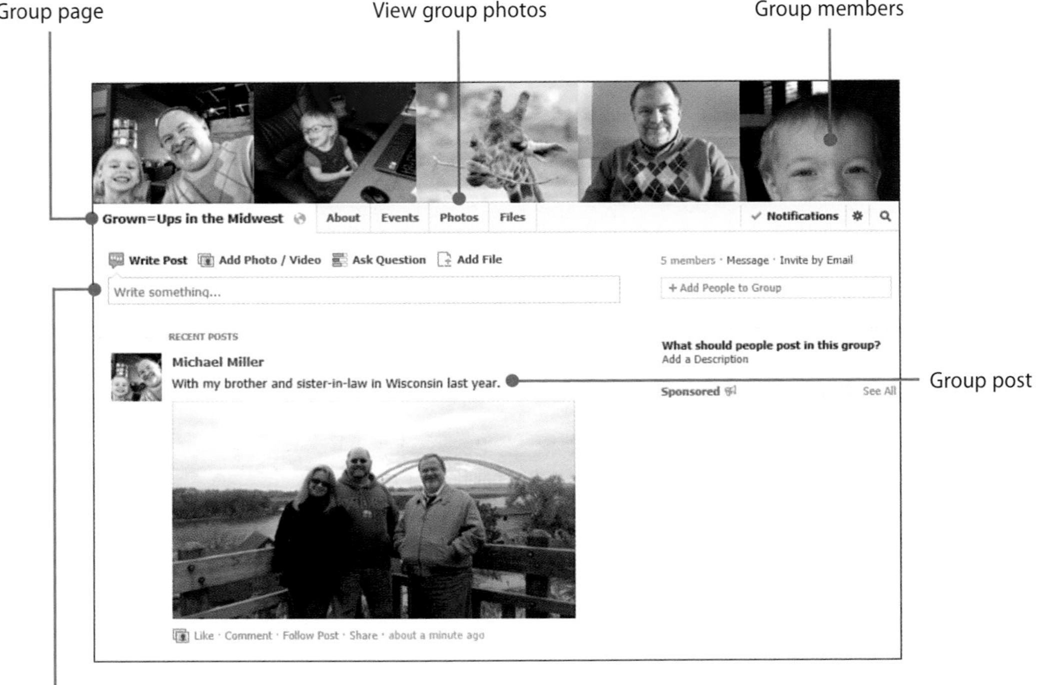

Post a message to the group

In chapter you find out how to find and participate in topic-oriented groups on Facebook.

→ Finding and Joining Facebook Groups
→ Participating in Facebook Groups
→ Managing Your Facebook Groups
→ Creating Your Own Facebook Group

12

Participating in Interesting Groups

As you read in the previous chapter, Facebook Pages are like fan clubs for companies and celebrities and other public figures. There are other kinds of "clubs" on Facebook, however, in the form of public *groups*. Facebook has groups for all types of interests, from quilting to photography to golf. You might even find groups dedicated to where you grew up or the people you knew back then.

A Facebook group is a way for you get together—virtually, of course—with others who share your interests. It's like an online club, in the form of a Facebook page!

Finding and Joining Facebook Groups

If you want to make new friends on Facebook, one of the best ways to do so is to search out others who share your interests. If you're into gardening, look for gardeners. If you're into recreational vehicles, look for fellow RVers. If you're a wine lover, look for other connoisseurs of the grape.

On Facebook, people who are interested in a given topic or hobby can socialize with each other in Facebook groups. A group takes the form of a special Facebook page, a place for people interested in that topic to meet online and exchange information and pleasantries.

Search for Groups

Facebook offers tens of thousands of different groups online, so chances are you can find one or more that suit you. The key is finding a particular group that matches what you're interested in—which you do by searching.

1. Go to the search box in the Facebook toolbar and enter one or more keywords that describe what you're looking for. For example, if you're interested in sewing, enter **sewing.** If you're interested in model airplanes, enter **model airplanes**. If you're looking for a group for the class of 1965, enter **class of 1965**.
2. As you type, Facebook displays a list of items that match your query. If you see an interesting group in this list, click it.
3. If you don't see any matching groups in this short list, go to the bottom of the list and click See More to expand the list.
4. Click the Groups Named entry to display a page of groups that match your query.

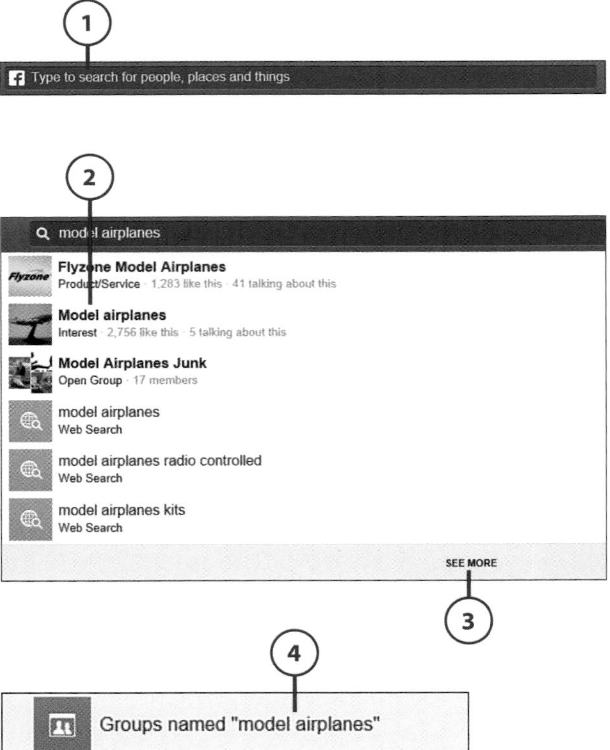

5. For each group listed you see a short description of the group and how many people are members. To view a group's Facebook page, click the name of the group.

Join a Group

After you find a group, you can officially join it—and then participate to whatever degree suits your fancy. You can join a group from the search results page, or from the group's Facebook page.

1. To join a group from the search results page, click the Join button.
2. To join a group from its Facebook page, click Join Group.

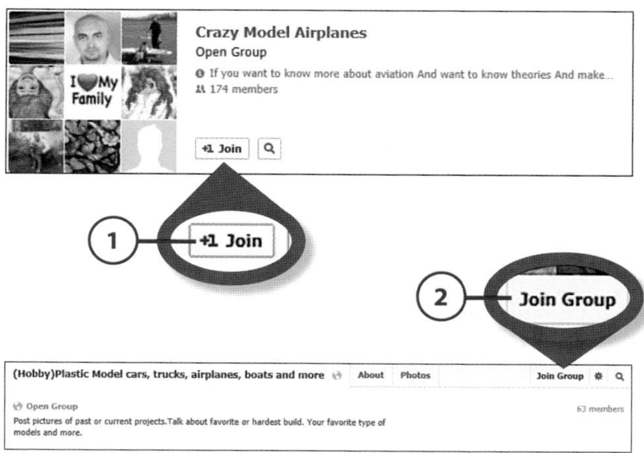

>>>Go Further

OPEN AND CLOSED GROUPS

Most groups are classified as Open groups, meaning they're open for all Facebook members to join. Some groups, however, are Closed groups, which require that the group administrator approve all requests for membership.

To join a Closed group, you must apply for membership, and hope that your request is granted. When you click the Join button, a request goes to the group administrator. If your request is granted, you receive a message that you've been approved and are now an official member of the group. If your request is not granted, you don't get any response.

Participating in Facebook Groups

What can you do in a Facebook group? Lots, actually. You can read the latest news, discover new information, view photos and movies, exchange messages with other group members, and engage in online discussions about the topic at hand. It's just like participating in a real-world club, except you do it all on Facebook.

Visit a Group Page

Although you can view a feed of messages from all your groups (covered later in this chapter), most people prefer to visit individual group pages. This enables you to partake in all of the resources available in a given group.

1. Go to your Timeline page and click More, Groups to display a list of all the groups you belong to.
2. Click the name of a group to open its Facebook page.

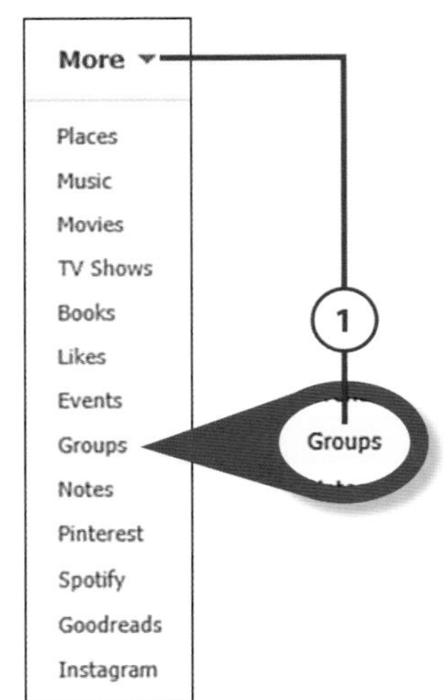

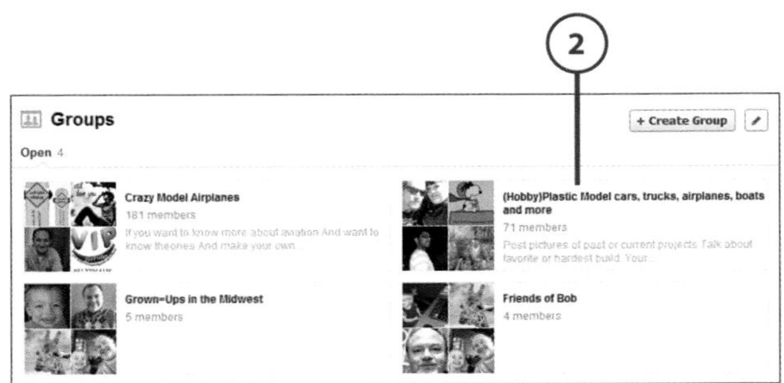

Read and Reply to Messages

After you open a group page, you can read messages posted by other members of the group and then like and comment on those messages as you would normal Facebook status updates.

Group Posts

Posts that you make on a group's Facebook page are only displayed on that page, not in individual members' News Feeds.

1. Open the group's page and scroll to the Recent Posts section to view posts from group members.
2. Click Like to like a particular post.
3. Click Comment to reply to a post and then enter your reply into the Comment box.
4. Click Share to share a post with your Facebook friends in your Facebook feed.

Post a New Message

Not only can you reply to posts made by other members, you can start a new discussion by posting a new message on the group's page. Other group members can then like and reply to your message.

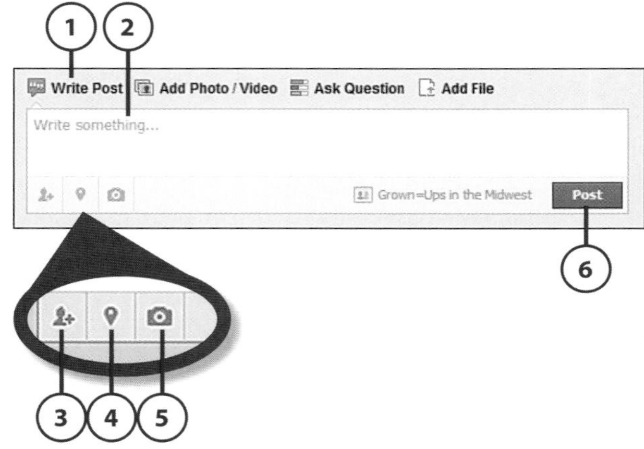

1. Open the group's page, scroll to the Publisher box, and click Write Post.
2. Enter your message into Write Something box; this expands the box.
3. Click the Who Are You With? button to tag another friend in this post.
4. Click the Where Are You? button to add a location to this post.
5. Click the Photos button to add one or more photographs to this post.
6. Click the Post button to post your message to the group.

View Group Members

Who belong to this particular group? It's easy to view all the members of a Facebook group.

1. Open the group's page and click About to display a list of group members.
2. To search for a particular member, enter that person's name into the Find a Member box and press Enter.
3. Mouse over a member's name to view more information about that person.
4. To send a message to a group member, mouse over that person's name and then click the Message button.
5. To add a group member as a friend, click Add Friend.
6. To view a person's Timeline page, click that member's name.

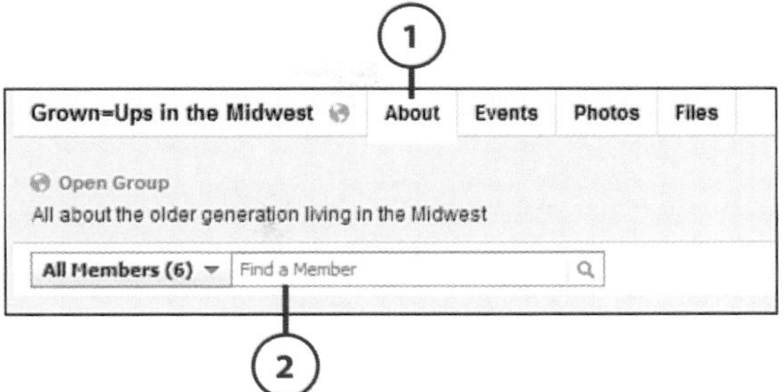

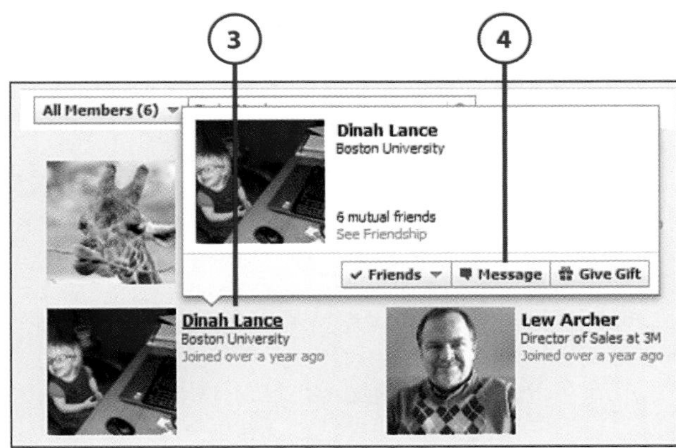

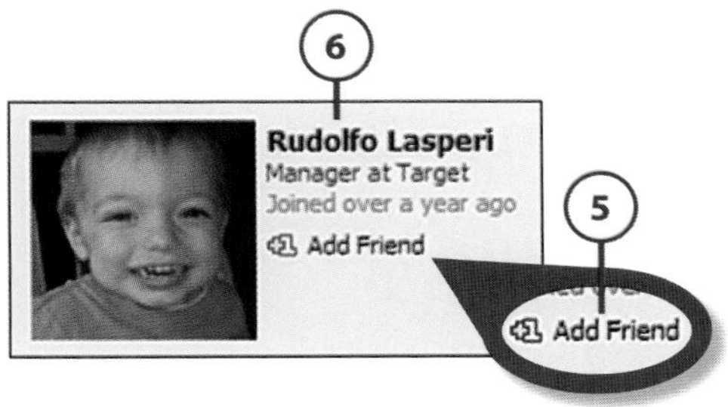

View Group Photos

Most groups let members post photos (and, in some cases, videos) of interest to other group members. If you're a member of a crafts group, for example, members might post photos of projects they've created. If you're a member of a group of old high school friends, members might post old photos from your school days. Viewing group photos, then, can be a fun activity.

1. Open the group's page and click Photos to display a list of group photos and photo albums.
2. Click a photo album to view all the photos in that album.
3. Click an individual photo to view that photo in a larger lightbox.

Upload Photos to the Group

You can upload your own photos to a group. This is a great way to share your activities with other group members.

1. Open the group's page and click Photos to display the group photos page.
2. Open the album to which you want to upload your photos.

No Album

If your group doesn't yet have any photo albums, click the Upload Photos button on the main photos page. After you choose the photo(s) to upload, you're prompted to create a new photo album.

3. Click Add Photos to display the Choose Files to Upload or Open dialog box.
4. Select the photo or photos you want to upload.
5. Click the Open button.
6. Enter a short description of the photo into the Say Something About This Photo box.
7. Click the Who Are You With? button to tag a person in this photo.
8. Click the Where Are You? button to add a location to this photo.
9. Click the Post Photos button to add these photos to the group.

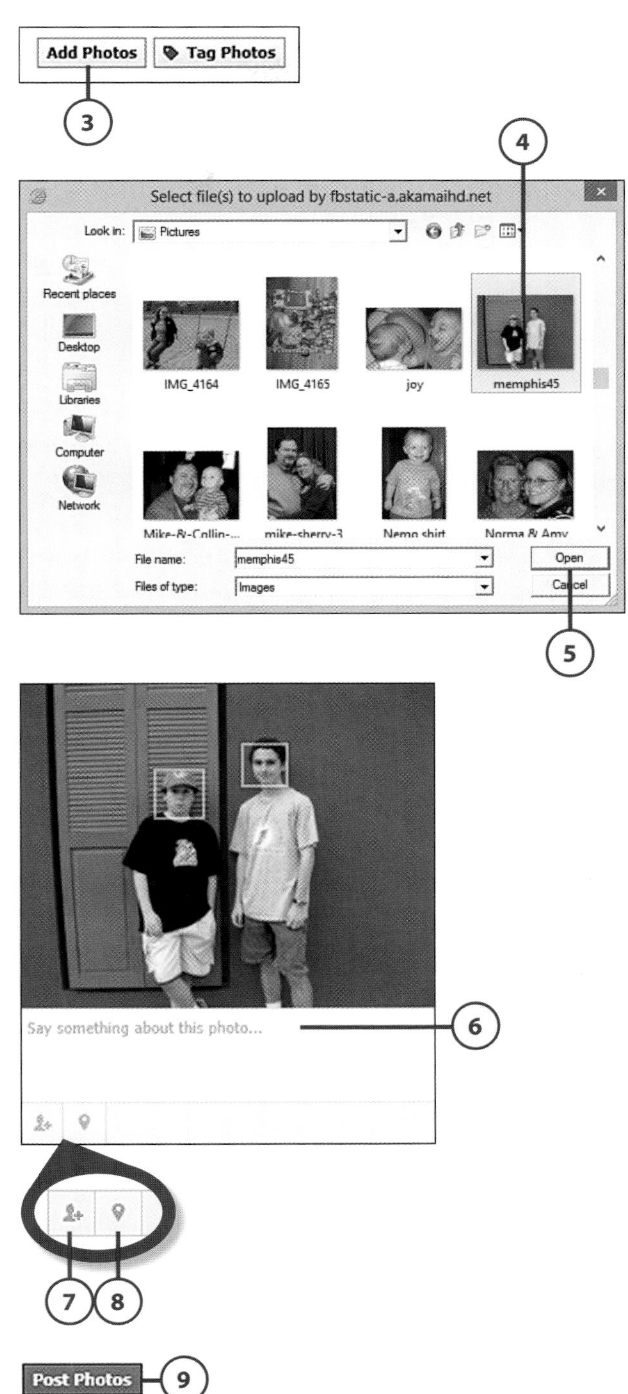

Uploading Videos

You can also upload your own videos to a group. Go to the main photos page, click the Upload Video button, and then proceed from there.

Get Notified of Group Activity

If you're active in a Facebook group, you might want to be notified when others post to the group. You can opt to receive notifications of each post made, or only of those posts made by your friends.

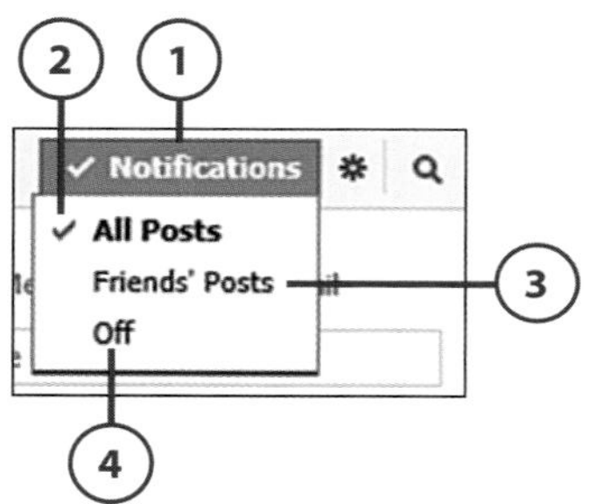

1. Open the group's page and click Notifications.
2. To receive a notification whenever a post is made to the group, select All Posts.
3. To receive a notification whenever one of your Facebook friends posts to this group, select Friends' Posts.
4. To not receive any notifications from this group, select Off.

>>>Go Further

USING GROUPS TO RECONNECT WITH OLD FRIENDS

On the surface, it's easy to think of Facebook groups as like 21st-century versions of the homeroom clubs you had back in high school. You know, chess club, knitting club, model airplane club, and the like.

While there certainly are a huge number of these club-like Facebook groups, there are also groups that are more about times and places than they are about hobbies and interests. As such, these groups attempt to reconnect people with shared experiences.

I belong to a number of groups that connect me back to the days of my youth. For example, I grew up on the west side of Indianapolis, and there's a Facebook group called Growing Up on Indy's Westside to which I belong. It's a fun little group, with people posting faded pictures of old haunts, and lots of discussions about the way things used to be and what we used to do back then. I can't say I contribute too often, but it's always fun to read what others post.

I also belong to a "Where is and/or who do you remember?" group for my high school. This is a great place to find out what my old classmates have been up to in the decades since graduation. Lots of posts asking about individual students, teachers, and events. It's a nice stroll through memory lane.

The point is, participating in Facebook groups can be a great way to reconnect with your past. You might even meet up with some of your old friends in these groups, or make some new friends you should have made way back then. It's kind of a virtual blast from the past, and we have the Facebook social network to thank for it.

Managing Your Facebook Groups

If you belong to several Facebook groups, you might need to manage your memberships at some point in time. Facebook lets you leave any group at any time, and also provides a way to view all your group messages in a single feed.

View Your Group Feed

By default, posts from your Facebook groups do not appear in your normal Facebook News Feed. To view your group messages, you can either go directly to each group's Facebook page, or display a special Groups feed on your home page. This Groups feed displays all the messages posted to all the groups to which you belong.

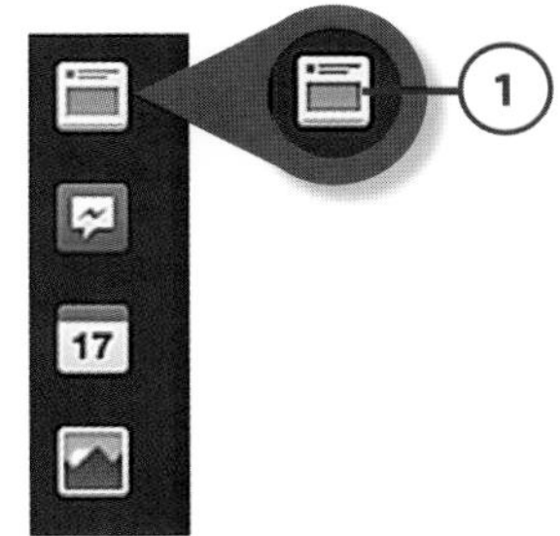

1. Click News Feed in the sidebar menu to open your Facebook home page.

2. Click Groups in the Feed list to display the Groups feed.

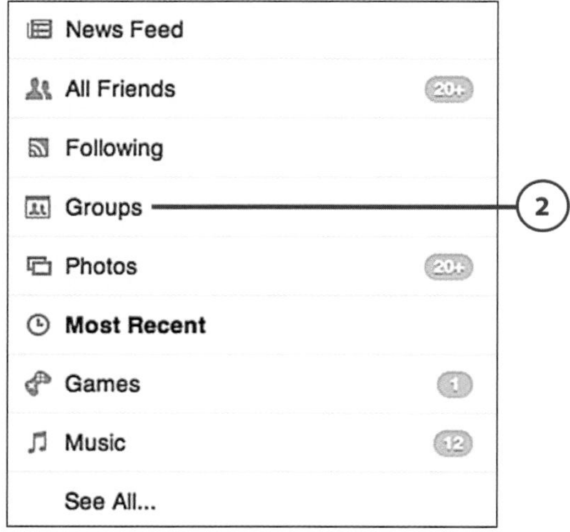

View All Your Groups

Not sure which groups you belong to? Then display a list of all your Facebook groups in a single place.

1. Go to your Timeline page and select More, Groups to display your Groups list.
2. Click any group name to open that group's Facebook page.

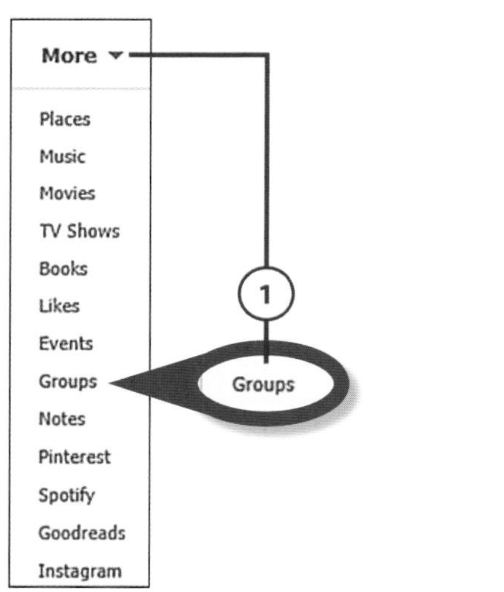

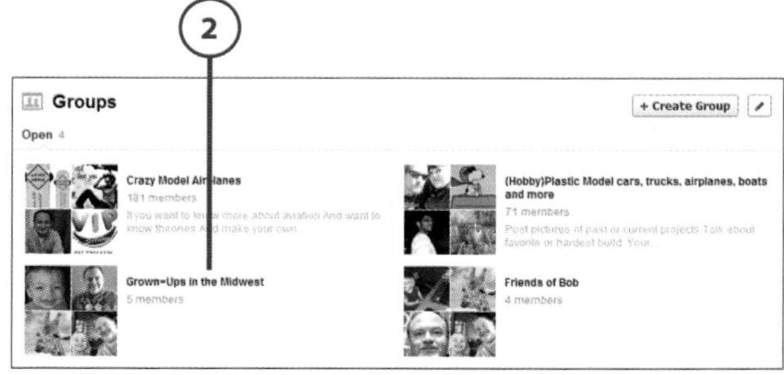

Leave a Group

If you grow tired of irrelevant or uninteresting posts in a given group, you can choose to unsubscribe from or leave a group.

1. Go to your Timeline page and select More, Groups to display your Groups list.
2. Click the Edit (pencil) button for the group you want to leave.
3. Click Leave Group to display the Leave *Group* dialog box.
4. Leave the Prevent Other Members of This Group from Re-adding You option checked.
5. Click the Leave Group button.

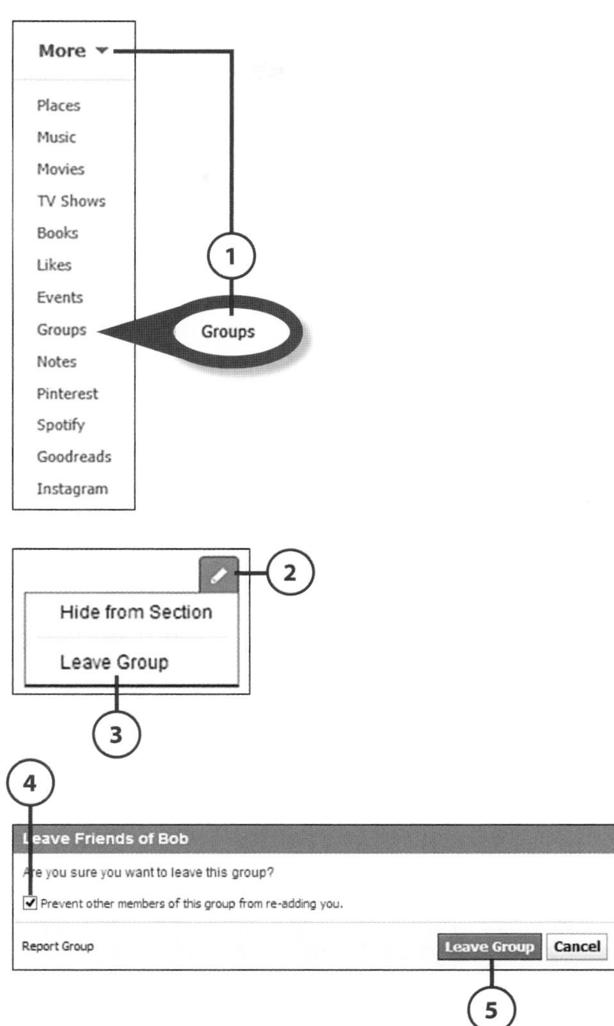

Creating Your Own Facebook Group

There are tens of thousands of groups already on Facebook, so chances are you can find one for whatever interests you. But if there isn't a group for your particular interest, you can create one—which is pretty easy to do.

Create a New Group

You can create a new group about any topic you like. You might want to create a group for a given hobby, event, or location. For example, if you're holding a class reunion, you could create a group to host posts and photos about the reunion.

1. From your Timeline page, click More, Groups to display the Groups page.
2. Click the Create Group button to display the Create New Group dialog box.
3. Enter the name of your new group into the Group Name box.
4. Enter the names of people you'd like to invite to your group into the Members box.
5. Choose whether you want the group to be Open to the general public, Closed to only those people whose membership requests you approve, or Secret to everyone except invited members.
6. Click the Create button.

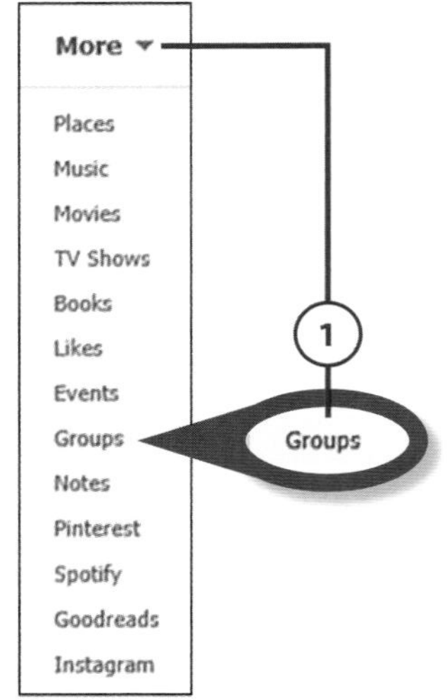

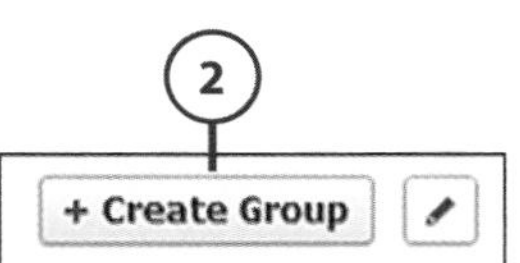

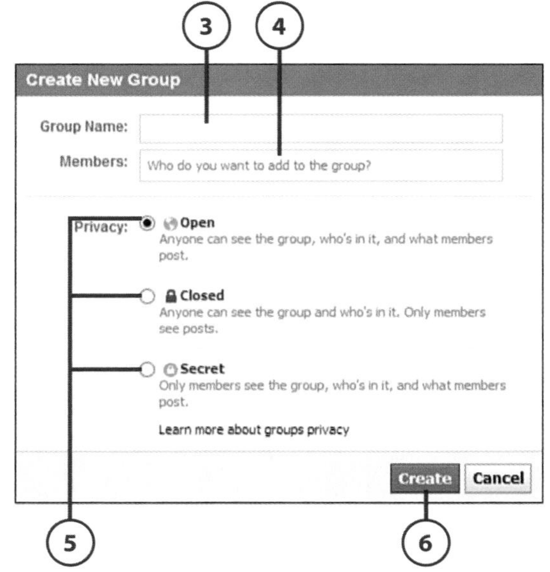

7. Click the icon you want to represent the group.
8. Click Okay to display the new group page.

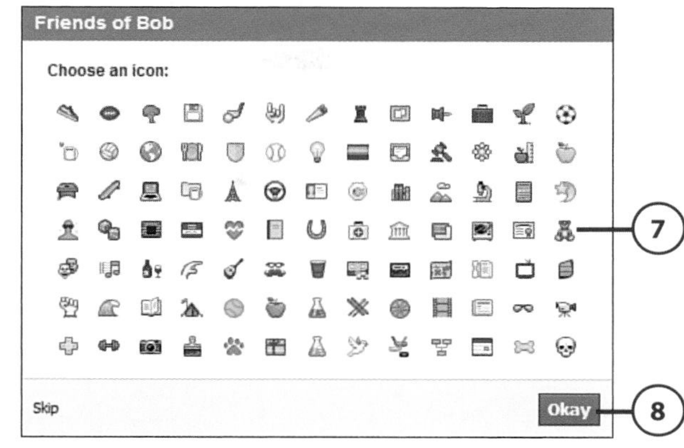

Invite Others to Join Your Group

After your new group is created, you might want to invite other people to join the group. (You can't rely just on people searching for your group to attract new members.) Chances are you have some Facebook friends who would probably like to participate; you can send them invitations to join.

1. Open your group's page and go to the Suggested Members section; these are friends who Facebook thinks you might like to invite.
2. Click the Add button to invite a given friend to the group.
3. Enter the names of any other Facebook friends you'd like to invite into the Add People to Group box and then press Enter.

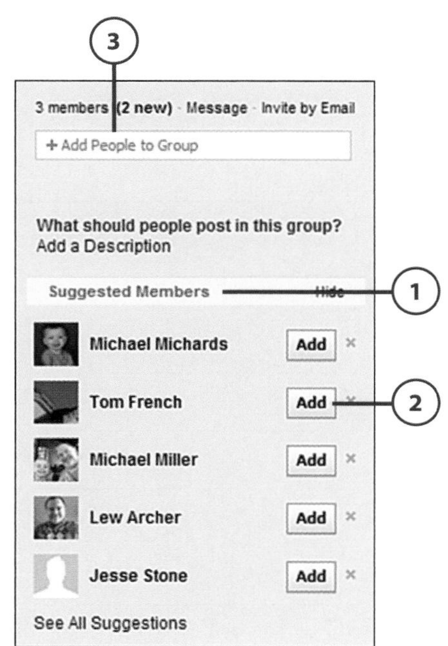

Send a Message to Group Members

As the administrator for your new group, you can send messages directly to all group members. This is a more direct means of communication than simply posting status updates to the group's Facebook page.

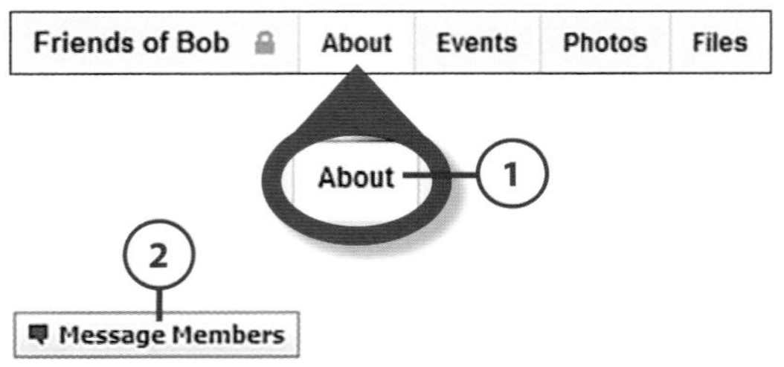

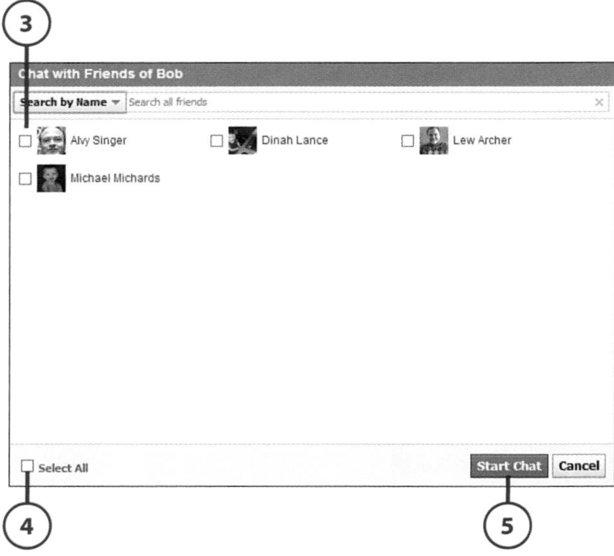

1. Open your group's page and click About to display the list of members.
2. Click the Message Members button to display the Chat With dialog box.
3. Check those members you want to send the message to.
4. To send the message to all members, check Select All.
5. Click the Start Chat button to open a group Chat pane.
6. Enter your message to the group into the bottom text box and then press Enter.

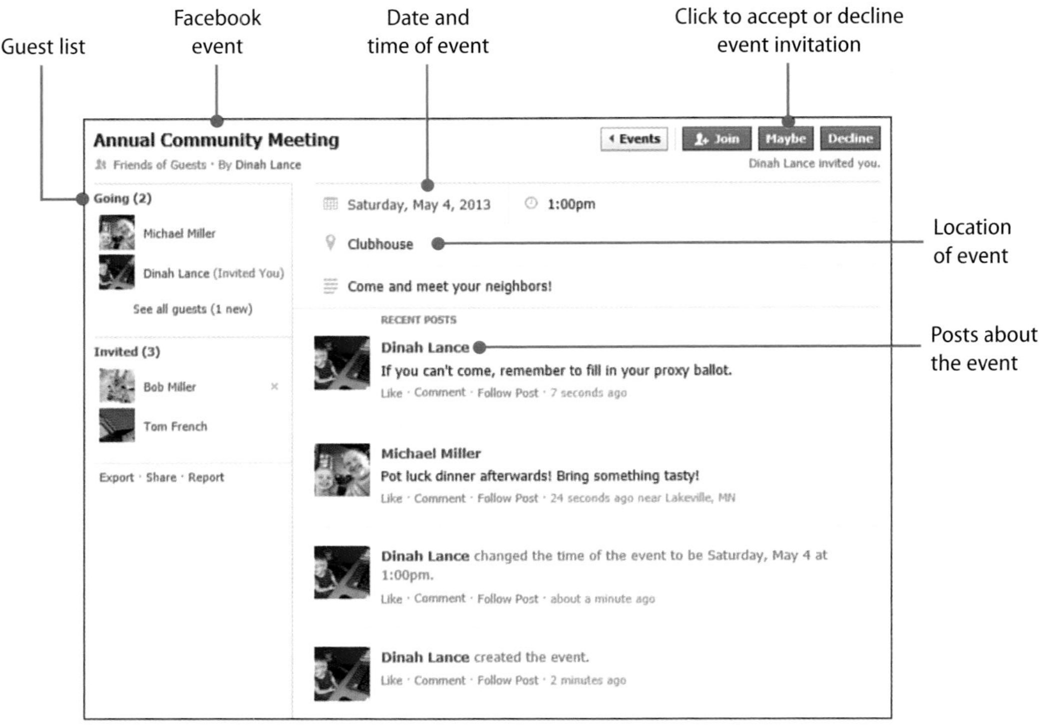

Guest list
Facebook event
Date and time of event
Click to accept or decline event invitation
Location of event
Posts about the event
Annual Community Meeting
Friends of Guests · By Dinah Lance
Events
Join
Maybe
Decline
Dinah Lance invited you.
Going (2)
Michael Miller
Dinah Lance (Invited You)
See all guests (1 new)
Invited (3)
Bob Miller
Tom French
Export · Share · Report
Saturday, May 4, 2013
1:00pm
Clubhouse
Come and meet your neighbors!
RECENT POSTS
Dinah Lance
If you can't come, remember to fill in your proxy ballot.
Like · Comment · Follow Post · 7 seconds ago
Michael Miller
Pot luck dinner afterwards! Bring something tasty!
Like · Comment · Follow Post · 24 seconds ago near Lakeville, MN
Dinah Lance changed the time of the event to be Saturday, May 4 at 1:00pm.
Like · Comment · Follow Post · about a minute ago
Dinah Lance created the event.
Like · Comment · Follow Post · 2 minutes ago

In this chapter you find out how to respond to event notifications and schedule your own events on Facebook—as well as celebrate your friends' birthdays online.

- → Dealing with Invitations to Events
- → Scheduling a New Event
- → Celebrating Birthdays

Attending Events and Celebrating Birthdays

Facebook enables you to do more than just post and read status updates to and from your friends and family. You can also use Facebook as a kind of event scheduler, so you can manage parties, meetings, reunions, and the like from within Facebook.

The most common type of event is a birthday, and Facebook helps out there, too. Facebook notifies you of your friends' and family members' upcoming birthdays and makes it easy for you to send your birthday greetings. Facebook even announces your birthday to your friends—so sit back and wait for those well wishes to arrive!

Dealing with Invitations to Events

You use Facebook to keep in touch with all your friends and family, so it's only natural to use Facebook to schedule events that might involve these same people. You're all online and on Facebook, after all; why not use Facebook to notify people of upcoming events?

Facebook's events feature lets you do just that—schedule events and invite your Facebook friends to those events, using Facebook's built-in messaging system. In effect, Facebook creates a new page for each event scheduled, and whomever creates the event can then invite people to view the page and attend the event. If you receive an invitation to a Facebook event, you can then decide to accept or decline the invitation.

Respond to an Event Invitation in Your News Feed

When you've been invited to an event, a status update to that effect appears in your Facebook News Feed. You can respond to the event directly from that status update.

No Obligation

You should feel no obligation to accept any specific event. Only accept those you genuinely want to and can attend.

1. Go to your News Feed and scroll to the status update that contains the event invitation.
2. Click Join to accept the invitation. (In Facebook terminology, when you accept an invitation you "join" the event.)
3. Click the name of the event to display the event page.

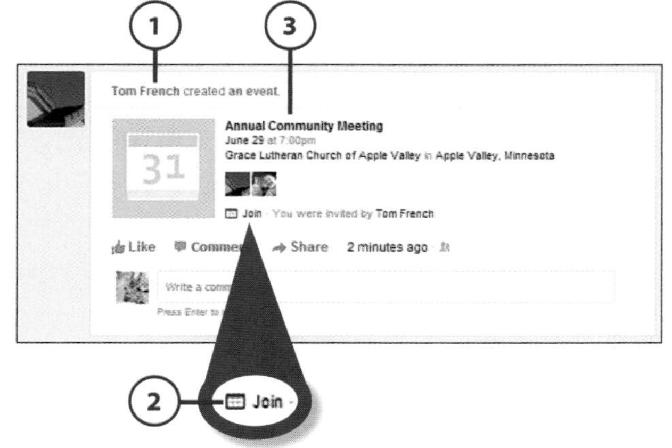

4. You can also respond to the event from the event page. Click Join to accept the invitation.
5. Click Decline if you don't want to accept the invitation.
6. Click Maybe if you're not sure whether or not you'll attend.

Respond to an Event Invitation in Your Notifications

Facebook also notifies you of upcoming events via its notification system. You can see all recent event invitations in the Notifications menu of the Facebook toolbar.

1. Click the Notifications button in the Facebook toolbar to see recent event invitations.
2. Click the event notification to display the event page.
3. Click Join to accept the invitation.
4. Click Decline if you don't want to accept the invitation.
5. Click Maybe if you're not sure whether or not you'll attend.

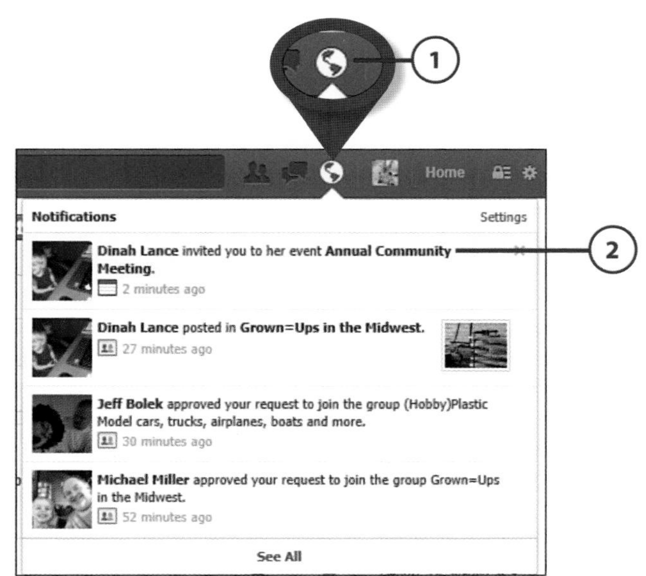

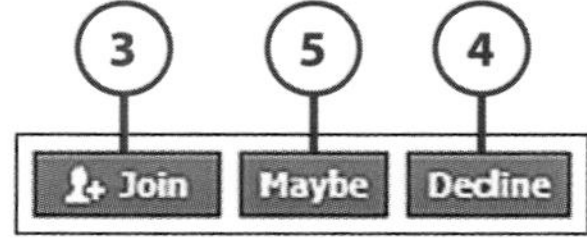

View an Event Page

When a friend schedules a new event, Facebook creates a page for that event. You can view the event page to learn more about the event.

1. Click Events in the sidebar menu to display the Events page.
2. All events to which you've been invited appear here, as do your friends' upcoming birthdays. Click the name of an event to view the page for that event.
3. The event page contains much useful information about the event. To view people attending the event, see the Going list on the left.
4. To view people who've been invited but haven't yet responded, see the Invited list.

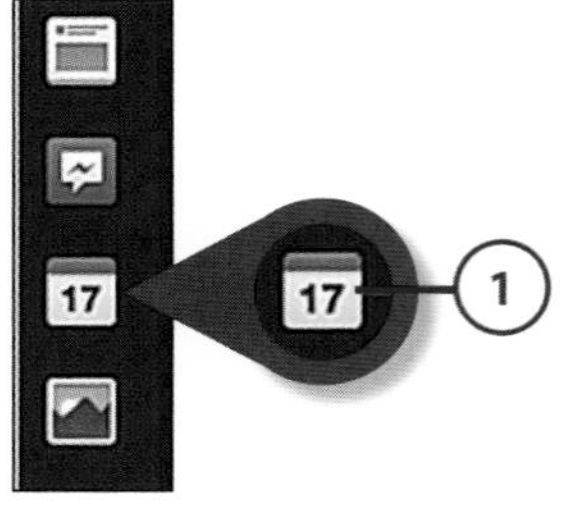

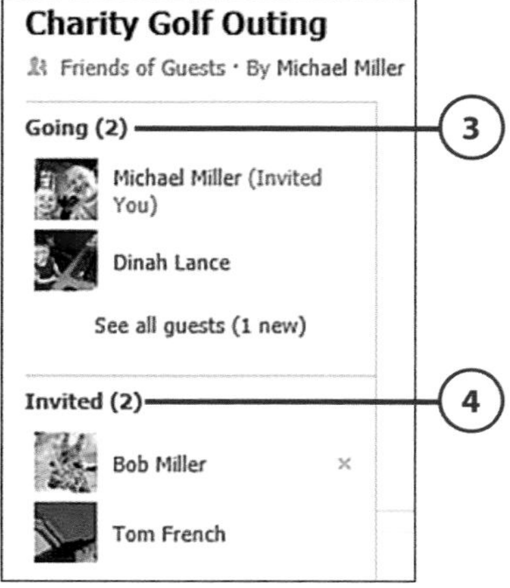

5. To view information about the event, see the date, time, and location at the top of the page.
6. To accept the invitation to this event, click the Join button.
7. To tell the host you won't be attending the event, click the Decline button.
8. If you're not sure whether or not you're attending the event, click the Maybe button.
9. To change your mind about attending, click the Going/Maybe/Not Going button and make another selection.
10. To post a message about this event, go to the Publishing box, click Write Post, enter your message, and then click the Post button.
11. View other messages about this event in the feed beneath the Publishing box.
12. To invite another friend to this event, click the Invite Friends button to display the Invite Friends dialog box.

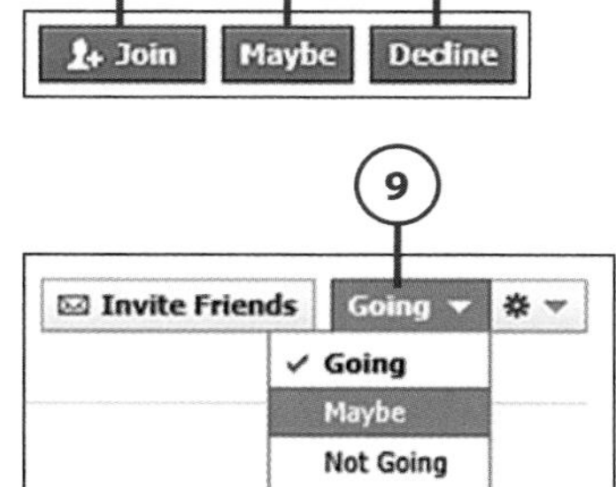

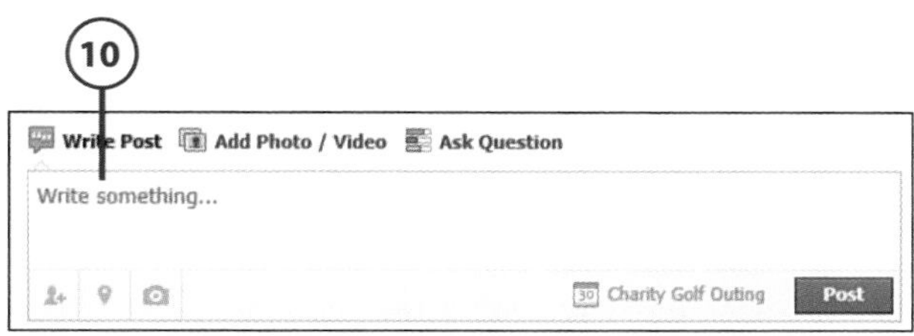

13. Check the names of those friends you want to invite.
14. Click the Save button.

>>>Go Further

FACEBOOK EVENTS

What exactly is an event? On Facebook, an event is any item on your personal schedule. Events can be small and private, such as a doctor's appointment or dinner with a friend. Events can also be large and public, such as a community meeting or family reunion.

This means that you can use Facebook events to invite friends to backyard BBQs, block parties, golf dates, and card games. You can also use Facebook events to invite family members to birthday parties, holiday gatherings, and family reunions.

The events you work with don't have to be real-world, physical events, either. You can schedule virtual events, such as inviting all your friends to watch a specific TV show or sporting event on a given evening. You can also schedule online events, such as seminars and conferences on sites that offer such options. In other words, you don't have to meet someone in person to share an event with them. It's all part of the social networking thing.

Scheduling a New Event

You don't have to wait to be invited to an event. You can also schedule your own Facebook events.

Maybe your neighborhood association has a meeting coming up. Maybe you're hosting a big party for some old friends. Or maybe you just want to let everyone know about an upcoming anniversary. Whatever the case, Facebook makes it relatively easy to create new events and invite some or all of your Facebook friends to these events.

Create an Event

Facebook lets you create all manner of events, from parties to community meetings, and invite selected friends to those events. You can then manage that event through the event's Facebook page.

1. Click Events in the sidebar menu to display your Events page.
2. Click the Create Event button to display the Create Event dialog box.
3. Enter the name of the event into the Name box.
4. Enter any additional details about the event into the Details box.
5. To specify the event's location, enter the location into the Where box.

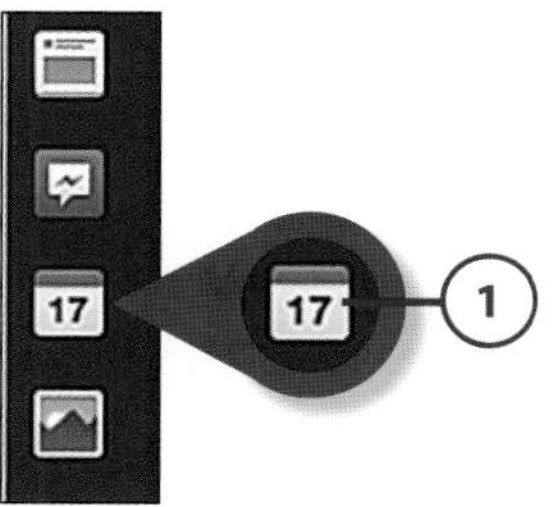

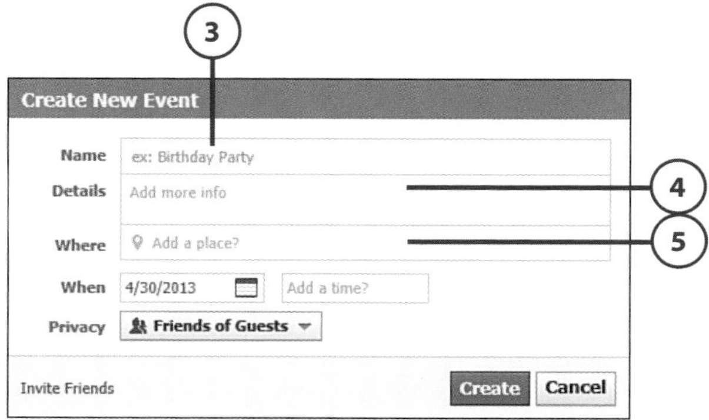

Location

You can enter an exact address as the event's location, a city or state, or even just "My House" or "Room 223 in the Henry Building."

6. Enter the date of the event into the When section, or click the calendar icon and select a date from the calendar.
7. Enter the start time of the event into the Add a Time? box.
8. If you entered a start time you can also enter an end time for the event. Click the End Time? link to display the End Time section, and then use the controls to set the end date and time.
9. To invite friends to your event, click the Invite Friends link to display the Invite Friends dialog box.
10. Check those friends you want to invite.
11. Click the Save button to return to the Create New Event dialog box.
12. To determine who can see a given event, click the Privacy button and select Public, Friends of Guests, or Invite Only.

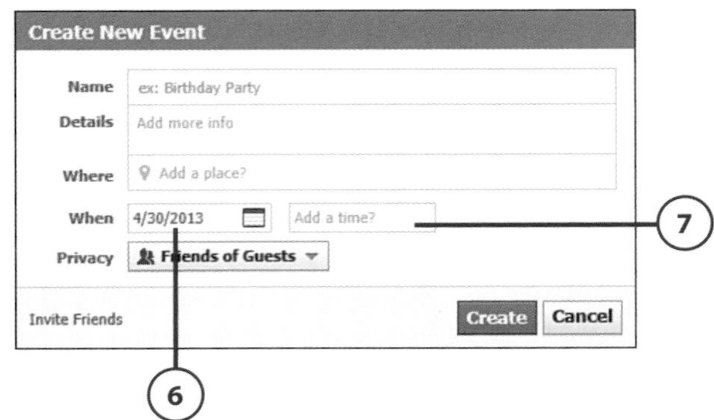

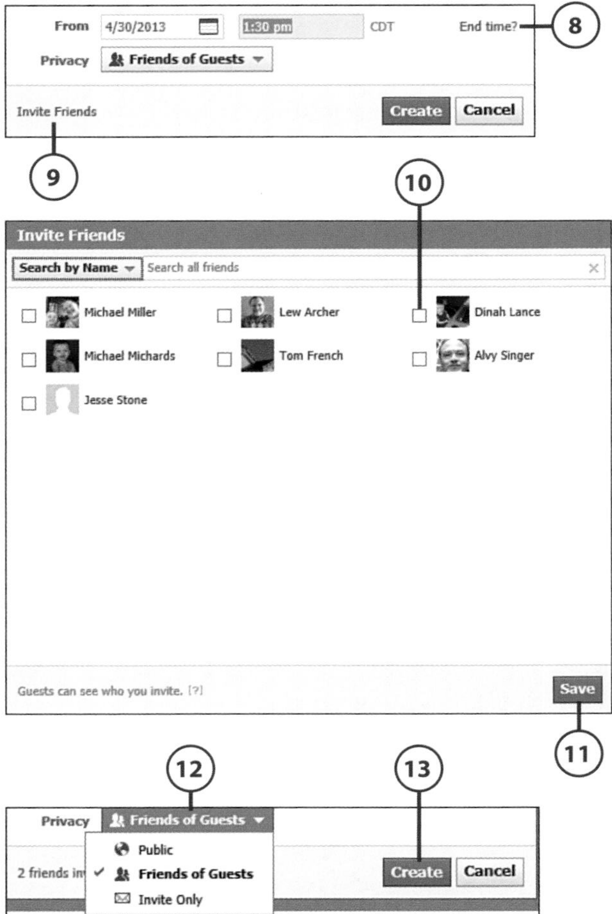

Public or Private

If you select Public, that event is visible to the general public. If you select Friends of Guests, it's visible to the people you invite and their friends. If you select Invite Only, the event is visible only to the people you invite.

13. Click the Create button to create the event and send out the desired invitations.

Edit an Event

You can, at any time, edit the information for an event you've created. You can invite additional people, add or change details about the location and timing, and even post messages about the event.

1. Click Events in the sidebar menu to display your Events page.
2. Click the event you want to edit to display its Facebook page.
3. Click the Add Event Photo to add a photo to accompany the event.
4. Click the Invite Friends button to invite additional friends to the event.
5. Click the Edit button to display the Edit Event Info dialog box.
6. Make the necessary changes to any of the information present.
7. Click the Save button to return to the event page.
8. To post a message about the event, go to the Publisher box, click Write Post, enter your message, and then click the Post button.

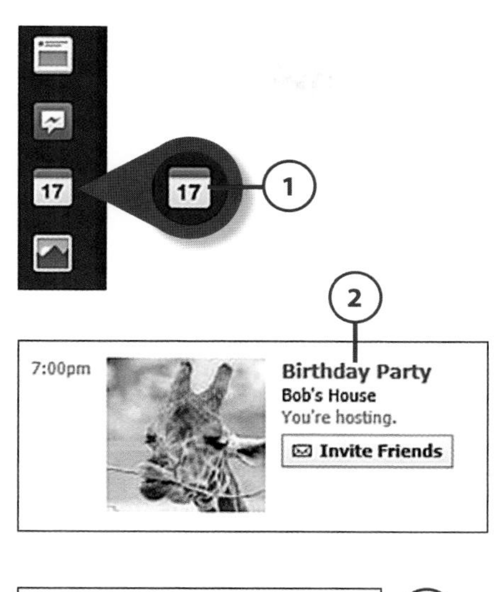

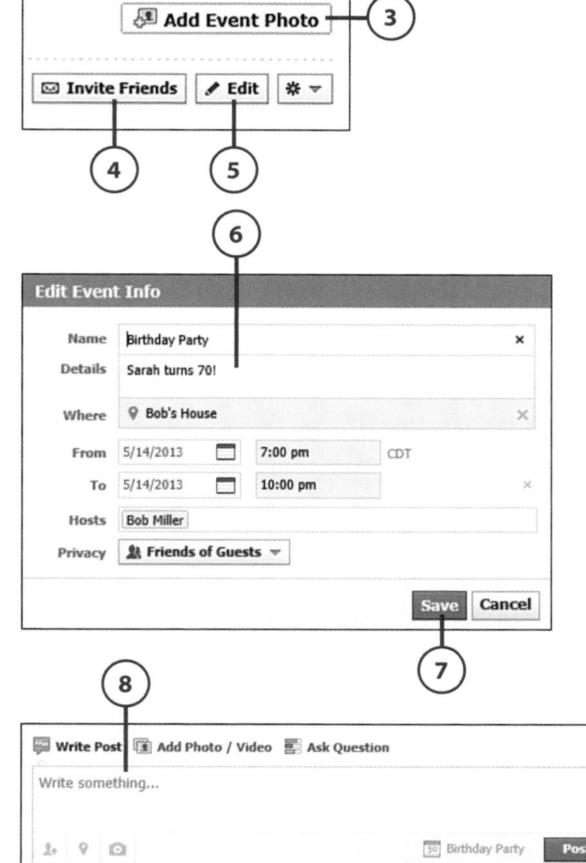

Cancel an Event

It happens. Even the best-laid plans go astray, and you may be forced to cancel a planned event. Here's how you do it.

1. Open the event page and click the gear button to display a menu of options.
2. Click Cancel Event.
3. When the Cancel Event? dialog box appears, click the Yes button.

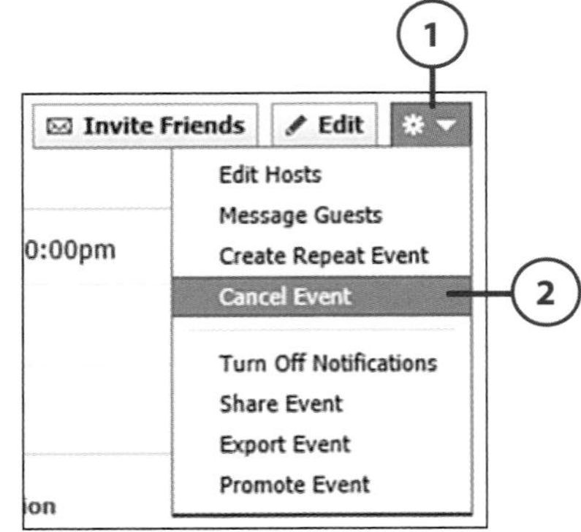

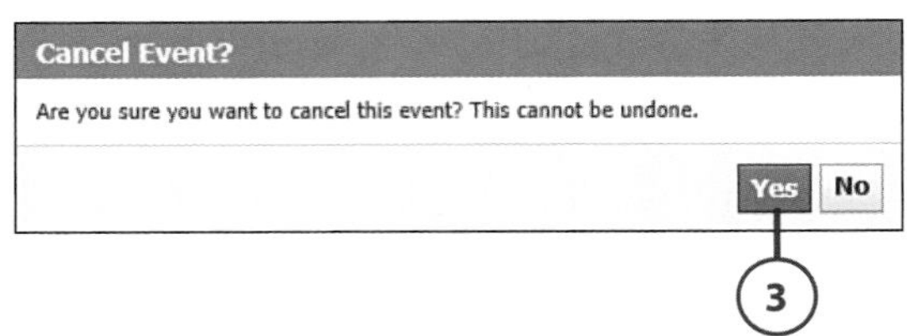

Celebrating Birthdays

Facebook knows a lot about you and your friends, including when you were born. To that end, Facebook does a nice social service by letting you know when someone's birthday is approaching—so that you can send your birthday wishes.

Personal Replies

Most people receive a lot of Facebook greetings on their birthdays. Don't be disappointed if you don't receive a personal thank you from the birthday baby.

View Today's Birthdays

Facebook notifies you when it's one of your friends' birthday. You can then leave that person a happy birthday message. It's what people do on Facebook!

1. Click News Feed in the menu sidebar to display your Facebook home page.
2. Today's birthdays are displayed in the notifications section near the top of the right-hand column. Click a birthday to display a pop-up panel about that person.
3. Enter your message into the Write a Birthday Wish box and then press Enter.

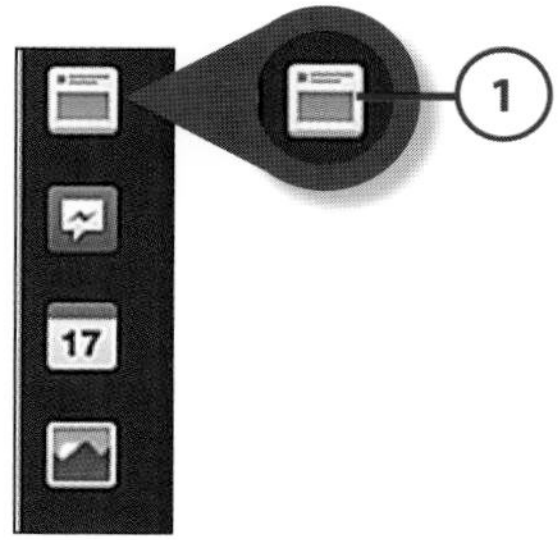

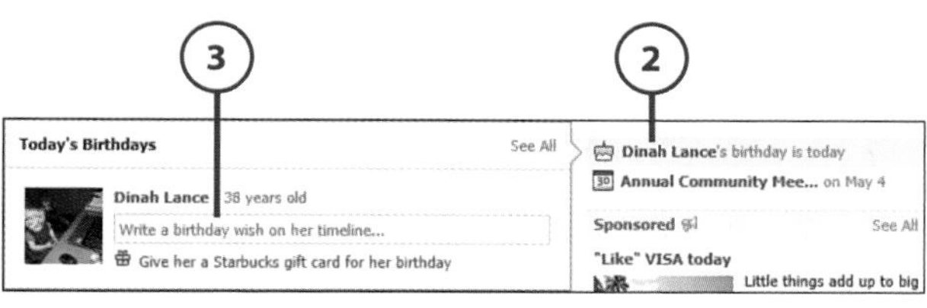

Public Only

Facebook only notifies you of birthdays from friends who have opted to make their birthdates public. Friends with private birthdays do not appear in the birthday list.

View Upcoming Birthdays

Facebook views a birthday as a kind of event and displays all upcoming birthdays on your Events page.

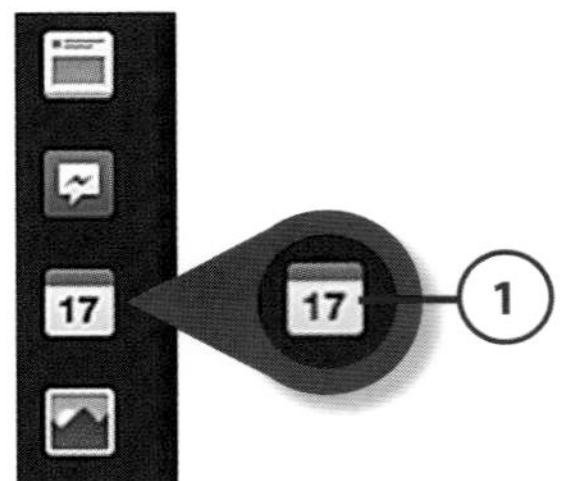

1. Click Events in the sidebar menu to display your Events page.
2. Click Calendar to view upcoming events in calendar view. Friends' birthdays appear as small thumbnail images on the calendar.
3. Mouse over a friend's thumbnail image to view that person's name and (in some cases) how old that person will be.
4. Click a friend's image to display that person's Timeline page.
5. Scroll to the Publisher box and click Post.
6. Enter your birthday greeting into the Write Something box.
7. Click the Post button to leave your birthday greeting.

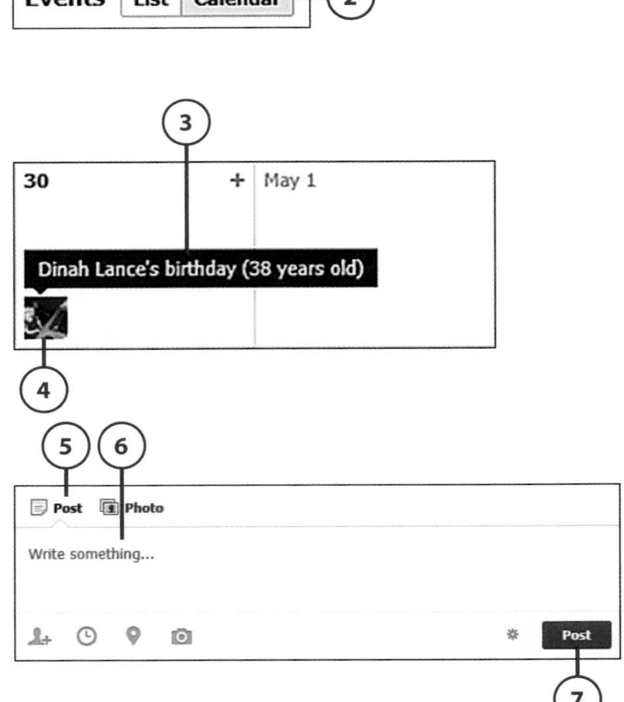

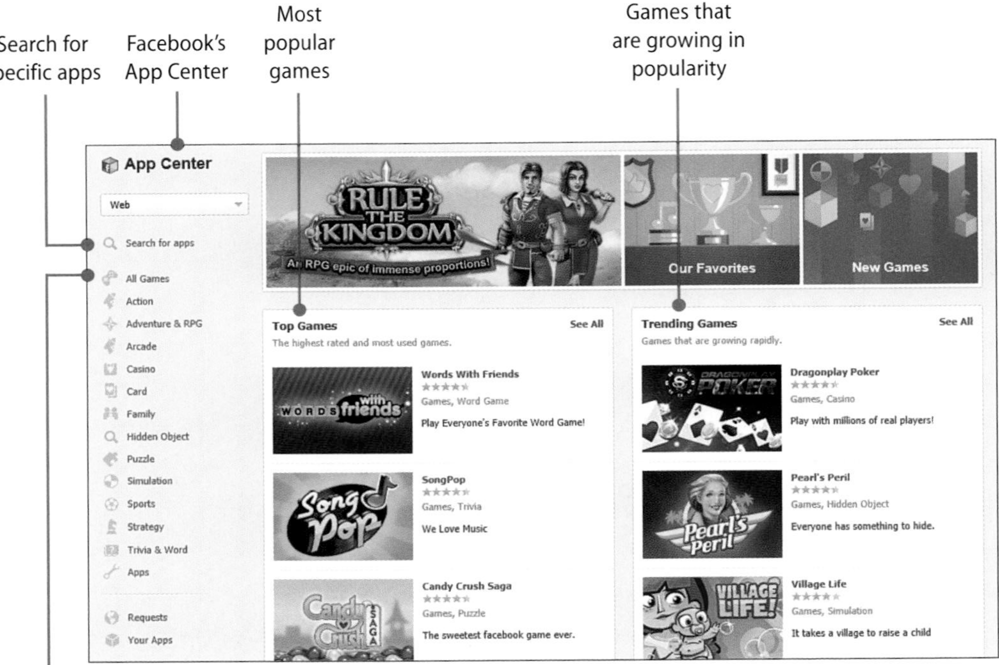

Search for specific apps
Facebook's App Center
Most popular games
Games that are growing in popularity
Browse by category
App Center
Web
Search for apps
All Games
Action
Adventure & RPG
Arcade
Casino
Card
Family
Hidden Object
Puzzle
Simulation
Sports
Strategy
Trivia & Word
Apps
Requests
Your Apps
RULE THE KINGDOM
An RPG epic of immense proportions!
Our Favorites
New Games
Top Games
See All
The highest rated and most used games.
Words With Friends
Games, Word Game
Play Everyone's Favorite Word Game!
SongPop
Games, Trivia
We Love Music
Candy Crush Saga
Games, Puzzle
The sweetest facebook game ever.
Trending Games
See All
Games that are growing rapidly.
Dragonplay Poker
Games, Casino
Play with millions of real players!
Pearl's Peril
Games, Hidden Object
Everyone has something to hide.
Village Life
Games, Simulation
It takes a village to raise a child

In this chapter you find out how to get more out of Facebook with useful apps and fun social games.

→ Discovering Apps and Games
→ Working with Apps and Games
→ Exploring Popular Apps and Games for Seniors

14

Using Apps and Playing Games

You can get more out of Facebook by using third-party applications or apps. An app is a service or utility that builds on Facebook's community and sharing features to offer additional functionality to you and other users.

While many apps are practical, others are more fun. There are a ton of social games you can play on the Facebook site, either by yourself or with your Facebook friends. It's a great way to pass the time while you're on Facebook!

Discovering Apps and Games

A Facebook app is a utility, service, or game that runs on the Facebook site. These apps are accessed from their own Facebook pages, and you use them while you're signed in to your Facebook account. Some apps build on the social networking nature of the Facebook site; others are designed for more solitary use. Some are strictly functional; others are more fun. There is a range of apps available—you're bound to find some that look interesting to you.

Third-Party Apps

Although some apps are developed by Facebook, most are created by third-party application developers. The vast majority of Facebook applications, including third-party apps, are available free of charge.

Browse for Apps and Games by Category

Facebook's App Center is the place to go when you're looking for new apps and games. You can browse the App Center by category to find what you're looking for.

1. Click App Center in the sidebar menu to display the App Center page.
2. Click a category on the left side of the page to display games in that category.
3. Click Apps to display app categories.
4. Click a category to display apps of that type.

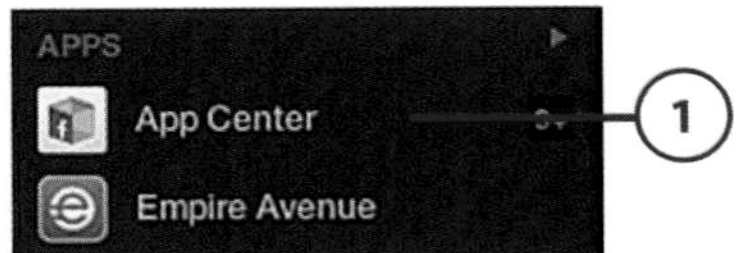

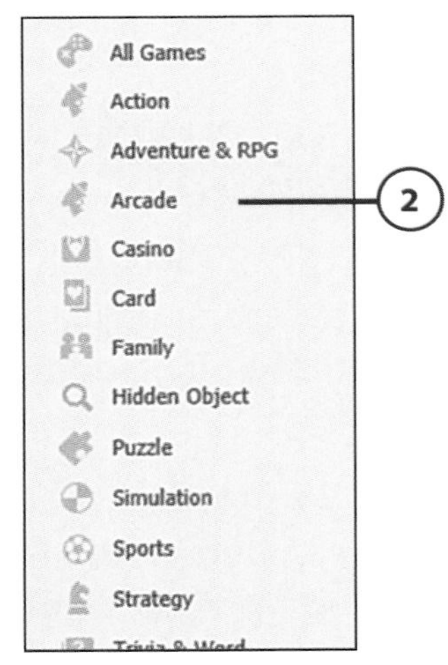

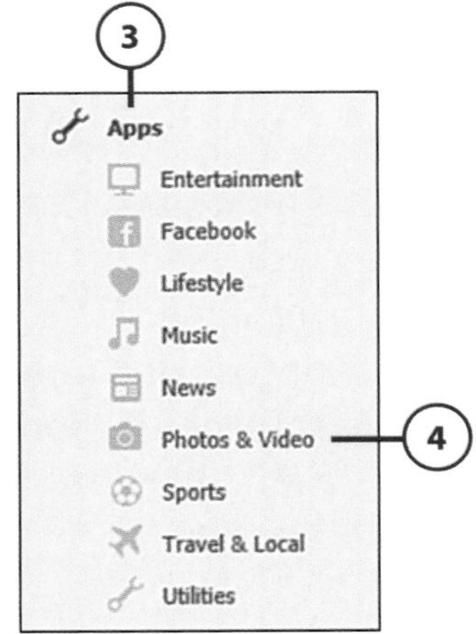

5. Click Suggested to view apps or games Facebook thinks you might like.
6. Click Top Rated to view those apps or games that have received the highest ratings from other users.
7. Click Trending to view those apps or games that are growing most in popularity.
8. Click Friends' to view those apps or games used by your friends.
9. Click the name of an app or game to view that item's Facebook page—and start using or playing it.

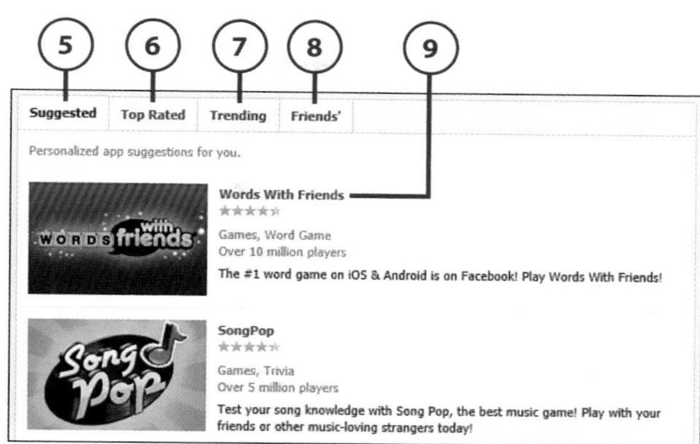

Search for Specific Apps and Games

Browsing is a good way to see what apps and games are available. But if you have a specific app or game in mind, you can search for it directly, which is quicker.

1. Click App Center in the sidebar menu to display the App Center page.
2. Click Search for Apps to display the search box.
3. Enter the name of the app or game into the search box and press Enter.

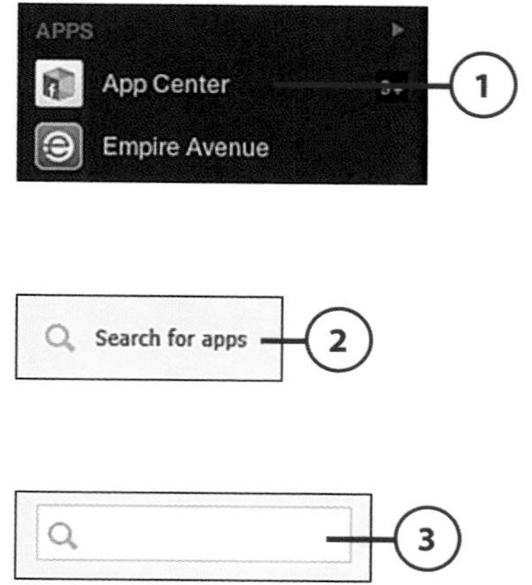

4. Facebook displays those apps or games that match your query. Click the name of an item to display its Facebook page.

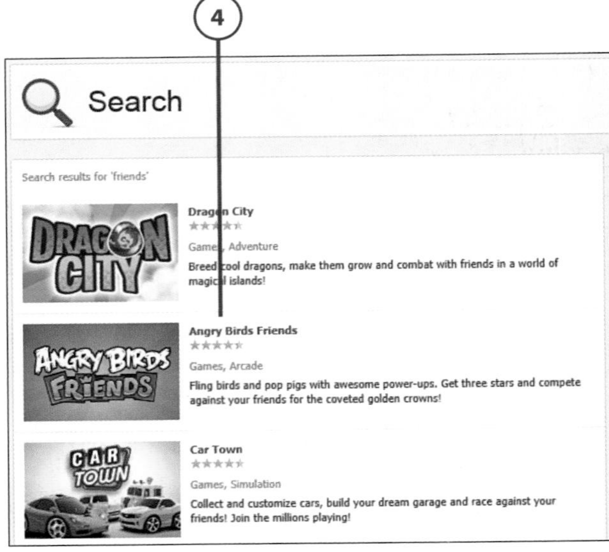

Working with Apps and Games

Every Facebook app is different. Some work within Facebook, others take you outside the Facebook site to their own websites. Some are relatively simple, others tie into your whole network of Facebook contacts to create a more compelling social experience.

That said, using a new app or game is typically a simple experience. It all starts when you go to that item's Facebook page.

Use a New App

After you've browsed or searched for a new app or game, you can learn more about the item—and start using it.

1. From the App Center, click the name of the app to open its Facebook page.

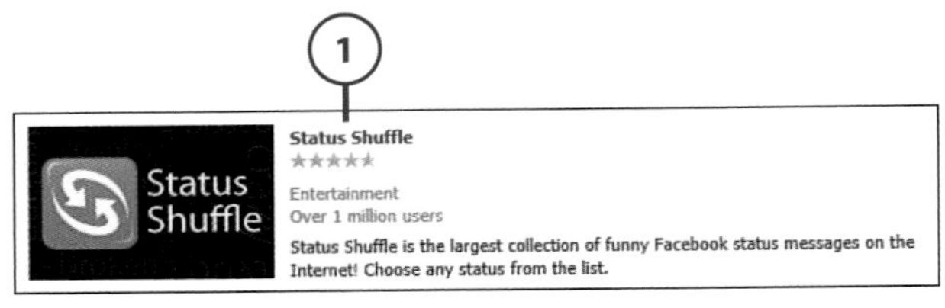

2. Some apps let you start using the app immediately from the app page. Click the Go to App button to start using this type of app.
3. Other apps are tied into the app's website. Click the Visit Website button to start using this type of app.

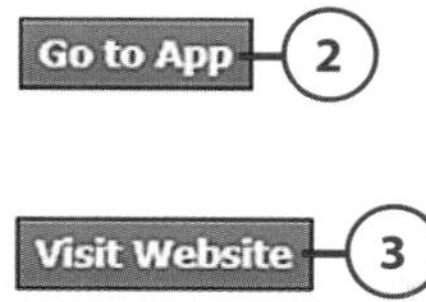

Its Not All Good

Social Apps and Privacy

Many Facebook apps are social in nature, in that they use your Facebook friends list to either obtain information about your friends or send information to them regarding your activity within the app. That's both good and bad.

One of the good things about a social app or game is that it helps to create a larger community of users by linking you together with your friends. The app might also use your friends' information to provide additional benefit to you. (For example, the Stik app helps you find trusted professional services, such as lawyers and accountants, by connecting you with friends and friends of friends who either offer or have used such services.)

The bad thing about a social app or game is that it makes a lot of personal information public. When you agree to share your information, including your friends list, with the app, you're relinquishing some degree of privacy. You're also betraying the trust of your friends by letting the app access some of their personal information, or post to their News Feeds. You might be comfortable doing that, and that's fine. But some users don't want to make everything public, and especially don't want to breach their friends' privacy. If that's how you think then don't sign up for social apps and games that request you share this information. If you don't join in then you won't be jeopardizing your privacy.

Play a Social Game

The most popular Facebook applications are actually games—social games, to be exact. These are single-player or multi-player games that you play on the Facebook site while you're logged in. Some of these games have millions of users on the Facebook site and can be quite addictive.

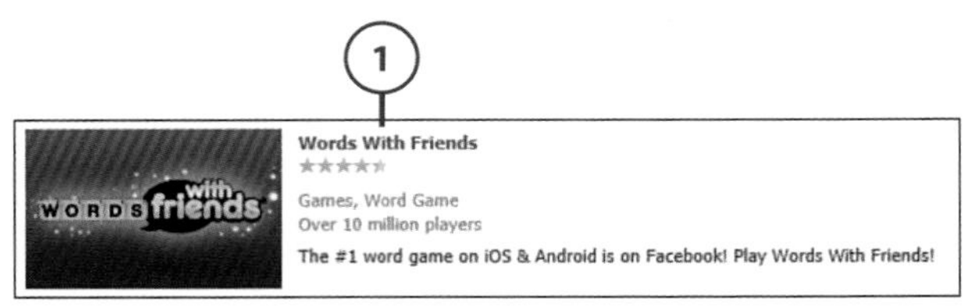

1. From the App Center, click the name of the game to open its Facebook page.
2. Click the Play Game button to begin playing the game.

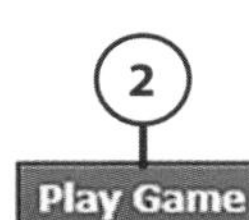

Manage Your Apps and Games

Want to see and manage the applications you're using? There are probably a lot more than you might remember.

1. Click App Center in the sidebar menu to open the App Center.
2. Scroll to the bottom of the left-hand column and click Your Apps.

3. Click the name of any app to view the page for that application.
4. To edit the settings for a particular app, click Settings to display the Edit Settings dialog box.
5. Make the desired changes and then click the Close button.

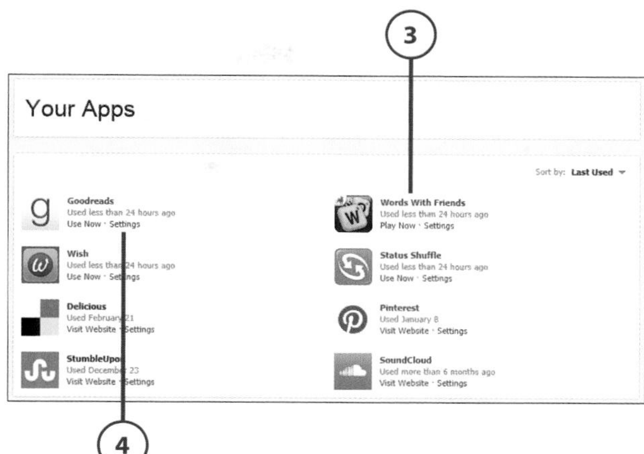

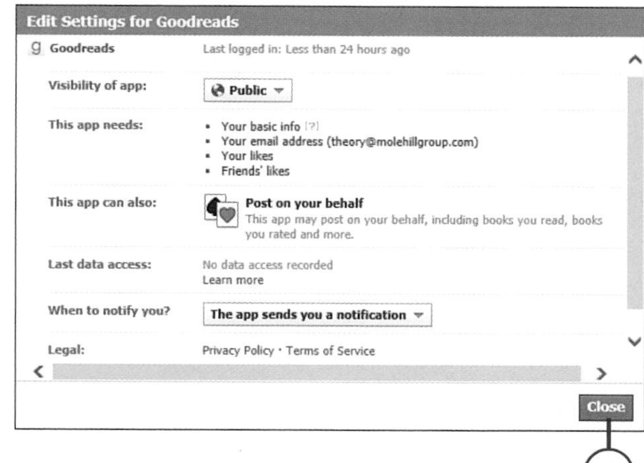

App Settings

Each app has different settings available in its Edit Settings dialog box. Some apps don't have any settings to configure.

Delete an App or Game

If you're no longer using a particular app or game, you can delete it from your personal list. This way you'll no longer receive notifications from the app.

1. Open the App Center and display your personal apps.
2. Go to the app you want to remove and click Settings to display the Edit Settings dialog box.

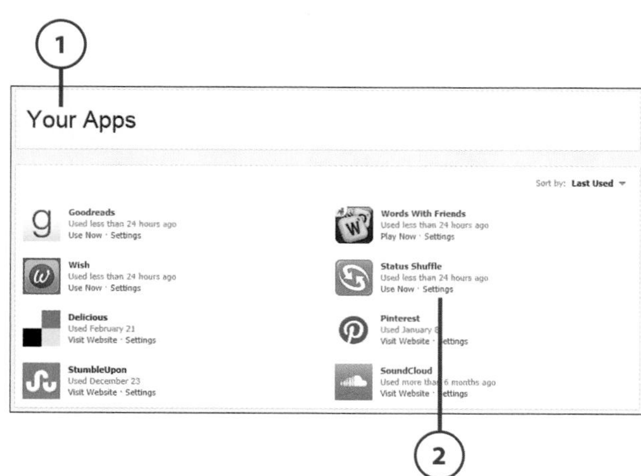

3. Click Remove App.
4. When prompted to confirm the removal, click the Remove button.

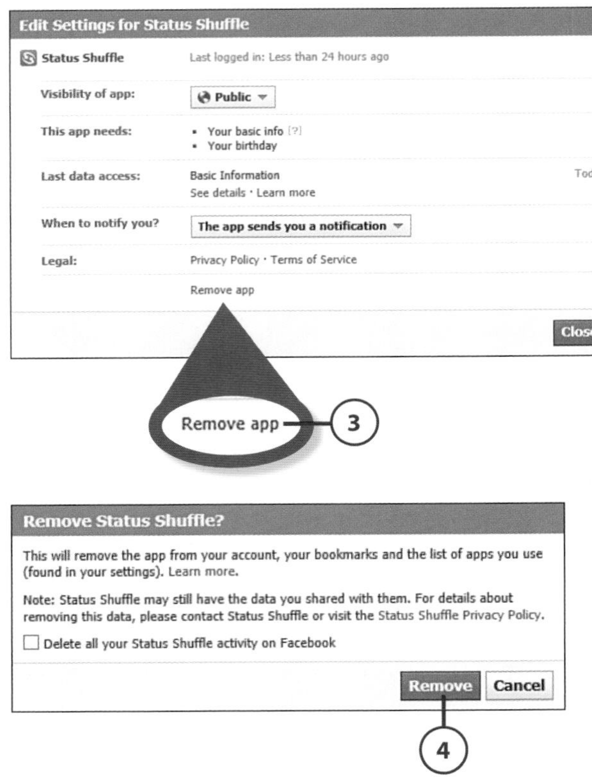

Exploring Popular Apps and Games for Seniors

Facebook offers apps and games for users of all ages. Some applications, however, are more popular with older users.

Seniors tend to gravitate toward apps that help do practical and interesting things. We like apps that help us connect to family members online, manage our schedules, track our favorite activities. It's a different bag of apps than what your kids or grandkids use.

With that in mind, here are some of the apps I find most useful or interesting to those of us of a certain age:

- **Birthday Calendar**—This app goes a few steps beyond Facebook's built-in birthday notifications, compiling all the birthdays of your friends and family members into a single calendar interface. It helps you plan ahead for upcoming birthdays, which is a good thing if you have a large family to deal with.
- **Family Tree**—A great tool for finding your relatives—and staying in touch with them.
- **GoodReads**—Helps you manage your book library, review books, and share your favorite books with your Facebook friends.
- **Groupon**—Enables you to purchase discount packages for products and services in your area.
- **iHeartRadio**—Enables you to listen to local radio stations online while you're using Facebook.
- **MyFitnessPal**—Provides real-time nutrition and fitness tracking, fitness advice, and community support. A great tool for anyone trying to stay in shape.
- **Team Stream**—Delivers scores and news items about your favorite sports teams.
- **TripAdvisor**—Offers hotel and vacation reviews online.
- **TripAdvisor—Cities I've Visited**—Creates an interactive travel map of places you've traveled, which you can then share with your Facebook friends.

Then there are the games. Although I'd like to say that older, more mature users are less likely to play Facebook's social games, I don't think that's the case. In fact, social games are a great way to fill those spare hours when you could be doing something more useful.

What types of games are most popular with senior users? Here's a short list:

- **Bejeweled Blitz**—A single-player puzzle game.
- **Bingo Blitz**—An online bingo game that you can play with your friends and other Facebook users.

- **DoubleDown Casino Slots and Poker**—All manner of online casino games, including virtual slot machines.
- **FarmVille**—One of the most popular games on Facebook, for users of all ages. Build and nurture your own virtual farm, complete with crops and animals.
- **Scrabble**—The classic word game, online in Facebook.
- **Scramble with Friends**—A challenging word-finding game.
- **Solitaire Blitz**—The classic single-player card game.
- **SongPop**—A pop music trivia game, for music lovers of all ages.
- **Texas HoldEm Poker**—Online poker with your Facebook friends.
- **Words with Friends**—An extremely popular word game that you play with your Facebook friends.

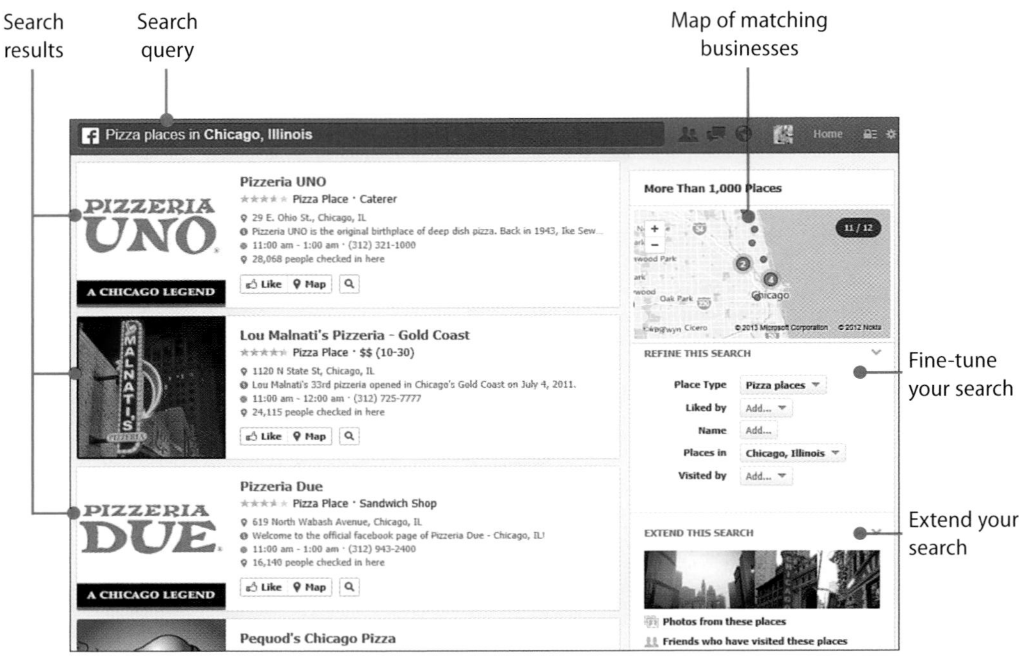
Search results
Search query
Map of matching businesses
Fine-tune your search
Extend your search
Pizza places in Chicago, Illinois
Home
Pizzeria UNO
Pizza Place · Caterer
29 E. Ohio St., Chicago, IL
Pizzeria UNO is the original birthplace of deep dish pizza. Back in 1943, Ike Sew...
11:00 am - 1:00 am · (312) 321-1000
28,068 people checked in here
Like
Map
PIZZERIA UNO
A CHICAGO LEGEND
Lou Malnati's Pizzeria - Gold Coast
Pizza Place · $$ (10-30)
1120 N State St, Chicago, IL
Lou Malnati's 33rd pizzeria opened in Chicago's Gold Coast on July 4, 2011.
11:00 am - 12:00 am · (312) 725-7777
24,115 people checked in here
Pizzeria Due
Pizza Place · Sandwich Shop
619 North Wabash Avenue, Chicago, IL
Welcome to the official facebook page of Pizzeria Due - Chicago, IL!
11:00 am - 1:00 am · (312) 943-2400
16,140 people checked in here
PIZZERIA DUE
Pequod's Chicago Pizza
More Than 1,000 Places
11 / 12
Chicago
REFINE THIS SEARCH
Place Type
Pizza places
Liked by
Add...
Name
Places in
Chicago, Illinois
Visited by
EXTEND THIS SEARCH
Photos from these places
Friends who have visited these places

In this chapter you find out how to search Facebook for people, places, and things.

- → Understanding Facebook's Graph Search
- → Using Facebook's Graph Search
- → Searching for Specific Things

Searching Facebook for Useful Information

If you think about it, Facebook knows an awful lot about you. Facebook knows where you live, where you have worked, where you went to school, and what you like. In addition, Facebook knows who your friends are, and it knows all those things about them, too.

It makes sense, then, to use Facebook as a search engine for useful and interesting information, much as you'd use Google or Yahoo! Yes, you can search Facebook for basic stuff, such as specific pages or groups or apps. But you can also search Facebook for more interesting connections, such as your friends who like a particular type of cuisine, or people in your hometown who watch a given TV show. Facebook is able to use what it knows about you and other users to create a huge database of information from which it can answer the most complicated search queries.

Understanding Facebook's Graph Search

There are more than one billion users of Facebook, and they all have their own histories, likes, and dislikes—all documented on the Facebook site. Facebook's new Graph Search takes this collective information and uses it to answer both basic and complex questions posed by you and other users.

Most web search engines, such as Google, require you to enter one or more keywords to conduct a search. Graph Search, in contrast, is a natural language search engine that lets you enter plain English questions. All you have to do is ask a question, as you would in real life, and Graph Search provides the answers.

Those answers come from Facebook connecting what it knows about its one billion users, and the relationships between them. In Facebook parlance, the "graph" is this database of user information, and when you search Facebook, you're searching the graph—hence the term Graph Search.

Facebook focuses Graph Search on the likes and interests you enter in your personal profile. When you like a particular Page or say you're interested in a given TV show, Facebook uses those pieces of information to answer somebody's future query.

For example, Facebook might know that you've listed gardening as an interest in your personal profile and that you currently live in North Carolina. If someone searches for gardening buffs in North Carolina, Facebook could identify you. Likewise, if you've liked the Starbucks Facebook Page and one of your friends searches for the best coffee in North Carolina, Facebook can put two and two together and use your recommendation to tell your friend about Starbucks.

By connecting these facts with your likes and interests, it's easy enough to discover friends who've read books by a given author, or find out what are your friends' favorite restaurants in your hometown.

This means you can use Graph Search to search for all kinds of things. The following are some examples of natural ways you can search on Facebook:

- Friends who like NCIS and CSI
- Friends who've read books by Hemingway
- Restaurants in San Diego
- Hotels in Orlando my friends like

- Photos of golf courses in Phoenix
- People in Des Moines who listen to Tony Bennett

The answers you receive will be both personal and pertinent.

Graph Search

Facebook introduced Graph Search in January, 2012, but by May, 2012, had only rolled it out to a few hundred thousand users—out of its total 1 billion person membership. So if you don't yet have Graph Search turned on for your personal Facebook account, just wait—you'll get it sooner or later.

Using Facebook's Graph Search

You use Graph Search via the search box in the Facebook toolbar at the top of every Facebook page. The results that Facebook returns differ depending on what you search for, however.

Perform a Basic Search

To conduct a search, you must enter one or more words that describe what you're looking for. The more words you enter, the more refined the results will be. And remember, Graph Search is a natural language search, which means you can enter complete sentences. Instead of searching for pizza, search for best pizza in Chicago; instead of searching for class photos, search for photographs of my college classmates.

1. Click within the search box in the Facebook toolbar and begin typing your query. As you type, a list of suggestions appears beneath the search box.

2. If one of the suggestions matches what you're searching for, click it.
3. Alternatively, click See More at the bottom of the list to display more search options and then click.
4. Click the search option that best matches what you're searching for.

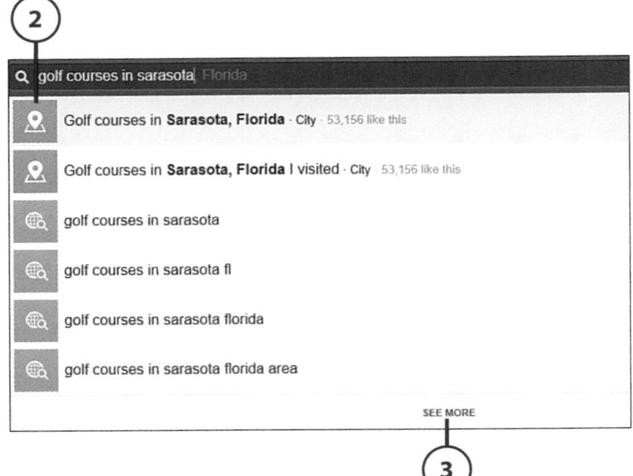

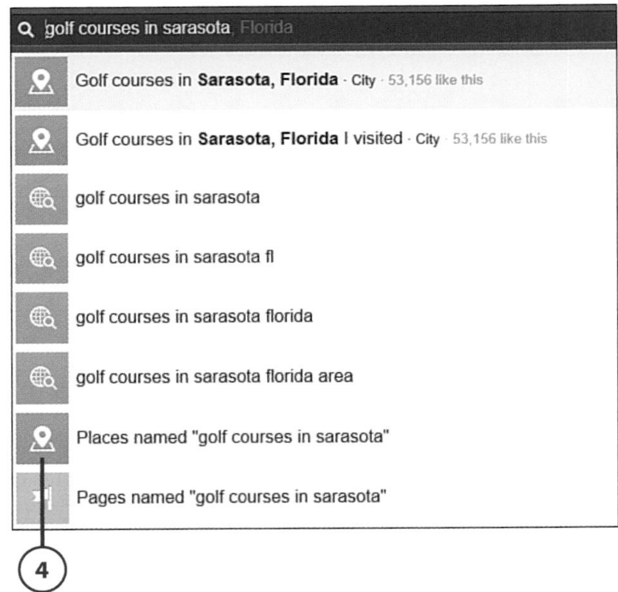

Understand Your Search Results

The search suggestions that Graph Search displays when you start typing in the search box are just that—suggestions. If you search for **favorite musicians**, for example, you see suggestions for My favorite musicians, Musicians, Favorite musicians of my friends, and Groups Pages, and Places named "favorite musicians." If you search for **restaurants in Phoenix**, you see several suggested place searches for just that.

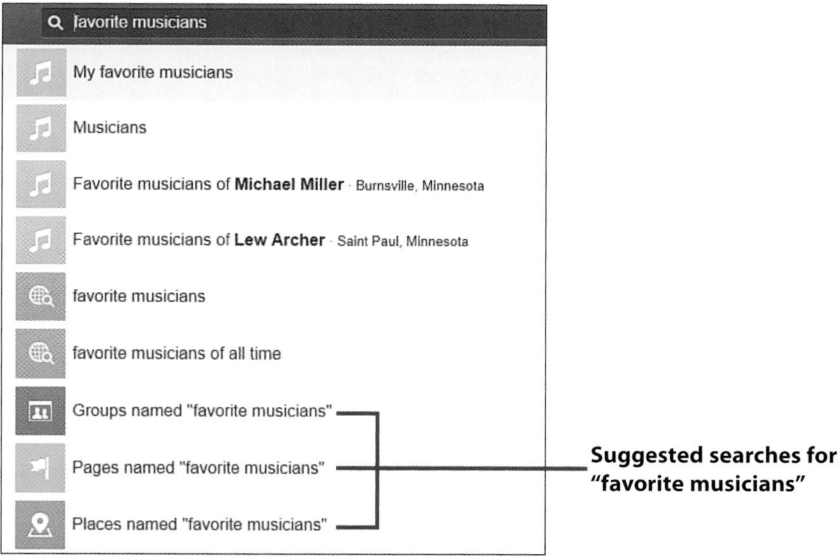

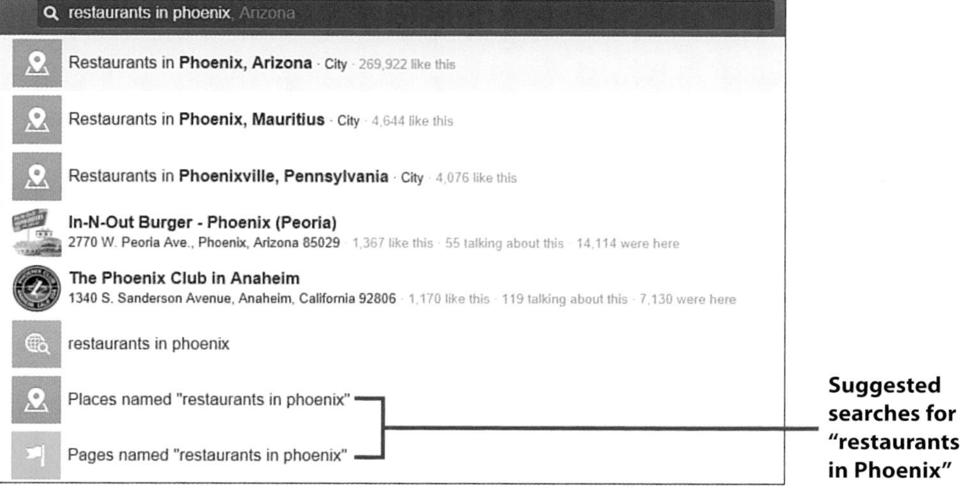

What you see when you click one of these suggestions differs by the type of suggestion. For example, clicking the **restaurants in Phoenix** suggestion displays a page of Phoenix restaurants popular among Facebook users. Each restaurant includes a star rating, price indication (number of dollar signs), and location, as well as how many people have checked in there and what other restaurants those people also liked. You can click the restaurant's name to go to its Facebook page, click the Like button to like the restaurant, or click the Map button to view a map of the restaurant's location.

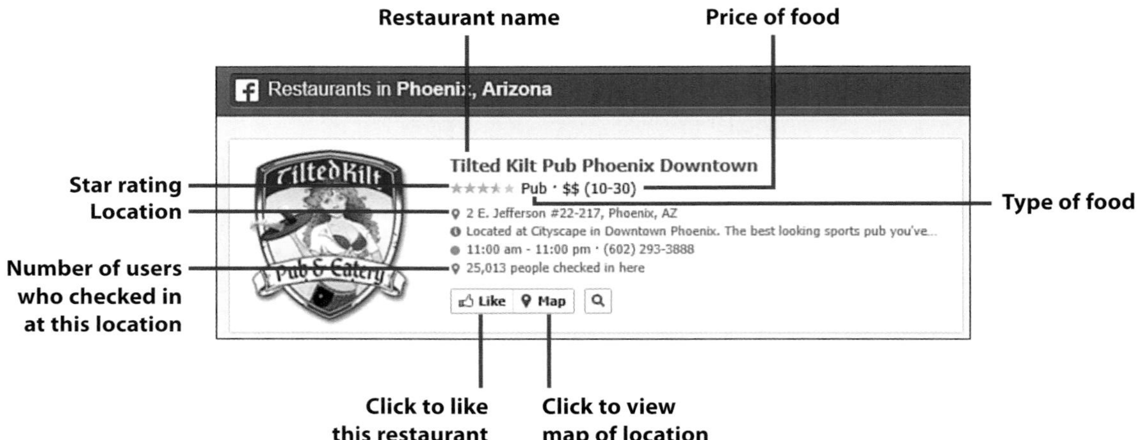

The results are much different for other suggestions, however. If you click the **Groups named "favorite musicians"** suggestion (for our first search example), you see a simple list of Facebook groups that have the phrase "favorite musicians" in their names. Click a name to view that group's page, or click the Join button to join the group. You can also click the People button to view members of that group, or click the Similar button to view a list of groups similar to this one on Facebook.

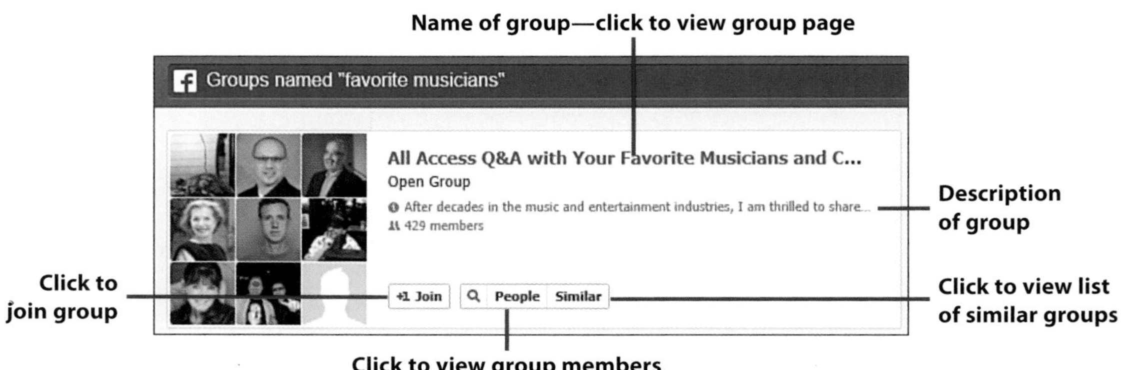

Other searches display more direct results. Let's say you searched for **photos of my friends in Minnesota**. Click this search suggestion and you see exactly what you searched for—photos of your friends that were taken in Minnesota. Click on any photo to view it larger in its own lightbox.

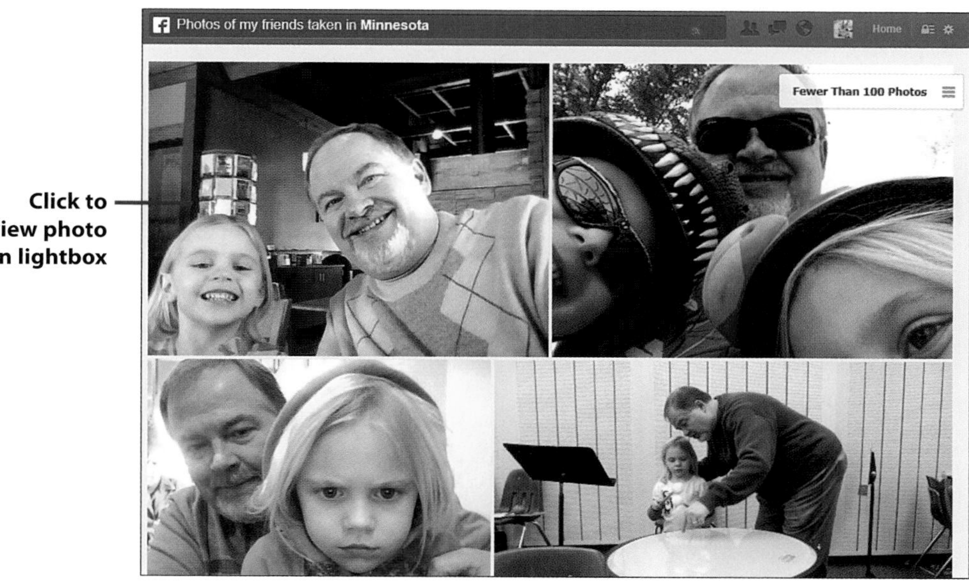

Fine-Tune Your Search Results

Many search results pages let you fine-tune the results. Look for a Refine This Search box on the right side of the search results page; the options available differ depending on what you're searching for.

Options

As an example, if you search for **restaurants in Minneapolis**, you find options to fine-tune your results by Place Type (Restaurant, Bar, and so on), Category (Asian, Barbeque, Burgers, Fast Food, and so forth), Liked By (specific friends), Name, Places In (location), and Visited By (specific friends). If you search for **friends in California**, you find options for Gender, Relationship (for example, Single or Divorced), Employer, Lives In, Hometown, School, and Friendship (My Friends, Friends of My Friends, and so forth).

---

1. Enter your query into the search box and click a search suggestion to display the search results page.
2. In the Refine This Search box, click the button for the option you want to fine tune and then make a selection from the resulting list. The search results are updated accordingly.

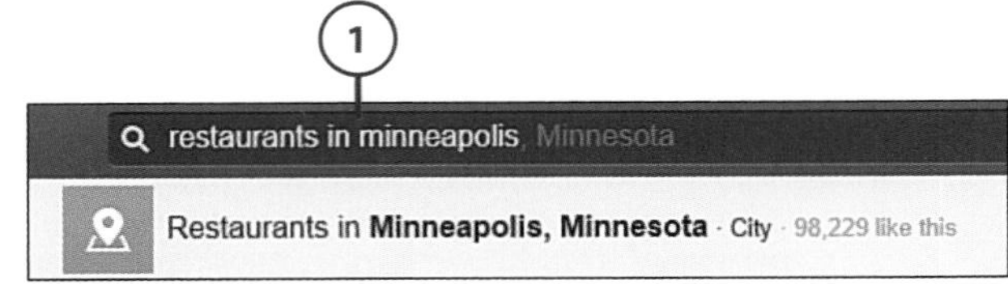

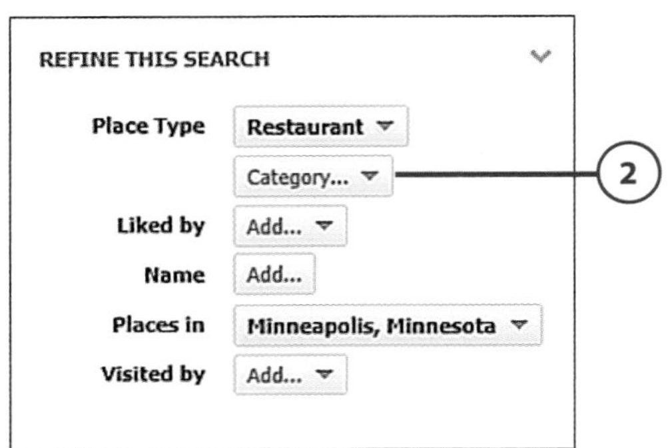

Extend Your Search

Some searches can be extended. That is, you start searching for one thing (hotels in Sarasota, for example) but then decide to see something else—photos of Sarasota, or maybe a list of friends who live there. Look for an Extend This Search box on the right side of the search results page.

1. Enter your query into the search box and click a search suggestion to display the search results page.
2. In the Extend This Search box, click the type of additional information you'd like to see.

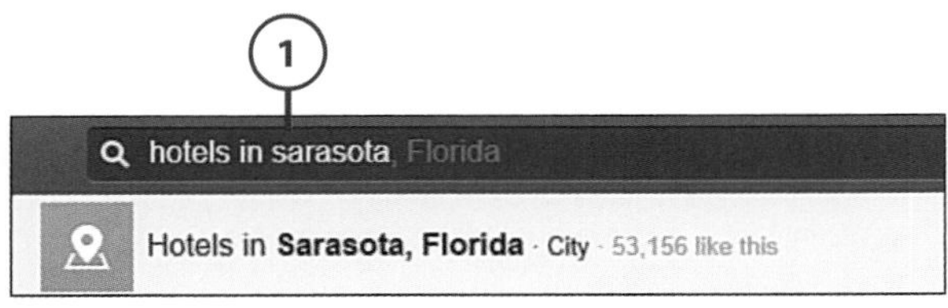

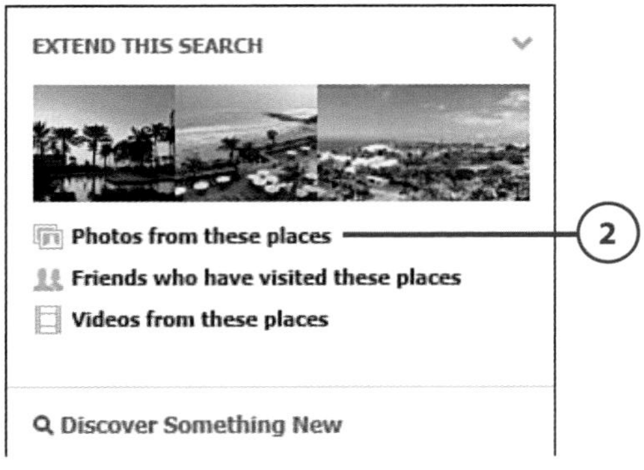

Search the Web

Facebook's Graph Search is tied into Microsoft Bing's web search. This means you can actually search the web from within Facebook.

1. Enter **web search:** into the Facebook search box, followed by the rest of your query. For example, if you're searching for hotels in Seattle, enter **web search: hotels in Seattle**. Press Enter and Facebook displays a page of search results from Bing.
2. Click the web page you want to view.

Web Search

You might see Web Search suggestions for other searches you make with Facebook's Graph Search. Click a Web Search suggestion to initiate the search with the Bing search engine.

Searching for Specific Things

Now you know how Graph Search works, and how to use it, in general terms. Let's take specific looks at some of the more popular types of searches you can make with Graph Search.

Search for Facebook Pages

Although you can use Graph Search for very sophisticated and personal searches, you can also use it to search for company or celebrity Pages on the Facebook site.

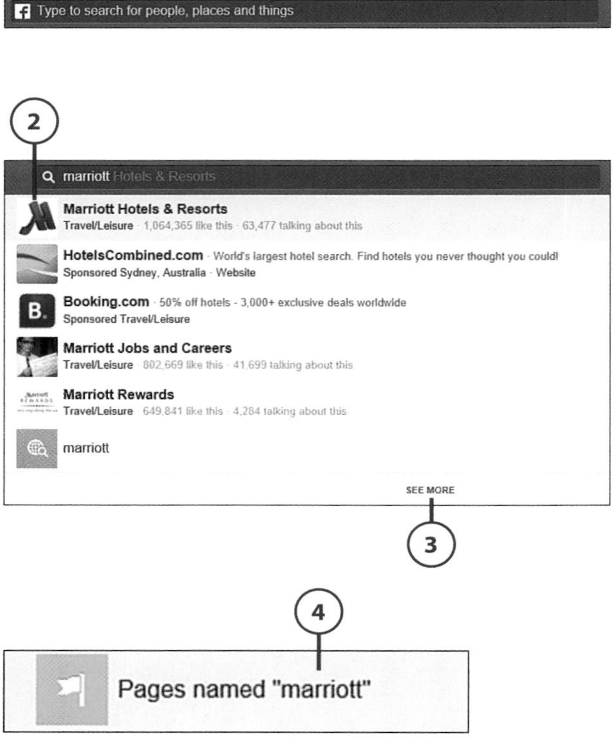

1. Click within the search box in the Facebook toolbar and begin typing the name of the company, product, or person. As you type, a list of suggestions appears beneath the search box.
2. It's likely that the Page you're looking for will appear near the top of the search suggestions. If so, click it to go to that Page.
3. Alternatively, click See More at the bottom of the list to display more search options.
4. Click the Pages Named option to view a list of suggested pages.
5. Click the Page you want.

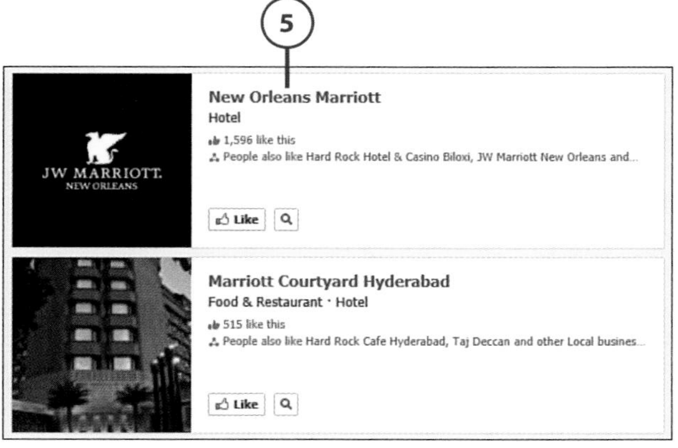

Search for Facebook Groups

Just as you can use Graph Search to look for Facebook Pages, you can also use it to look for interesting Facebook groups.

1. Click within the search box in the Facebook toolbar and begin typing the name of the group or words that describe what the group is about. As you type, a list of suggestions appears beneath the search box.
2. It's likely that one of the suggestions will be a group in which you're interested. If so, click the name of that group to go to that group's page.
3. Alternatively, click See More at the bottom of the list to display more search options.
4. Click the Groups Named option to view a list of suggested groups.
5. Click the group you want.

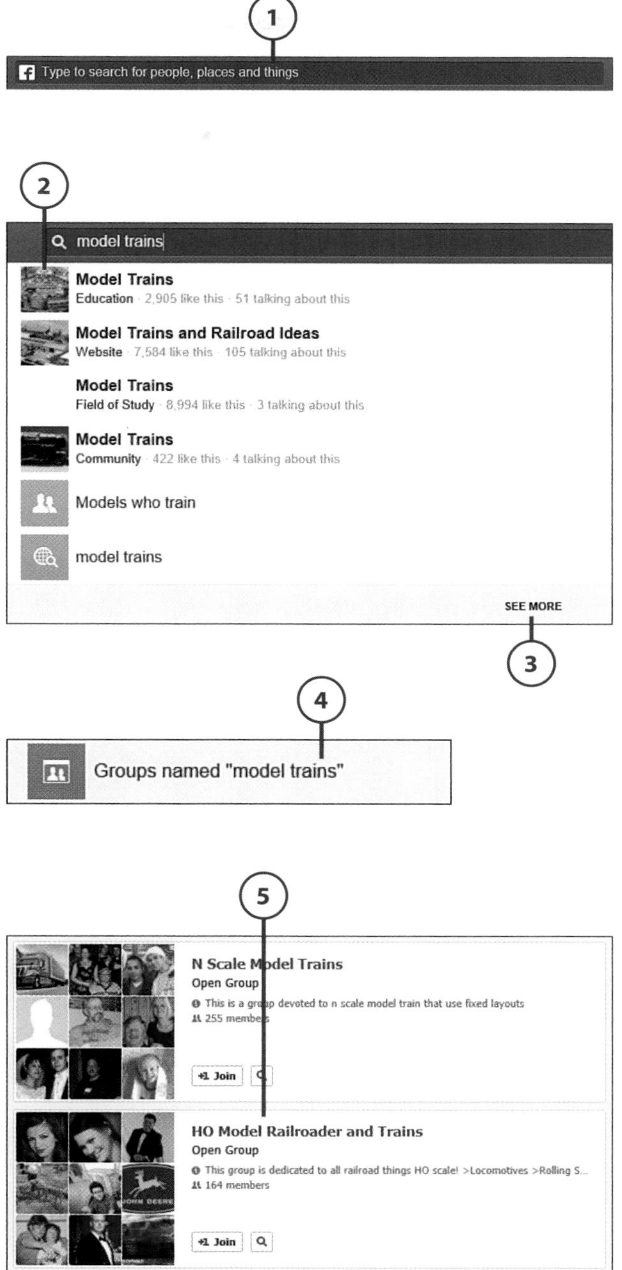

Search for Apps and Games

You can also use Graph Search to search for apps and games you might want to use and play.

1. Click within the search box in the Facebook toolbar and begin typing the name of the app or game.
2. It's likely that one of the suggestions will be the app or game you're looking for. If so, click that item to go to the app's Facebook page.
3. Alternatively, click See More at the bottom of the list to display more search options.
4. Click the Apps Named option to view a list of suggested apps and games.
5. Click the app or game you want.

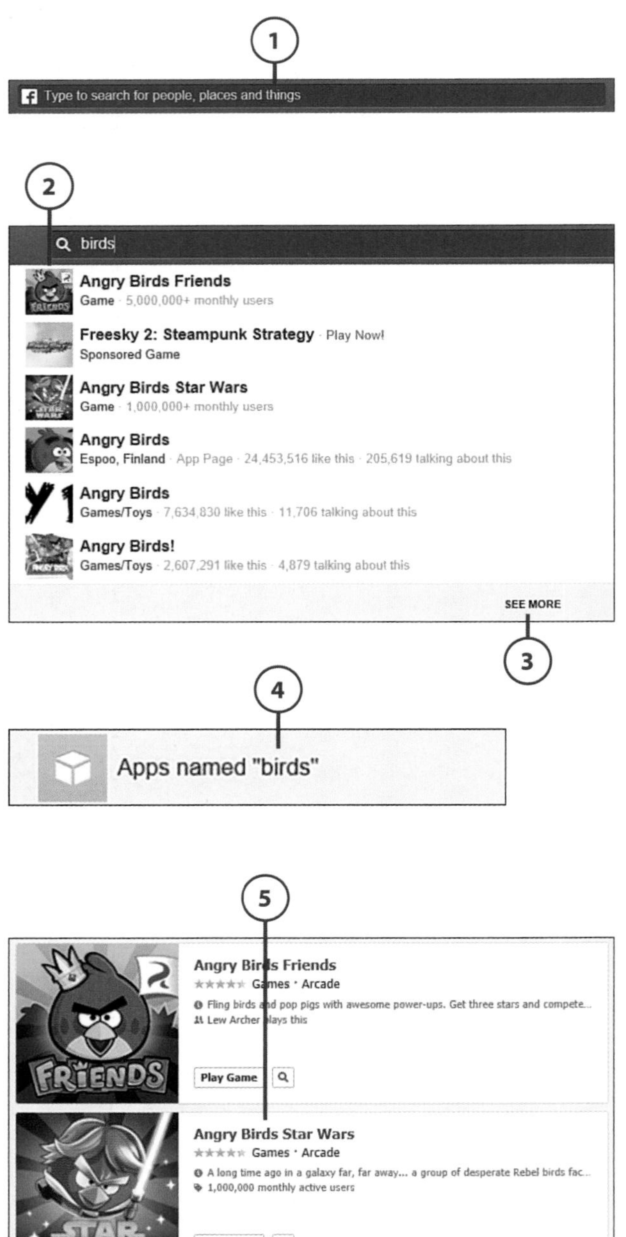

Search for People

One of the more popular uses of Graph Search is to look for specific friends on Facebook. We've discussed how to search for old friends previously in this book, but Graph Search gives you even more options for tracking down long-lost friends—particularly in establishing connections between other friends you already know of.

1. To search for a person by name only, enter that person's name, like this: **people named john doe**.
2. To search for a person by name and current location, enter the person's name and location, like this: **people named john doe in minneapolis**.
3. To search for a person by where they grew up, enter the person's name and hometown, like this: **people named john doe who lived in kokomo**.
4. To search for a person by where they went to school, enter the person's name and school, like this: **people named john doe who went to school at indiana university.**
5. To search for a person by where they used to work, enter the person's name and company, like this: **people named john doe who worked at general motors**.

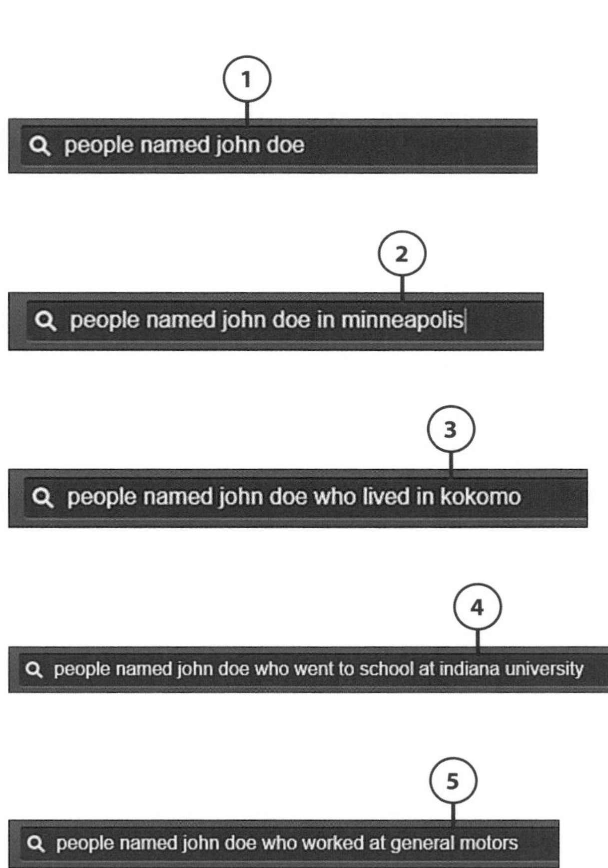

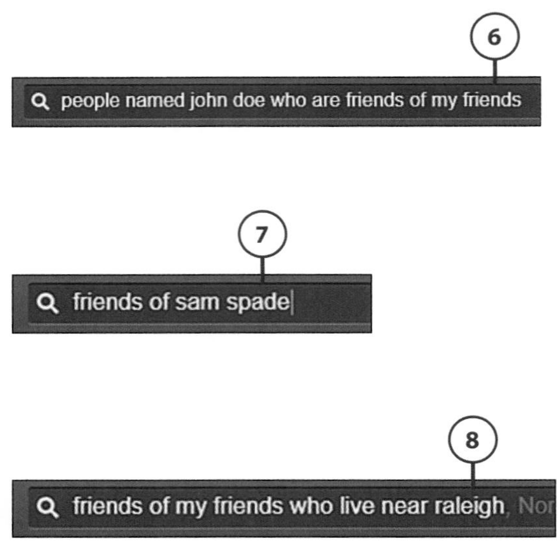

6. Sometimes the best approach is to search through friends of your friends. To search for a person in your friends' friends lists, enter the person's name like this: **people named john doe who are friends of my friends**.
7. Or, you can just search through all the friends of a specific friend, like this: **friends of sam spade**.
8. To search for friends of your friends who currently live near you (or any specific location), enter the location like this: **friends of my friends who live near raleigh**.

Search for Local Businesses

Are you looking for a good Italian restaurant to have dinner at? Or maybe a decent local hardware store? What about a hotel to stay at on an upcoming vacation? Facebook's Graph Search can help you find all these businesses, and more.

1. To search for a type of business near your current location, enter this: ***business* nearby**. For example, to search for a nearby hardware store, enter: **hardware stores nearby**.

2. To search for a business in another location, enter the location and type of business, like this: ***business* in location**. For example, to look for an Italian restaurant in Topeka, enter: **italian restaurants in topeka**.

3. To narrow your search to businesses that your friends like, add **my friends like** to your query. For example, to look for nearby grocery stores that your friends like, enter **grocery stores nearby my friends like.**

Search for Books, Movies, and Music

Graph Search can be a good way to find other things you might like. For example, if a lot of your friends like a particular book, you might like it too. The nice thing about this type of search is that Facebook shows you which of your friends liked a particular item; you can then base your decision on who liked what.

1. To search for books you might like, enter **books my friends like** or **authors my friends like**.

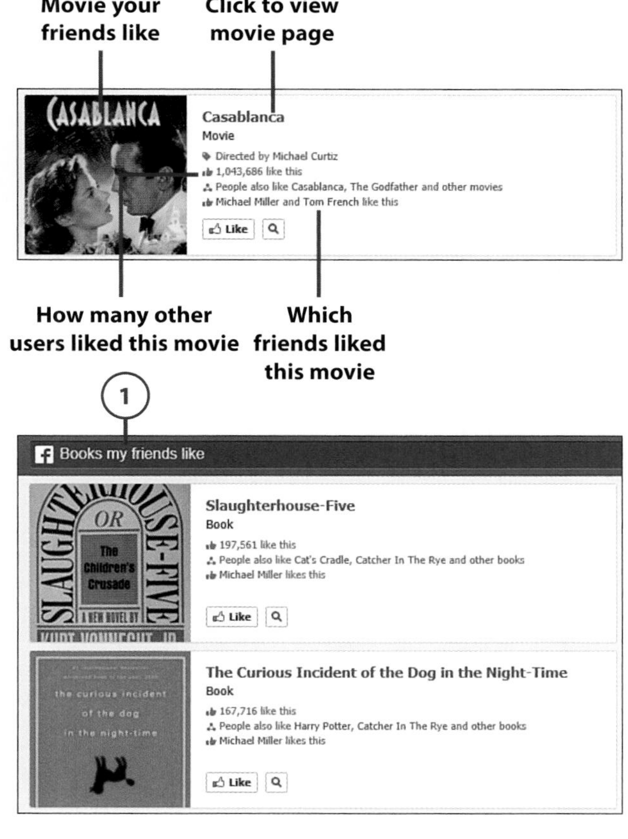

2. To search for movies you might like, enter **movies my friends like**.

3. To search for TV shows you might like, enter **TV shows my friends like**.

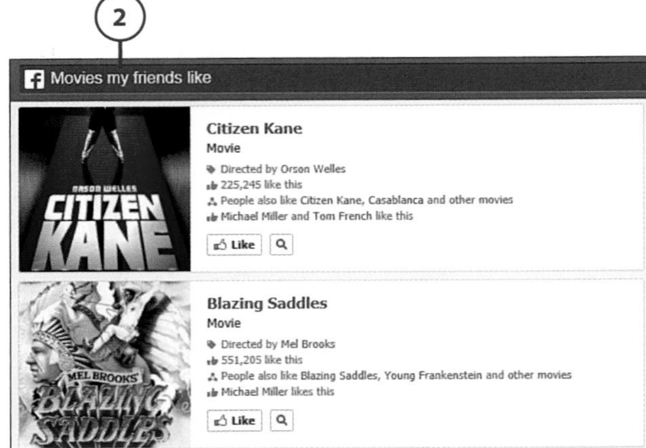

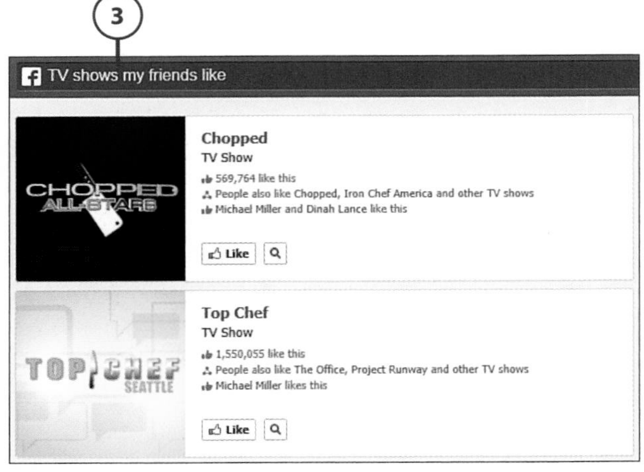

Search for Photos

Facebook is the largest photo-sharing site in the world, but it can be tough to find those specific pictures you're looking for. That's where Graph Search comes in. Just enter a detailed description of what you're looking for, and Graph Search finds the best photos that match your query.

1. To search for photos of a particular location or landmark, enter **photos of location**. For example, to see photos of the Statue of Liberty, enter **photos of Statue of Liberty**.

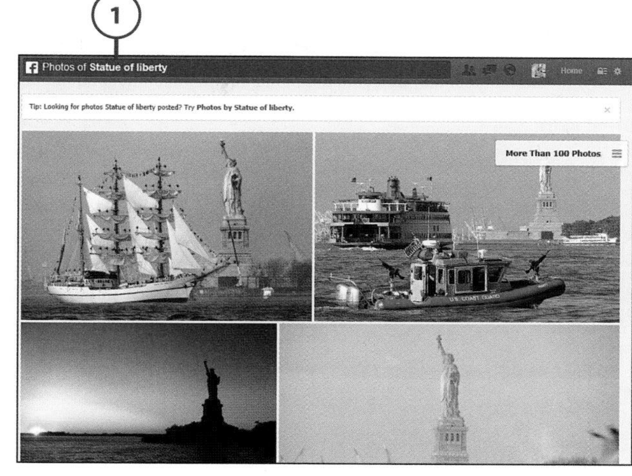

2. To search for photos taken in a particular city or state, enter **photos taken in *location***. For example, to see pictures taken in Orlando, enter **photos taken in Orlando**.

3. To view photos of a particular item or object, enter **photos of *object***. For example, to view photos of parrots, enter **photos of parrots**.

4. To view photos of a particular location or object taken by your friends, add **uploaded by my friends** to your query. For example, to search for photos your friends have taken in La Jolla Cove, enter **photos of La Jolla Cove uploaded by my friends**.

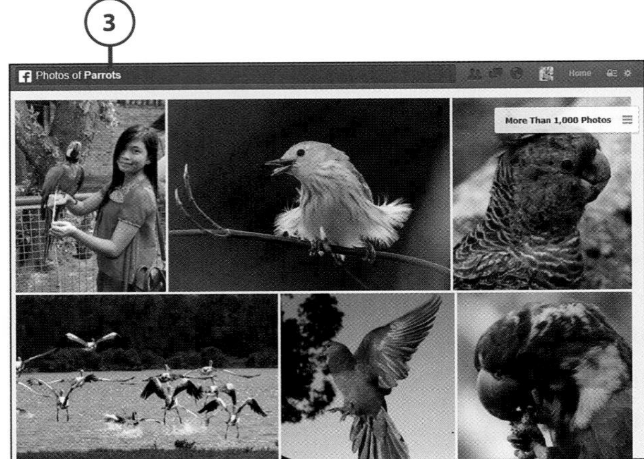

Picture posted by grandkids

In this chapter you discover the best ways to use Facebook to get closer to the youngest members of your family.

→ How to Engage Your Grandkids on Facebook
→ Responding to Your Grandkids' Posts
→ Five Things *Not* to Do with Your Grandkids on Facebook

16

Using Facebook to Keep in Touch with Your Grandchildren

As popular as Facebook is among seniors, it's even more popular among younger generations. This makes Facebook an ideal place to meet up with your grandkids, especially those who don't live nearby. There's nothing better than signing into your Facebook account and seeing a new message, photo, or video from your favorite grandchild.

How to Engage Your Grandkids on Facebook

It's likely that your grandchildren are on Facebook. (The older ones, anyway; you have to be 13 years old to sign up.) That means that you can add your grandkids to your Facebook friends list, and see their posts in your News Feed.

Using Facebook to keep in touch with your grandkids isn't as simple as all that, however. That's because younger people tend to use Facebook differently than do older ones. You need to take care to nurture a comfortable relationship with your grandkids, without stepping over any boundaries they might set up. There are rules to follow.

Make Friends with Your Grandkids

The first step in using Facebook to connect with your grandkids is to add them to your friends list. It shouldn't be too hard to find your grandchildren on Facebook and then send out the necessary friend requests. When your grandkids are on your friends list, every post they make should show up in your News Feed.

It's Not All Good

Selected Posts

By default, your grandkid's posts are visible to all their Facebook friends, including you. More tech-savvy youngsters, however, might figure out how to fine-tune their privacy settings and exclude you (and other family members) from some or all of their posts. This means you *don't* see everything they post in your News Feed. There's no way around this.

1. Facebook might suggest your grandchildren (and other family members) as friends when you first sign up or when you click the Friend Requests button on the toolbar—especially if you have their addresses in your email contacts list. If so, click the Add Friend button.

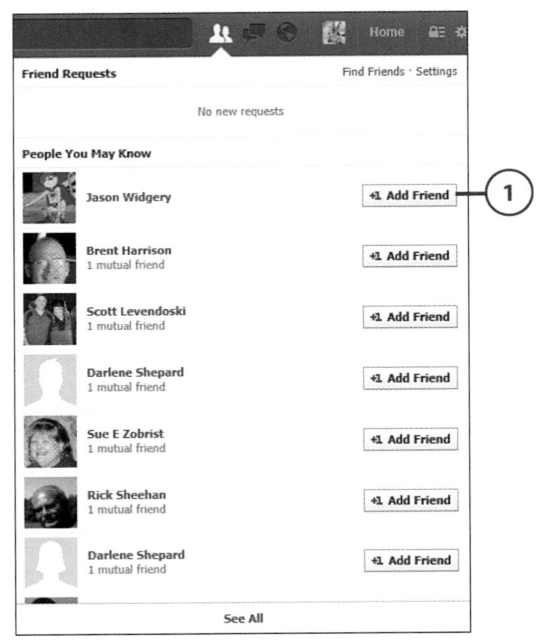

Finding Friends

Learn how to find family and friends on Facebook in Chapter 2, "Finding Old (and New) Friends."

2. Alternatively, you can do a simple search for your grandkids on the Facebook site. Use the search box in the Facebook toolbar to search for **people named *john doe*** and your grandchild's name should pop up.

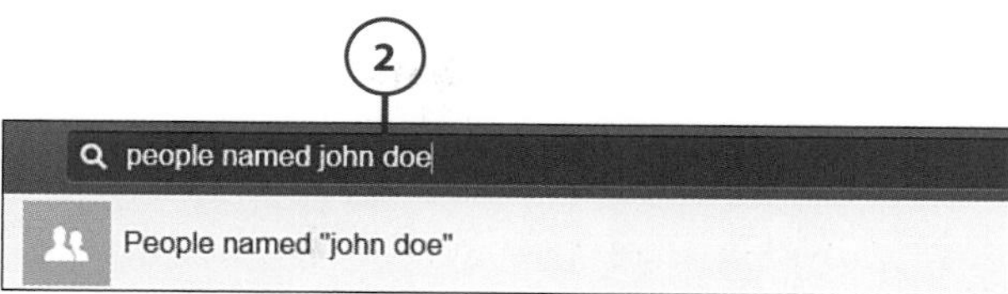

It's Not All Good

Rejected

Most grandchildren embrace the opportunity to get closer to their grandparents via Facebook and readily accept a friend request from a grandparent. Some grandkids, though, might be less than thrilled that their grandparents are intruding on what they might view as their personal social network. If this happens to you, don't take it personally; to that child, it just isn't "cool" to have old people as friends on Facebook.

Share Your Posts—Selectively

Just as you can read your grandkids' posts on Facebook, they can also read your status updates in their News Feeds. However, your grandkids might not be interested in everything you post, especially those posts that deal with issues of interest to seniors.

The solution to posting items that might turn off your grandkids is to not send all your posts to the youngsters. You can use Facebook's lists and privacy functions to send only certain posts your grandkids' way—so they'll be spared the embarrassment of having to read about your elder moments.

Its Not All Good

They Love You, But...

Depending on what you post on Facebook, your grandkids might find your status updates charming. Or they might find them embarrassing or even totally uninteresting. Let's face it; the kinds of things that interest someone our age aren't likely to be engrossing to the average teenager. Sure, you played a good round of golf today, or got a good deal at the local discount store, but do your grandkids really care about that? For that matter, all those words of wisdom and inspiration that you like to post are likely to be roundly ignored by youngsters with more immediate things on their minds.

In other words, don't expect your grandkids to like and comment on everything you post. At best, they might read your posts and then move on. At worst, they might figure out how to block your posts—or even unfriend you.

1. Start by creating a new Facebook friends list that contains all your grandchildren. Go to the Timeline page for your first grandchild, click the Friends button, and then click Add to Another List.
2. Click New List.

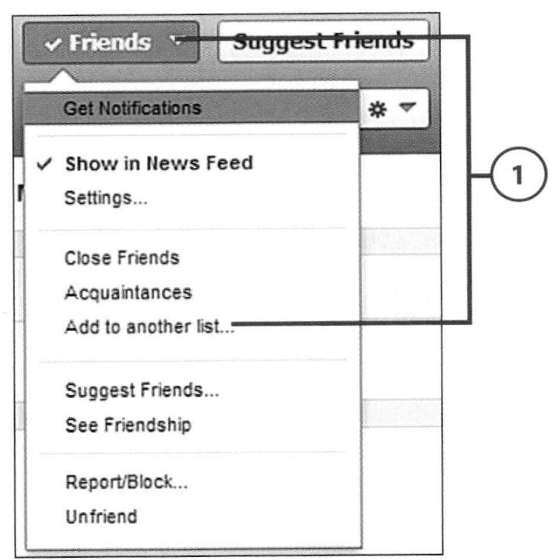

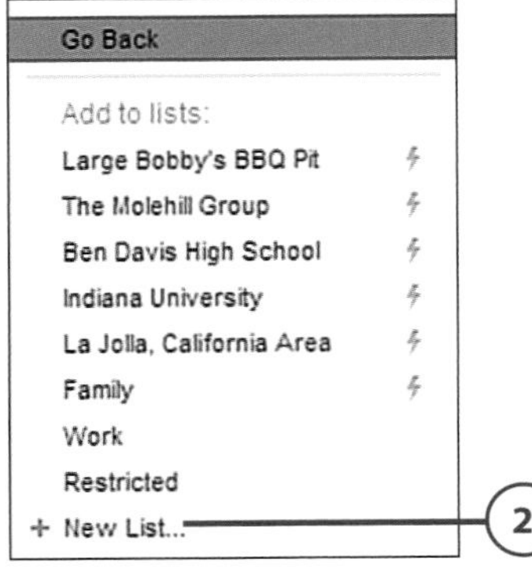

3. Enter **Grandkids** into the New List box and press Enter to create the list.

4. For each of your other grandchildren, go to his or her Timeline page, click the Friends button, and then click Add to Another List.

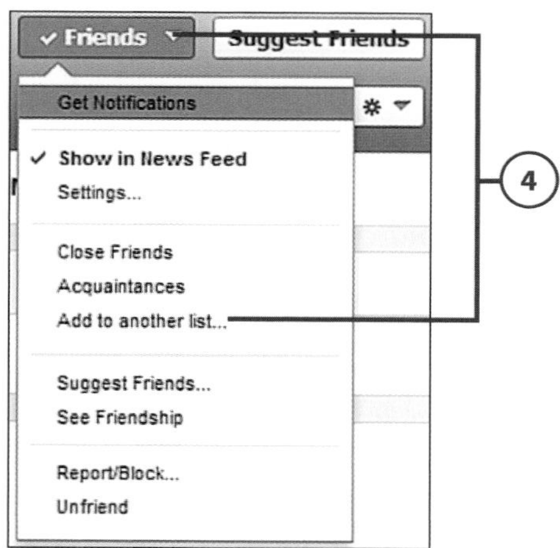

5. When the menu changes, check Grandkids.

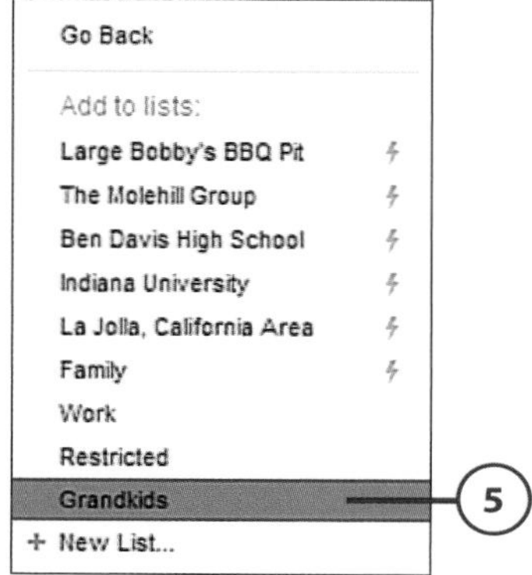

Custom Friends Lists

Learn how to create and use custom friends lists in Chapter 8, "Organizing Your Friends into Lists."

6. Now you can configure your privacy settings so that your grandkids don't see the bulk of your posts. Click Privacy Shortcuts on the Facebook toolbar, select Who Can See My Stuff?, and then go to the Who Can See My Future Posts? section.
7. Click the privacy button and select Custom to display the Custom Privacy dialog box.
8. Go to the Don't Share This With section and enter Grandkids into the These People or Lists box.
9. Click the Save Changes button.
10. By default, all new posts you make are sent to all of your friends *except* your grandkids.

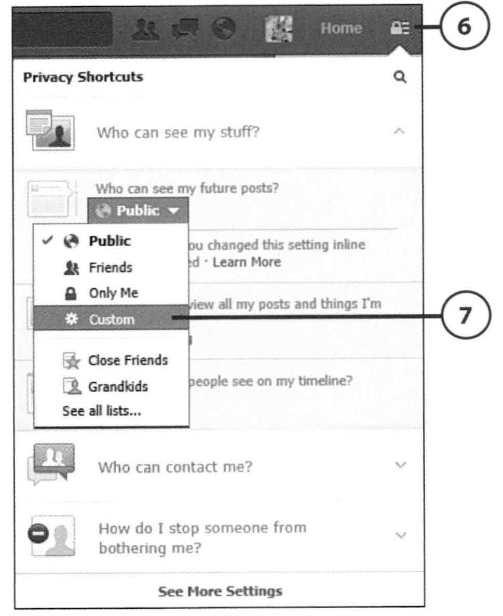

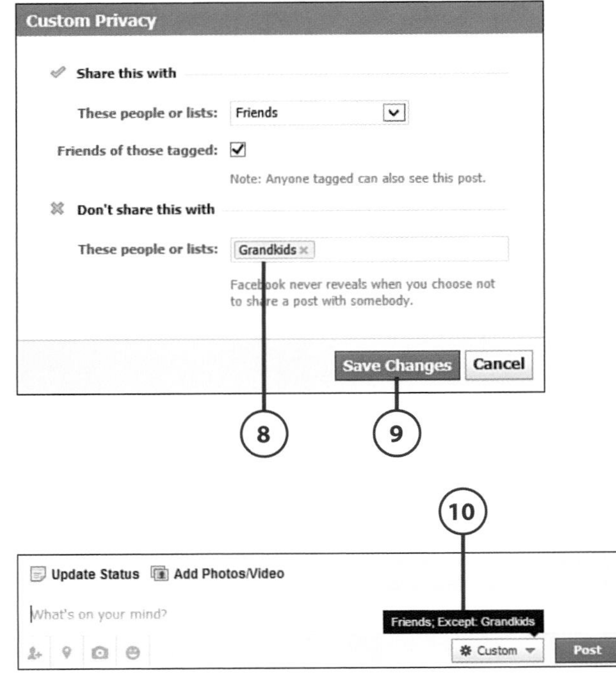

11. To send a post to your grandkids only, click the privacy button and select Grandkids.

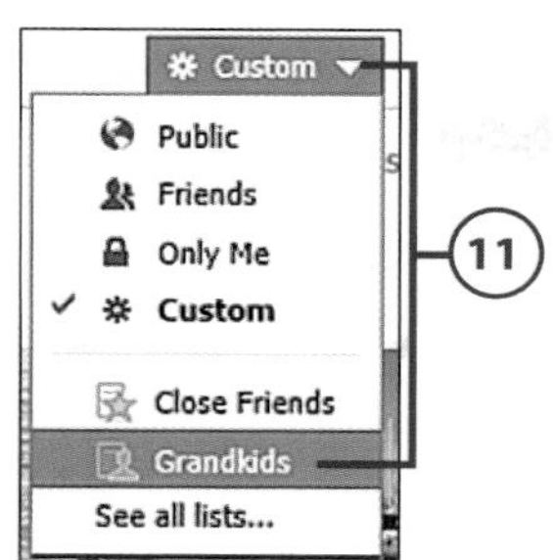

12. To send a post to all your friends, including your grandkids, click the privacy button and select Friends.

Custom Privacy

Learn about Facebook's privacy settings in Chapter 18, "Keeping Private Things Private."

Send a Private Message

Facebook status updates are public, but sometimes you want to send a more personal message to your grandkids. That's where Facebook's private messaging system comes in. You can easily send a private message to your favorite grandchild, and no one else will see it.

1. Click Messages on the Facebook toolbar to display the menu of options.
2. Click Send a New Message to display the New Message dialog box.

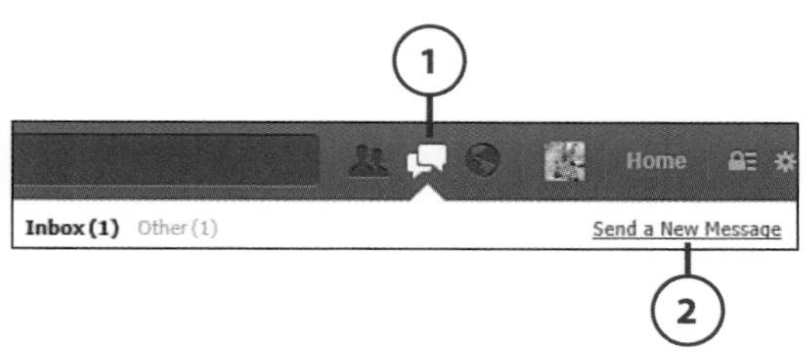

3. Enter the name of your grandchild into the To box.
4. Enter your message into the Write a Message box.
5. Click Send to send the private message.

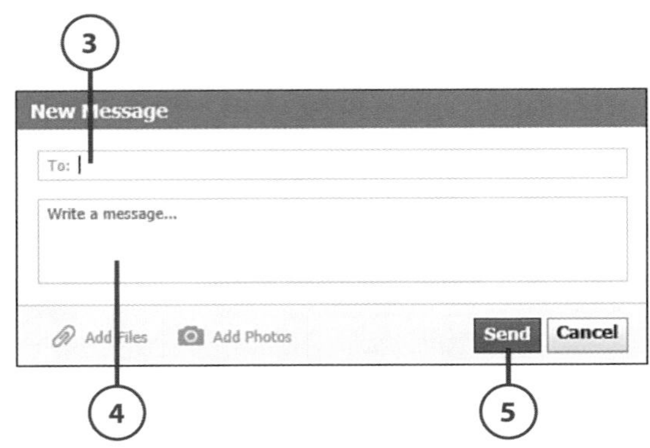

Private Messages

Learn how to send and receive private messages in Chapter 9, "Exchanging Private Messages."

Share Photos and Videos

Just as you can read each other's status updates, Facebook also lets you share photos and videos with your grandkids.

1. Encourage your grandkids (or their parents) to post photos and videos of themselves to Facebook. This provides you a constantly updated photo album of your loved ones.

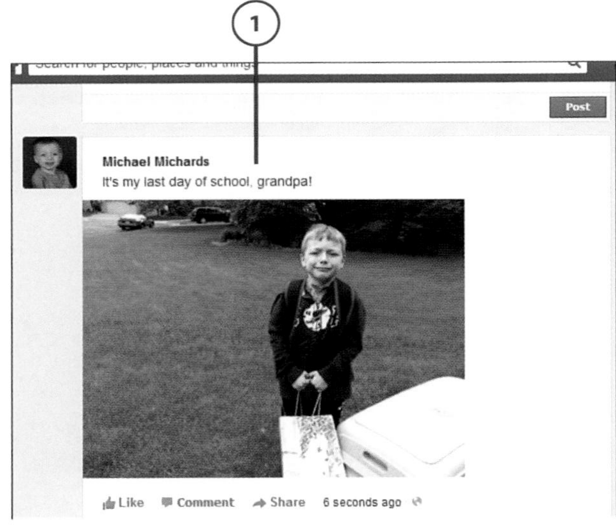

2. Make sure you post the occasional photo or video of yourself, for your grandkids to see. Don't limit yourself to posed pictures, either; your grandkids will get a big kick out of any crazy or silly picture or video you upload.

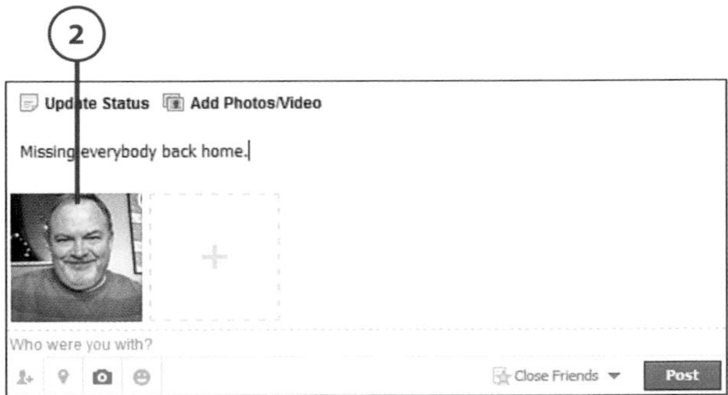

Pictures and Movies

Learn more about sharing photos in Chapter 5, "Viewing and Sharing Family Photos." Learn more about sharing videos in Chapter 6, "Viewing and Sharing Home Movies."

Chat via Text and Video

If you're on one side of the country and your grandkids are on the other, or even if you're only a few states away, you might only see your grandkids in person one or two times a year. Now, with Facebook text and video chat you can visit with each other several times a week, if you like. It can truly bring together distant families.

1. Schedule time for a weekly video chat with each of your grandchildren. This is especially great for talking to your younger grandkids who are sure to appreciate the one-on-one time with their favorite grandpa or grandma.

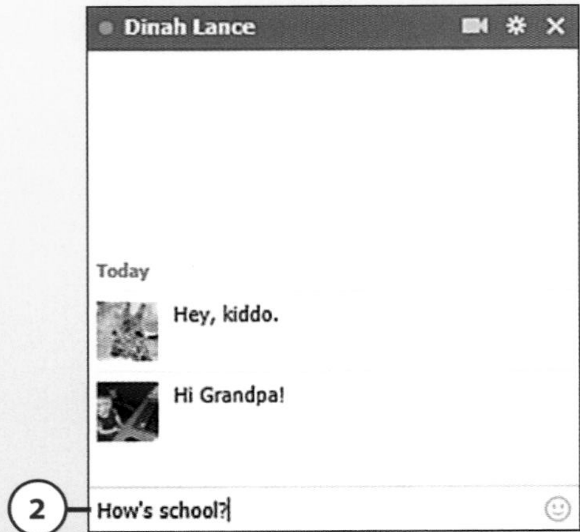

2 For the teenagers in your family, Facebook's text chat might be more up their alley. Chatting on Facebook is just like texting on a mobile phone, and you know your grandkids are down with that. Next time you're on Facebook, check to see if your favorite grandchild is also online (she probably is) and then open a text chat and say hi. If she wants to turn it into a video chat, you always have that option.

Facebook Chat

Learn more about text and video chatting in Chapter 10, "Chatting with Friends and Family in Real Time."

Play Games Together

Here's one you might not have thought of. If your grandkids are like mine, they love to play games—board games, card games, video games, you name it. Well, Facebook is chock full of social games that you can play with other Facebook users. That means all you have to do is pick a game and then invite your grandkids to play it with you, online.

>>>Go Further

FAMILY GAMES

What games are best for playing with your family online? Here's a list of games to start with:

- Are You Smarter Than a 5th Grader?
- Backgammon Live
- Chess
- Gin Rummy
- Ludo Playspace
- Monopoly
- Scrabble
- The Price is Right Game
- Who Wants to Be a Millionaire
- Words with Friends
- Yahtzee!

Just go to the App Center page and search for any or all of these games by name.

1. Go to Facebook's App Center and search for social games you think your grandkids will like.

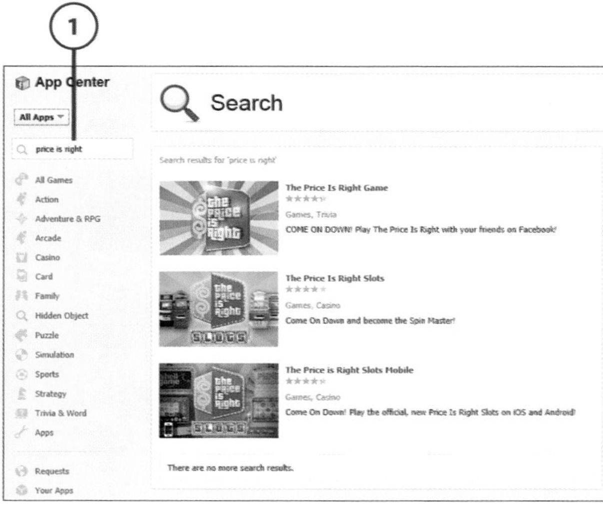

2. Open the game and then invite your grandchildren to play with you, in real time.

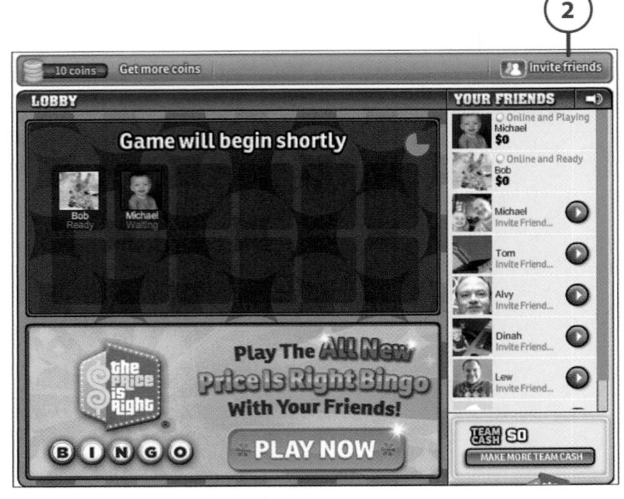

Facebook Games

Learn more about finding and playing Facebook games in Chapter 14, "Using Apps and Playing Games."

Consider Using Other Social Media

Facebook used to be the cool place for kids to hang out online. Things change, however, and Facebook is less cool than it used to be—especially now that everybody's grandparents are also signing up. (It's a double-edged sword!) This means that some teenagers are migrating away from Facebook to other social media, so you might need to look elsewhere to connect with your grandkids online.

Seniors on Twitter?

I'll be honest. You won't find a lot of seniors on most of these newer social networks—which is why they're so appealing to younger users. Still, if you know you grandkids are big on Twitter or Tumblr and you want to stay in touch, you might want to investigate.

1. Instagram (www.instagram.com) is a photo-sharing smartphone app that's very popular among the high school crowd. Kids use Instagram as a kind of mobile visual social network.

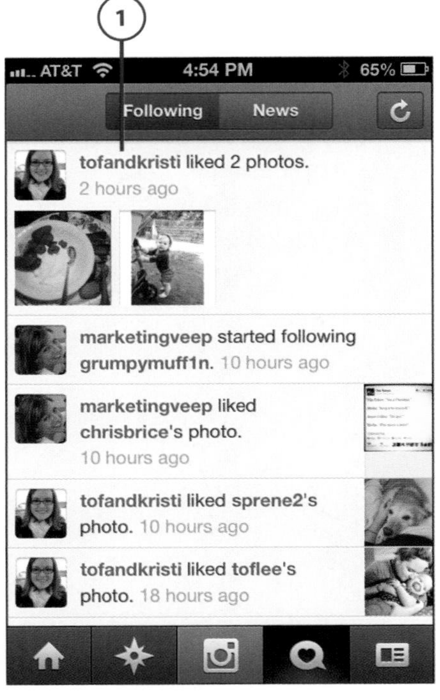

2. Tumblr (www.tumblr.com) is a microblogging network, where users create their own personal blogs, and post short text messages or photos there. Teens like Tumblr because they can personalize their blogs much more than they can with their Facebook Timeline pages.

3. Twitter (www.twitter.com)is a social medium that is especially popular among older teens and people in their twenties. Users post short "tweets" (140 characters or less) that are then viewed by their online "followers." It's more like text messaging than posting on Facebook, which makes it more suited for mobile use.

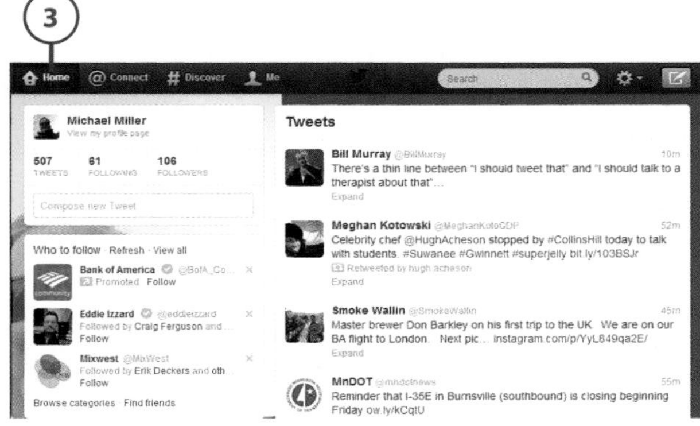

>>>Go Further

BRIDGING THE GENERATION GAP

I find it fascinating that technology is helping to bring together families that, up until recently, were increasingly drifting apart.

Baby boomers and Gen X'ers alike are more mobile than preceding generations, resulting in families spread over larger distances. The days of multiple generations cohabitating in the same town (or under the same roof!) are long gone, which has led to a splintering of the extended family.

That's changed, however, thanks to the Internet in general and social networks in particular. Today physical distance matters less, because we can use Facebook and other Internet-based technologies to keep in touch with family members, no matter where they live. Facebook has been particularly effective in bringing generations together; when there's news to spread, it's easier to post a single Facebook status update than it is to make a dozen phone calls to family members here and there.

In addition, Facebook lets you communicate with your grandchildren in a way that's familiar and comfortable to them. Instead of forcing the youngsters to sit down for a physical visit or endure a boring phone call, you instead engage them on their own terms, via short Facebook status updates. That's how they like to communicate, and now you can do it, too.

It's true; Facebook is helping our generation reconnect with our younger relatives—including those sons and daughters who moved away many years ago. A status update can never replace a hug, but I know that grandparents on Facebook are closer to their children and grandchildren than they were just a few short years ago, before social networking.

Responding to Your Grandkids' Posts

Most communication on Facebook is via status updates, displayed in users' News Feeds. That's true of communication with your grandchildren, as well—which means you need to learn how to deal with what they post.

The reality is that younger people, teenagers especially, are prone to publicly posting whatever is currently on their minds. This results in a lot of angry, revealing, embarrassing status updates. (And photos!) If you're a teenager, you're used to seeing this sort of thing from your friends. But if you're a grandparent (which you are), you might be shocked or dismayed by what your teenaged grandkids post on Facebook. How you respond will determine whether you stay your grandkids' "friend" on Facebook, or whether you get silently unfriended.

Don't Criticize

One of the things that younger people hate about older people (their parents and grandparents, especially), is their tendency to criticize. Teens don't like adults coming down on them, even inadvertently or in a well-intentioned way.

So if your grandson posts that he blew off class today, resist the temptation to admonish him. If your granddaughter posts a photo of her new outfit, don't leave a negative comment about how the color doesn't flatter her eyes, or that the skirt is too short. There will be plenty of other opportunities in life to get in your little digs; don't spoil the social connection by incessantly offering your opinions on what your grandkids are doing.

Don't Hijack the Conversation

You also don't want to jump in the middle of an ongoing conversation between your grandchild and her friends. Teenagers view Facebook as kind of a private forum (although we all know it's not) and thrive on the comments that friends leave to their posts. You'll see a lot of back and forth between a handful of friends, resulting in a thread of messages and comments.

The worst thing you can do is interrupt this sort of conversation in process. Resist the urge to chime in with your two cents' worth, which could completely disrupt the flow of messages. Feel free to read, but don't hijack the conversation for your own means.

If nothing else, your jumping into the middle of a conversation could severely embarrass your grandchild. Don't expect your comments to be in sync with what her peers are saying, and don't expect your humor to translate to the younger generation. Chances are your comment will stick out like a sore thumb, and teenagers do not like to stand out like that. Just avoid commenting and you'll avoid embarrassing your grandkids.

Don't Respond at All

In fact, the best way to comment on your grandkids' Facebook posts is not to comment at all. While it's great to read their posts to see what they're up to, you don't necessarily want to remind them that you're looking in. You don't want your grandkids to feel as if you're monitoring them; they want to be free to post whatever it is they want to post, without worrying about whether or not grandma is watching.

What you want to do, then, is read your grandchildren's status updates and view their photos, but not "like" them or comment on them. Most young people on Facebook, for whatever reason, are surprisingly open about what they post; you get to see who your child is hanging out with, hear about her latest fight with her boyfriend, read about how much she hates her classes this semester or likes her new job or is creeped out by the guy who works at the pizza stand at the mall. They won't be near as open if they think they're being watched.

That means that when it comes to reading your grandkids' posts, you need to keep your Facebook presence muted. That is, you don't want to remind your grandchildren that you're reading what they write—which means not commenting on their posts. You need to stay pretty much invisible, as far as your grandkids are concerned, so they don't know that you're there.

Don't Stop Your Own Posting

Just because you shouldn't comment on your grandkids' status updates doesn't mean that you can't post your own status updates. Chances are the kids won't equate your occasional post showing up in their News Feeds with the fact that you're eyeballing everything they post online.

If you can't resist the urge and do post a comment to one of your grandkids' status updates, let me tell you what is likely to happen. First, your grandchild will become much less open on Facebook; the number of posts she makes will drop dramatically. Then she'll get smart and figure out how to configure Facebook so that you—and you alone—can't read her status updates. Then she'll go back to posting frequently, but you'll never know because you won't be able to see a thing she posts. You'll be locked out, which is not what you want.

This is why you want to remain a silent observer, as far as your grandkids are concerned. Yes, you'll be listed as one of their Facebook friends, but you'll be one of those silent friends they soon forget about. You can watch, but you shouldn't be heard.

Ignore What You See

The good thing about viewing your grandchild's status updates is you'll see what she's doing and what she's thinking. It's a great way to get closer to a distant grandchild, just by observing her activities online.

The bad thing about this is that you get exposed to *everything* your grandkids are doing. You don't see only what's important, you also see the most mundane posts (maybe she's having a bad hair day, or a fight with one of her friends). Even worse, you might be exposed to some information or behavior that you'd rather not know about. It's a matter of TMI (too much information), which teenagers in particular are prone to post. If you want to keep intact that vision of your grandchild as a starry-eyed angel, maybe it's better *not* to connect on Facebook.

To be fair, your younger grandkids' posts probably won't be too shocking; they're just kids, after all. But with older teenagers, prepare to be shocked. Teens today tend to post anything and everything that goes through their minds, and that might be a lot of stuff you might not want to know.

This means you need to steel yourself for both mundane and profane posts from your grandkids. You have to resolve not to get upset by anything you might see in their feeds. Remember, you shouldn't be commenting on or criticizing what they post; that's not your role, and could drive them away from participating in Facebook.

So if you see something offensive or disturbing in your grandkids' posts, just ignore it. On the other hand, if you find something particularly worrisome, such as suicidal threats or signs of bullying, you have an obligation to respond—but not publicly on Facebook. Send your grandchild a private message, or pick up the phone and give her a call. But don't jump in publicly; reserve advice for a more private conversation.

Five Things ***Not*** to Do with Your Grandkids on Facebook

Facebook can be a wonderful way to keep in touch with your grandchildren, but only if you avoid some common missteps.

Don't Do These Things

With that in mind, here are some important things not to do when posting and responding to your grandkids.

1. Don't friend your grandkids' friends. Your grandkids like to keep their friends and family separate, so a family member getting friendly with one of their peers is a big social no-no. Resist the urge to send a friend request to one of your grandchildren's Facebook friends. It's okay for you to accept a friend request if one of her friends invites you, but it's not okay for you initiate the contact. In general, you should keep your circle of friends to your friends and immediate family, not to your grandchildren's friends.
2. Don't post unflattering photos of your grandkids. Family photos that you think are funny might not seem so funny to your grandkids—especially when their friends see them. The problem comes if you upload an embarrassing photo to Facebook and tag a grandchild in it. Thus tagged, all her Facebook friends will see the photo, with the resulting mortification. Think twice before you post those "cute" photos of your grandkids, especially as they get older. And if you must post the photos, don't tag your grandchildren by name. If they're not tagged, their friends probably won't see the photos—which is best for all concerned.
3. Don't use your grandchild's photo as your profile picture. I know you're really proud of your grandkids, but you shouldn't appropriate their photos as your own. Many grandparents use photos of their grandkids as their own profile pictures, or as the cover images on their Timeline pages. That's not fair to your grandkids—and, to be fair, looks kind of weird. Post your own photo as your profile picture, and be done with it.

4. Don't post too much personal information. Facebook is a great forum for keeping friends and family up-to-date on what's happening in your life, but that doesn't mean you need to post every little detail about what's happening. Your grandkids, especially, will be embarrassed or even grossed out if you post all the fiddly details about your latest medical exam or (God forbid) romantic interlude. There's just some stuff that kids don't want to know, and you need to know that.

5. Don't try to be cool. I know, you want to fit in with the young generation today, but let's face it—you're not that young, and you're not that cool. Don't embarrass yourself by trying to use today's hip lingo, or even common Facebook abbreviations, such as LOL (laughing out loud). No matter how hip you think you might be, you'll still come off as an old fogey trying to act younger than you really are. Bottom line, when you're posting on Facebook, act your age. You've earned the privilege.

Photo
Short text message
Lew Archer
Had a wonderful time visiting with all our old friends in San Diego last week.
Great weather and great conversations all week long!
Like
Comment
Share
7 seconds ago
Write a comment...
Press Enter to post.

In this chapter you discover the types of things you should share on Facebook—and those you shouldn't.

- → What's Good to Post on Facebook
- → What *Not* to Post on Facebook
- → Learning Facebook Etiquette

What You Should—and Shouldn't—Share on Facebook

Facebook is not your own private diary or soapbox. It's a public website, where what you post is visible to all your friends and family—and, potentially, millions of other users.

As such, it's important to make your posts interesting to the people who'll be reading them. It's also important not to post certain types of information; with everyone you know reading everything you post, it's easy to get yourself in trouble with a few taps of the computer keyboard.

What's Good to Post on Facebook

If you've been on Facebook for any time at all, you've seen your share of boring, self-indulgent, and just plain useless status updates from friends. Not everyone has the knack of posting updates that you really want to read.

It's important to post interesting status updates. But what exactly qualifies as something worthwhile to post about?

Post Interesting Information

The best advice I can give for what to post on Facebook is anything that your friends and family are likely to find interesting. Not things you might find interesting, but what others might find interesting about you.

Interesting Topics

To make sure your updates get read, focus on interesting and unique topics. The fact that you went to a concert or read a good book is interesting; that you woke up with a headache or just had a cup of tea is not.

1. Post things that your friends and family want to know about. Friends typically want to know if you've done or seen something interesting, been ill, met a mutual friend, and such. If you think someone's interested in it, post it.
2. Post things you want to share with your friends. These are moments and events that are important to you, but you think your friends might care about, too.
3. Post about major life events—things in your life that your friends and family *need* to know about. These are important moments and events, such as anniversaries, birthdays, celebrations, and the like.

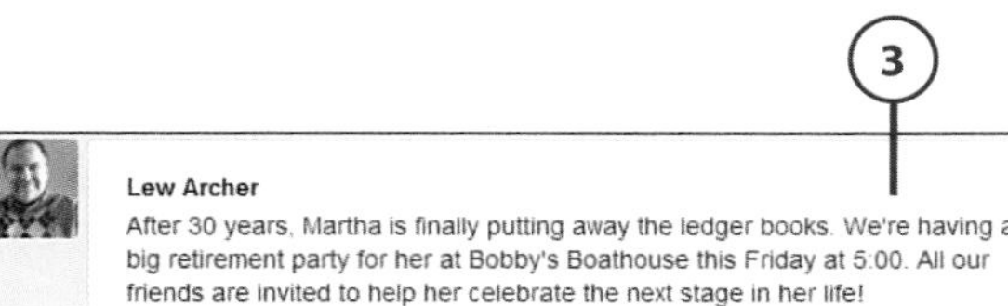

4. Post interesting thoughts. Look, you've come this far in life, you've earned your opinions. Share your wisdom with your friends and family via Facebook status updates.

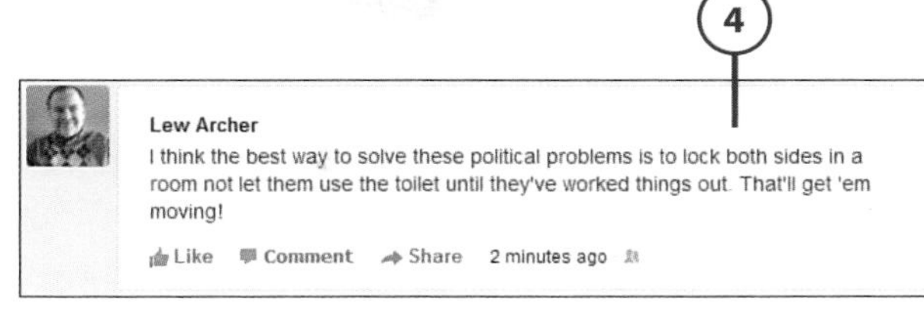

Post Important Information

Many people use Facebook as a kind of bulletin board for their families and friends. One post can inform a large number of people about something important; it's a lot more efficient than sending out dozens of emails or making tons of phone calls.

1. Post if something has happened to you. If you've been ill or hospitalized, lost your job, moved to a new house, or whatever, use Facebook to let everyone know about it.

2. Post if something has happened to your spouse. Many of your friends are likely mutual friends of your spouse, so if anything major has happened to your spouse, include that information in your status update—especially if your spouse can't post herself, for whatever reason.

3. Post if something has happened to another family member. You might know something about a cousin or nephew that others in your family might not know about. Share your information with other family members via a Facebook post.

4. Post if something has happened to a mutual friend. It's tough to keep track of all your old friends. Start the chain going by posting what you know, and let your other friends pass it on to their friends, too.

What ***Not*** to Post on Facebook

There are some things you probably shouldn't post on Facebook. Many of the posts you see from friends are mundane and uninteresting; some are inflammatory and offensive. And then there are those posts that just contain too much information about personal matters you'd rather not know.

It's important, then, to think before you post. Remember that Facebook is not a private diary; it's a public website with more than 1 billion users. Some things simply shouldn't be shared with all those people.

Avoid Uninteresting or Unwise Posts

Remember, by default, Facebook status updates are public for all to read. Post only that information that you'd want your friends (or spouse or grandkids) to read.

- Don't complain. The last thing your Facebook friends want to find in their news feeds is your private griping. It's okay to grouse and be grumpy from time to time (you're entitled, at your age), but don't use Facebook as your personal forum for petty grievances. If you have a personal problem, deal with it; whining gets old really fast.

- Keep your opinions to yourself. In particular, avoid getting overly political or controversial in your posts. It's true that some people like to use Facebook as a platform for their opinions, but that's a sure fire way to get "unfriended" by friends who disagree with you. Although it might be okay to share your opinions with close real-world friends, spouting off in a public forum is not only bad form, it's a way to incite a flame war—an unnecessary online war of words.
- Don't post confessions. Facebook is not the place to come clean about past indiscretions; it's a public forum, not a private confessional. If you need to confess something to someone, do it in a more private way.
- Don't get too personal. Facebook is definitely not the best place to share intimate details about your life. Most people get a little awkward when someone discloses just a little too much about his or her personal life. A good rule of thumb is that if you don't want your grandkids to know about it, don't share it on Facebook. (And let's hope you're somewhat discrete around your grandkids!)
- Don't post anything that anyone—including lawyers or the police—could use against you. When you post a status update, it's there for everyone to see, friend or foe. It gets back to that confessional thing; if you think something could come back to bite you, don't post it.
- Don't post embarrassing photos of yourself or others, and don't tag anyone else who's in those photos—especially your children or grandchildren. You don't want to humiliate yourself or your family online.
- Don't post just to get attention. Here's something new to Facebook: *vague-booking*. This is the practice of posting a message that's intentionally vague but hints at some personal problem or crisis. People vaguebook to get their friends to respond with worried inquiries about what's wrong; it's highly manipulative and sure to create enmity over time. If you really have sort of problem, it's better to call a friend instead of posting about it publicly to everyone on Facebook
- Don't post if you don't have anything interesting to say. Posting too many meaningless updates will cause friends to start ignoring everything you post.

Avoid Posting Personal Information

There's a whole other class of information you shouldn't post on Facebook—personal information that could be used by identity thieves to hijack your bank accounts or site memberships online. If you don't want to become a victim of identity theft then avoid posting too many personal details to your Facebook account.

- *Don't* post your personal contact information—phone number, street address, email address, and so forth. You don't want complete strangers to contact or harass you.
- *Don't* post location information when you're away from home. This can tip off burglars that your house is empty, or notify stalkers where you can be found. Wait till after you get home to tell your friends where you had dinner or vacationed.
- *Don't* post the layout of your house. You don't want to give potential burglars a roadmap to all your goodies.
- *Don't* post your social security number (SSN). Ever. If your SSN gets in the wrong hands, identity theft will result.
- *Don't* post other pieces of information that could be used to gain access to your online accounts—your birthdate, birthplace, mother's maiden name, and so forth. This information is typically used for "challenge questions" if you forget your password on a website; if you post this information where potential thieves can see it, they might be able to reset your password and gain access to your online accounts.

Learning Facebook Etiquette

Your status updates on Facebook should be not only interesting but also easy to read. Not that each post has to be letter perfect, but there are some guidelines you should follow.

Carefully Compose Your Status Updates

Facebook status updates are not long, thought-out missives. A status update is more immediate than an email, and less well-constructed than a handwritten letter.

That said, you can ensure more satisfied readers if you follow some simple posting guidelines. Your status updates don't have to be perfect, but they do need to be in the ballpark.

- Be personal and personable. Your writing on Facebook should be light and informal, not stiff and professional. Write as you'd talk, in your own personal voice. Make it sound like you—and be as friendly as you know how to be.
- Keep your posts short. Facebook users, even your dear old friends, don't have the attention span, the patience, or the inclination to read long tomes. They want quick bits of information, something they can scan without necessarily reading. Keep each status update to a paragraph, no more than a few sentences—and the shorter the better. Even older Facebook users expect short posts.
- Include links and photos in your posts. A Facebook status update doesn't have to be just text. You can—and should—include photos and links to other websites in your posts. In fact, most posts today have some sort of visual element. Nothing wrong with text-only posts; it's just that users are drawn to—and tend to expect—more visually interesting posts. If you can illustrate your point with a photo, or a link to a picture on another web page, then do so.

Know the Shorthand

As your grandchildren will no doubt attest, writing a Facebook status update is a bit like sending a text message on your cell phone. You do it quickly, without a lot of preparation beforehand or editing afterwards. It's an in-the-moment communication, and as such you can't be expected to take the time to create a grammatically perfect message.

For this reason, Facebook status updates do not have to—and seldom do—conform to proper grammar, spelling, and sentence structure. It's common to abbreviate longer words, use familiar acronyms, substitute single letters and numbers for whole words, and refrain from all punctuation.

For example, instead of spelling out the word "Friday," you can just write "Fri." Instead of saying "See you later," just say "later." Instead of spelling out "New York City," use the abbreviation "NYC."

Misspellings

It's also acceptable, at least to some users, to have the occasional misspelling. It's not something I personally like to do or see, but I'm a professional writer and pickier about these things than many people; most people will let it slide if you get the spelling or grammar wrong once in a while.

Younger users, especially, like to use a sort of online shorthand (or "Facebook grammar") to pack as much as possible into a short status update. These are the same acronyms and abbreviations that have been used for decades in text messaging, instant messaging, and Internet chat rooms. You might not be familiar with this shorthand, much of which is detailed in Table 17.1. It may be a tad unseemly for older folks to use this hip lingo, but it certainly helps to know what everything means when you're reading posts from your grandkids.

Table 17.1 Common Facebook Acronyms

Acronym	Description
AFAIK	As far as I know
ASAP	As soon as possible
ASL	Age/sex/location
B/W	Between
B4	Before
BC	Because
BFN	Bye for now
BR	Best regards
BRB	Be right back
BTW	By the way
CU	See you
Cuz	Because
FB	Facebook

Acronym	Description
FTF	Face to face
FWIW	For what it's worth
FYI	For your information
GM	Good morning
GN	Good night
HTH	Hope that helps
IDK	I don't know
IM	Instant message
IMHO	In my humble opinion
IRL	In real life
JK	Just kidding
K	Okay
L8	Late
L8r	Later
LMAO	Laughing my ass off
LMK	Let me know
LOL	Laughing out loud
NSFW	Not safe for work
OH	Overheard
OMG	Oh my God
Pls *or* Plz	Please
Ppl *or* peeps	People
R	Are
Rly	Really
ROFL	Rolling on the floor laughing
SD	Sweet dreams
Tht	That
Thx *or* Tnx	Thanks
TY	Thank you
TTYL	Talk to you later

Acronym	Description
U	You
Ur	Your
WTF	What the f**k
WTH	What the hell
YMMV	Your mileage may vary
YW	You're welcome
Zzz	Sleeping

>>>Go Further

HOW OFTEN SHOULD YOU POST?

How often should you update your Facebook status? That's an interesting question, without a defined answer.

Some of my Facebook friends post frequently—several times a day. Some only post occasionally, once a month or so. Most, however, post once a day or once every few days. So if there's an average, that's it.

Some of the more frequent posters are justified, in that they post a lot of interesting information. Others I find more annoying, in that their posts are more personal and less practical; every little tic and burp is immortalized in its own update. That's probably posting too much.

On the other hand, my friends who only post once a month or so probably aren't trying hard enough. I'd like to hear from them more often; certainly they're doing something interesting that's worth posting about. After a while, I tend to forget that they're still around.

So you need to post often enough that your friends don't forget about you, but not so often that they wish you'd just shut up. I suppose your update frequency has something to do with what it is you're doing, and how interesting that is. But it's okay to post just to let people know you're still there—as long as you don't do so hourly.

Click to configure privacy settings
Privacy Shortcuts button
Home
Privacy Shortcuts
Who can see my stuff?
Click to configure contact settings
Who can contact me?
How do I stop someone from bothering me?
See More Settings
Click to manage block list

In this chapter you find out how to keep your private information from becoming public on the Facebook site.

→ Determining Who Sees What You Post
→ Limiting Contact from Other Members
→ Controlling Tagging
→ Controlling Who Sees What on Your Timeline

18

Keeping Private Things Private

Facebook is a social network, and being social means sharing one's personal information with others. In Facebook's case, you share your information by default—both with your friends and with Facebook and its partners and advertisers.

Unfortunately, all this sharing poses a problem if you'd rather keep some things private. If you share everything with everyone then all sorts of information can get out—and be seen by people you don't want to see it. Keeping personal information personal on Facebook is possible, but it requires some work on your part.

Determining Who Sees What You Post

Many seniors worry about their privacy online, and for good reason. Not only is the Internet rife with would-be identity thieves, there are also a lot of companies that would like to get hold of your private information to contact you for advertising and promotional reasons.

This is why many seniors are cautious about getting on Facebook; they're afraid that the information they post will be needlessly shared with the wrong people. There's a basis to these fears, as Facebook likes to share all your information with just about everybody on its social network—not just your friends or their friends, but also advertisers and third-party websites.

Fortunately, you can configure Facebook to be much less public than it is by default—and thus keep your private information private. You just have to know which settings to tweak.

Configure Facebook's Default Privacy Settings

The first step to ensuring your Facebook privacy is to determine who, by default, can see all the posts you make. You can do this in a positive fashion, by telling Facebook precisely who can view your new posts. You can take a more negative (or defensive) approach, by telling Facebook who can't see your status updates.

Public Sharing

Facebook makes your information and status updates public by default. This is because Facebook believes it can better connect users with one another and build a stronger community by making public all of a user's likes and dislikes. The more Facebook knows about you, the more connections it can recommend and make.

---

1. Click the Privacy Shortcuts button on the Facebook toolbar to display the pull-down menu.
2. Click the down arrow next to Who Can See My Stuff? to expand the menu.

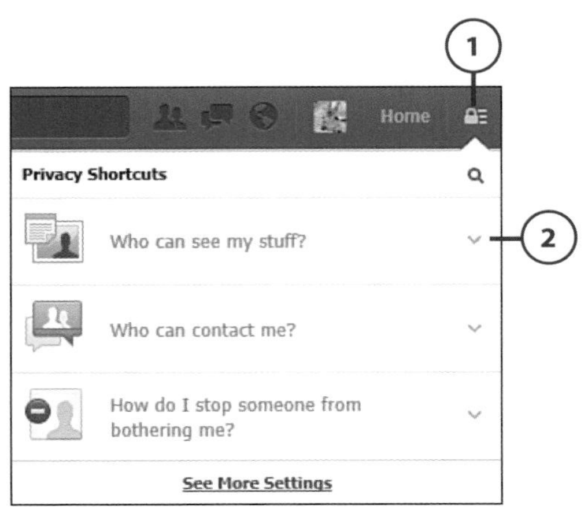

3. Go to the Who Can See My Future Posts? section, click the down arrow, and select one of the resulting options.
4. Click Public to let anyone on Facebook see your posts.
5. Click Friends to restrict viewing to only people on your Facebook friends list.
6. Click Only Me to keep your posts totally private—that is, to keep anyone from seeing them.
7. Click Custom to create a custom list of people who can or can't see your posts. The Custom Privacy dialog box displays.
8. Pull down the Share This With list and select Only Me to hide your information from everyone.
9. Pull down the Share This With list, select Specific People or Lists, and then enter the names of those Facebook users (or the name of a custom friends list) you want to see the info if you want to make your information visible only to specific people.
10. Enter names into the Don't Share This With box to prevent specific people from viewing your posts.
11. Click the Save Changes button.

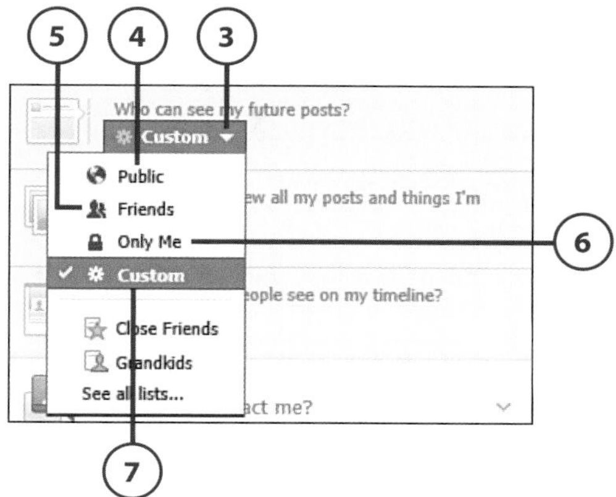

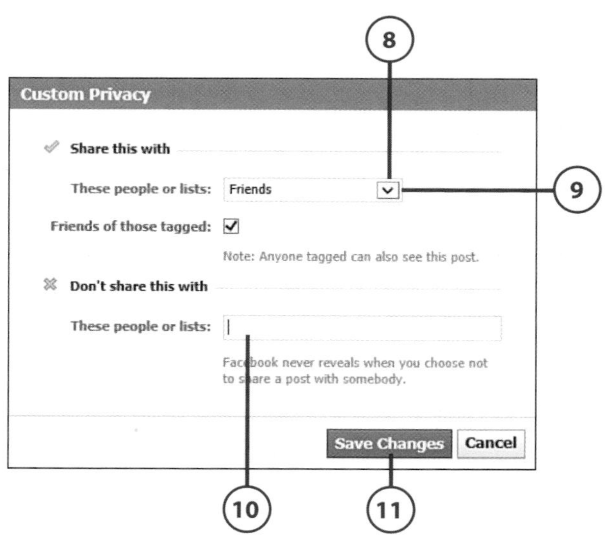

Select Who Can See (or Not See) Individual Posts

Even after you set these global posting privacy settings, you can change the privacy setting for any individual post you make. That is, any given post can be sent to a specific list of people that overrides the global settings you made previously.

For example, you might have set your global privacy settings so that your friends can see your posts. But if you have a new post that you only want your immediate family to see, you can configure that single post to go to only to your family members, not to everyone else on your friends list.

1. Go to your Facebook Home page and start a new status update as normal.
2. Click the Post Privacy Setting button and select one of the following options.
3. Click Public to make this post visible to any Facebook user.
4. Click Friends to make this post visible to everyone on your friends list.
5. Click Only Me if you want no one but yourself to see this post (which is kind of silly, but still).
6. Click a list name (if you've previously created any friends lists) to send the post to members of that list.
7. Click Custom to open the Custom Privacy window to specify the people who can see this post.

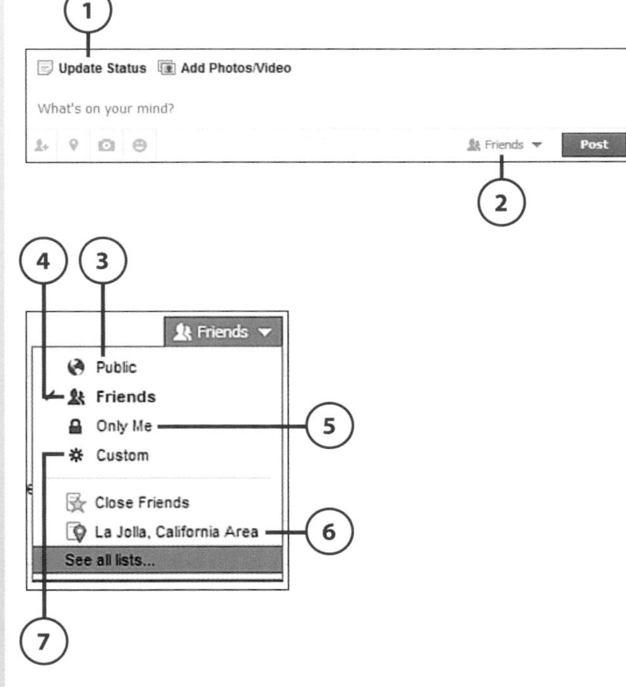

8. Select the necessary options to make this post visible to or hide it from specific people or lists.
9. Click the Save Changes button.

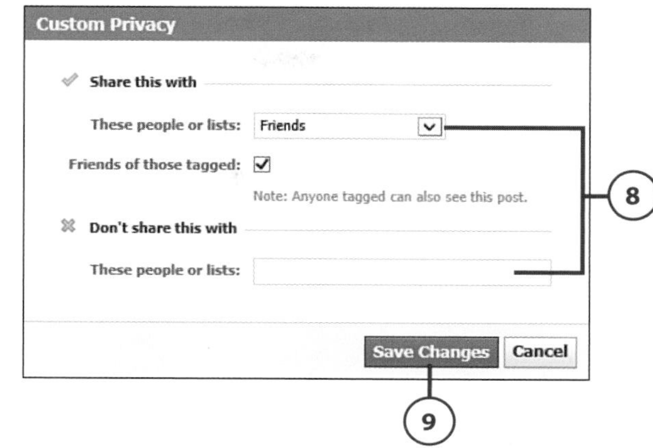

Limiting Contact from Other Members

Are you getting private messages or friend requests from people you don't know? It's time to reconfigure your privacy settings to limit contact from complete strangers.

Control Who Can Contact You

By default, just about anybody who Facebook thinks you might know can send you private messages. If you'd rather not be contacted by complete strangers, you can tell Facebook to only let your friends send you messages.

1. From the Facebook toolbar, click the Privacy Shortcuts button to display the drop-down menu.
2. Click the down arrow next to Who Can Contact Me? to expand this section.

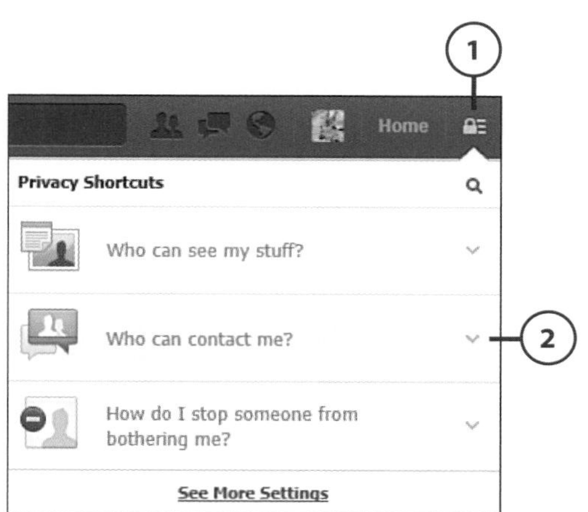

3. Select Strict Filtering to see private messages only from people on your friends list.

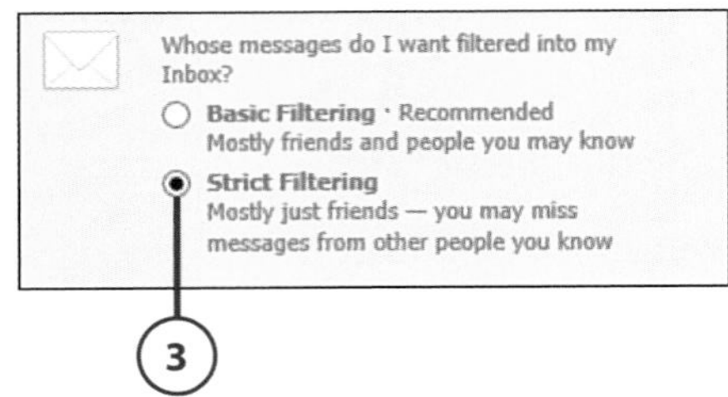

Control Who Can Send You Friend Requests

You can also limit who on Facebook can request to be your friend. By default, anyone on Facebook can friend you; you might not want to see friend requests from people you don't know, however.

1. From the Facebook toolbar, click the Privacy Shortcuts button to display the drop-down menu.
2. Click the down arrow next to Who Can Contact Me? to expand this section.
3. Go to the Who Can Send Me Friend Requests? section and click the Privacy button. (By default, the button says "Everyone.")
4. Click Friends of Friends to limit friend requests to people who know the people you know—people who are friends with your Facebook friends.

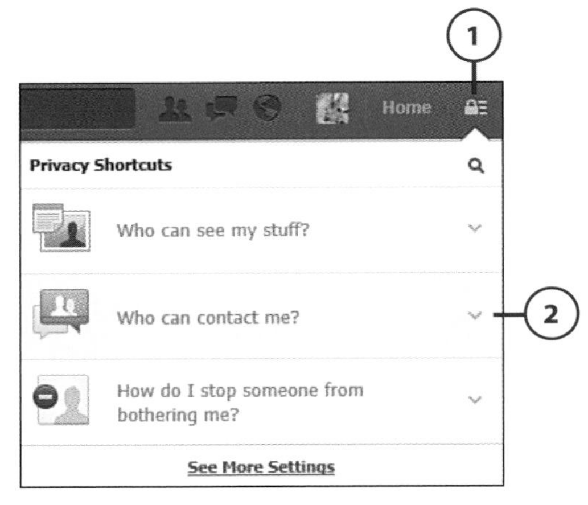

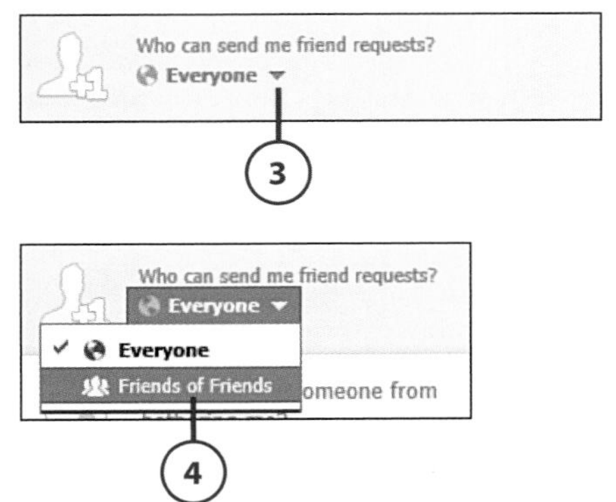

Controlling Tagging

Facebook likes to connect people with each other. This is often done via "tagging," where one user can tag ("who are you with?") another user in a status update or photo without asking the other person. When you're tagged, you're connected to that post or photo, whether you want to be or not—which can be an invasion of your privacy.

Restrict Who Sees Tag Suggestions in Photos That Look Like You

One of the ways that Facebook encourages tagging is by suggesting people to tag when someone posts a photo. Facebook does this via facial recognition technology; it compares a given photo with the millions of other photos uploaded to its site, and tries to match a new face with one it already knows.

So if someone uploads a picture of someone that looks like you, Facebook suggests that you be tagged in that photo. That's fine, unless that's not really you—or if the photo is one you'd rather not be associated with. Fortunately, you can turn off these photo tag suggestions.

It's Not All Good

You Can Still Be Tagged

Just because you turn off Facebook's ability to suggest your name when someone uploads a photo, that doesn't mean you can't be tagged in that photo. The person who uploaded the photo can still manually tag you, even if your name isn't automatically suggested.

1. From the Facebook toolbar, click the Settings (gear) button to display the menu of options.
2. Click Account Settings to display the Account Settings page.

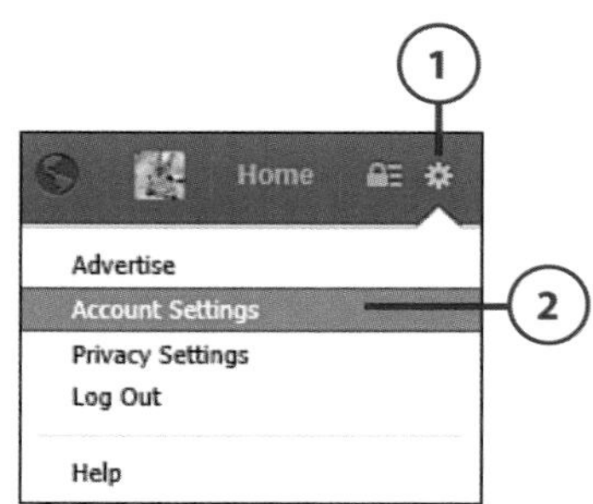

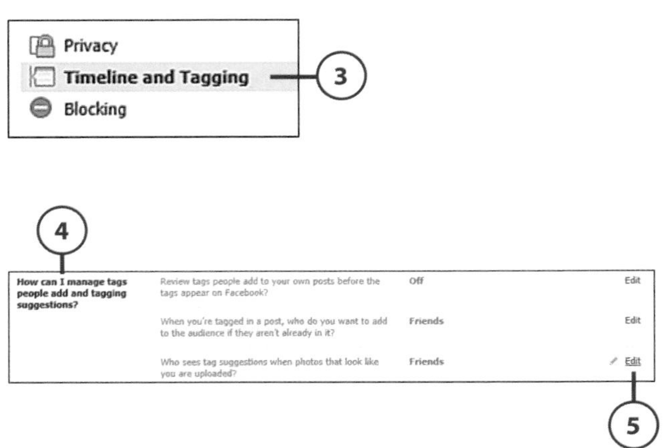

3. Click Timeline and Tagging in the left-hand column to display the Timeline and Tagging Settings page.
4. Go to the How Do I Manage Tags People Add and Tagging Suggestions? section.
5. Go to the Who Sees Tag Suggestions When Photos That Look Like You Are Uploaded? option and click Edit.

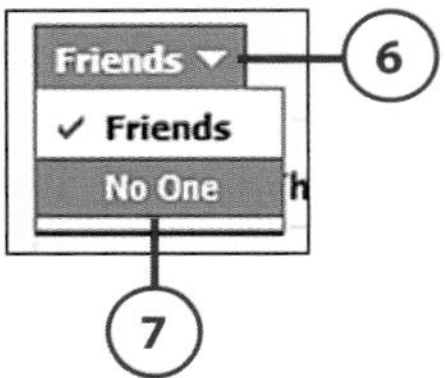

6. Click the Privacy button to see the list of options.
7. By default, any of your friends will see your name in their tag suggestions. Click No One to keep your name from appearing as a tag suggestion for anyone, including your friends.

Limit Who Can See Posts You're Tagged In

As noted, there's nothing to stop friends from manually tagging you in the posts they make and the photos they upload. What you can do, however, is keep anyone else from seeing those tags—in effect, hiding your name when tagged.

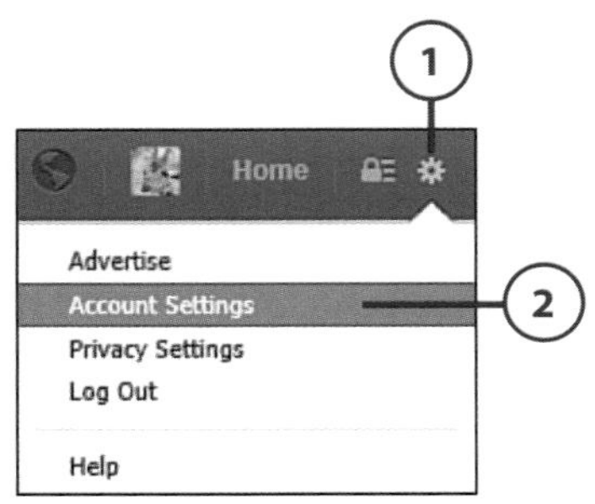

1. From the Facebook toolbar, click the Settings (gear) button to display the menu of options.
2. Click Account Settings to display the Account Settings page.

3. Click Timeline and Tagging in the left-hand column to display the Timeline and Tagging Settings page.
4. Go to the Who Can See Things on My Timeline? section.
5. Go to the Who Can See Posts You've Been Tagged In On Your Timeline? option and click Edit.
6. Click the Privacy button to display the list of options.
7. Click Friends to limit your exposure to only people on your friends list.
8. Click Only Me to hide your name from everyone on Facebook.

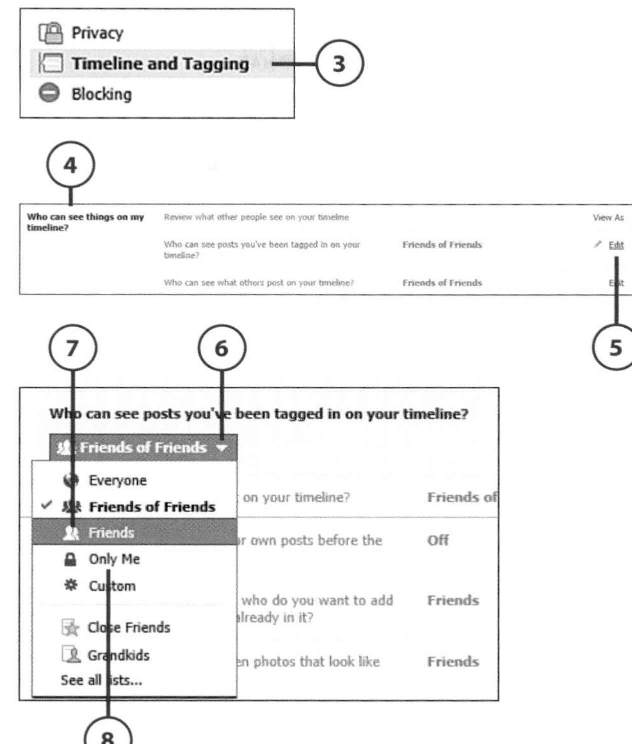

Approve Tags People Add to Your Posts

Here's a real invasion of your privacy. You post a picture to Facebook, and someone tags himself in your photo—even if it's not really a picture of him! Fortunately, Facebook gives you the option of reviewing all tags that people add to the posts you make and the photos you upload—so you can restrict who "associates" with you online.

1. From the Facebook toolbar, click the Settings (gear) button to display the menu of options.
2. Click Account Settings to display the Account Settings page.

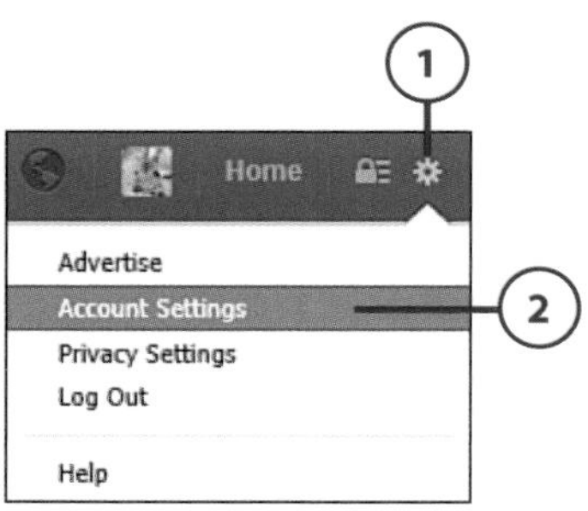

3. Click Timeline and Tagging in the left-hand column to display the Timeline and Tagging Settings page.
4. Go to the How Do I Manage Tags People Add and Tagging Suggestions? section.
5. Go to the Review Tags People Add to Your Own Posts Before the Tags Appear on Facebook? option and click Edit.
6. Click the Privacy button to see the list of options.
7. Click Enabled. You are notified whenever someone tries to add his or her tag to one of your posts or photos, and you have the option of approving or rejecting that tag.

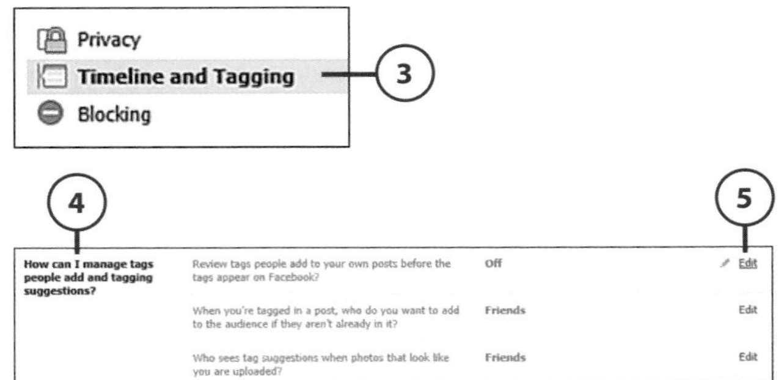

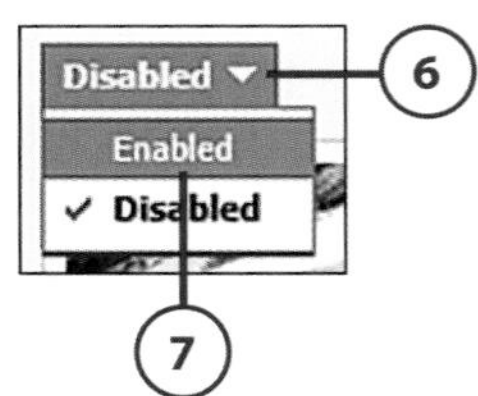

Controlling Who Sees What on Your Timeline

Another place that Facebook displays personal information is on your Timeline. Fortunately, you can limit who can see specific information there—and hide entire sections, if you like.

Control Who Sees Specific Information

Any given section in your Timeline has its own privacy settings. That is, you can configure different parts of your Timeline to be visible to different groups of people. For example, you can configure your Timeline so that everyone on Facebook can see your About section, but limit viewing of your Photos section to only people on your friends list.

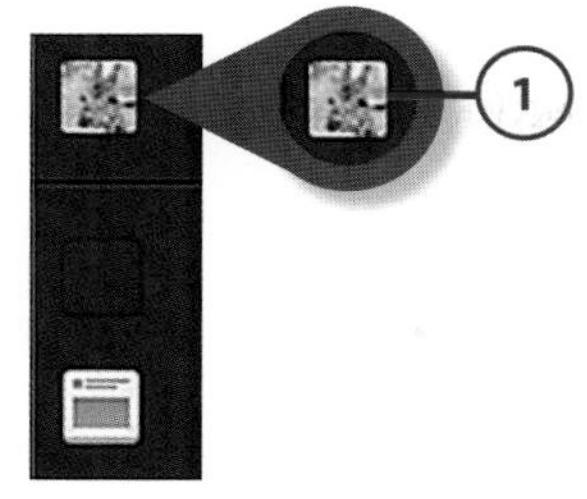

1. Click your picture in the sidebar menu, or your name on the toolbar, to display your Timeline page.

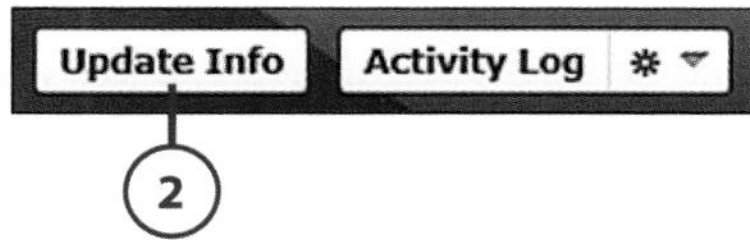

2. Click the Update Info button.

3. Click the Edit button for the section you want to configure.

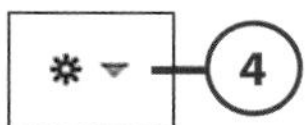

4. Click the Privacy button for the piece of information you want to configure.

5. Select who can see this information: Public (everyone on Facebook), Friends (people on your friends list), Only Me (no one can see it), Custom, or one of your customized friends lists.

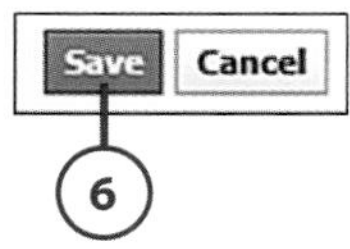

6. Click the Save or Done Editing button.

Hide Sections of Your Timeline

In addition to setting privacy options for individual pieces of information, you can also choose to hide entire sections of your Timeline. For example, if you don't want anyone to see the Places you've been or Music you've listened to, you can hide those sections.

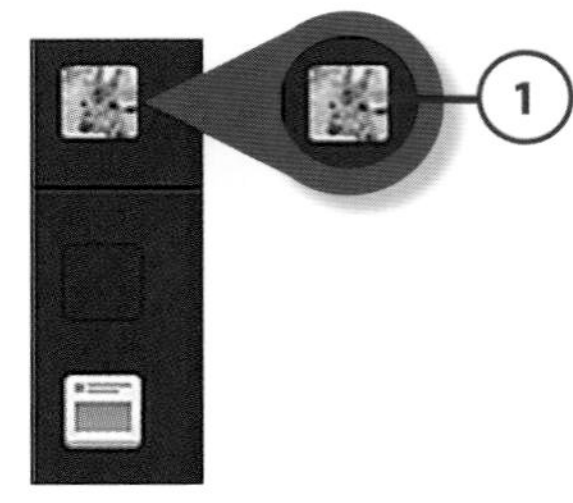

1. Click your picture in the sidebar menu to display your Timeline page.

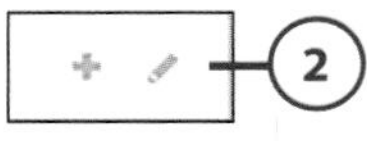

2. Click the Edit or Remove (pencil) button for the section you want to hide.

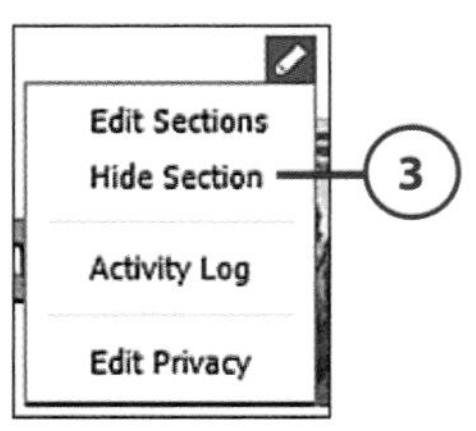

3. Click Hide Section.

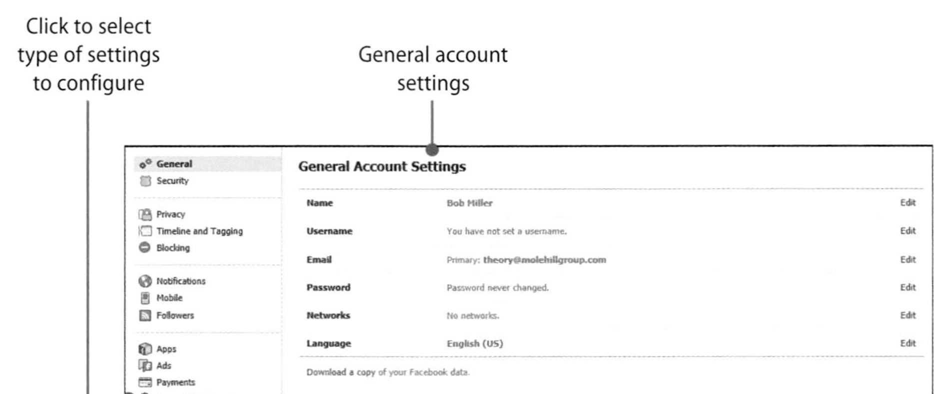
Click to select type of settings to configure
General account settings
General
Security
Privacy
Timeline and Tagging
Blocking
Notifications
Mobile
Followers
Apps
Ads
Payments
Support Dashboard
General Account Settings
Name
Bob Miller
Edit
Username
You have not set a username.
Edit
Email
Primary: theory@molehillgroup.com
Edit
Password
Password never changed.
Edit
Networks
No networks.
Edit
Language
English (US)
Edit
Download a copy of your Facebook data.

In this chapter you find out how to configure various aspects of your Facebook account.

- → Changing Your Account Settings
- → Leaving Facebook
- → Dealing with Death

Managing Your Facebook Account

Your Facebook account contains your basic personal information—your name, email address, password, and the like. What do you do if you move, get a new email account, or find that your password is compromised? Fortunately, Facebook enables you to easily change any and all of this information, at any time.

Changing Your Account Settings

You can change all your Facebook settings from the Account Settings page, which you access from the Facebook toolbar. The Account Settings page has a dozen different tabs, each of which hosts a specific type of information.

Configure General Account Settings

When you want to change your Facebook username, email address, or password, select the General Account Settings tab.

1. Click the Gear button on the far right of the Facebook toolbar to display the menu of options.
2. Click Account Settings to display the Account Settings page.
3. Click the General tab in the left column to display the General Account Settings.
4. Click Edit in the Name section to change your name on Facebook.
5. Click Edit in the Username section to set or change your official Facebook username.
6. Click Edit in the Email section to change the email address you've inked to your Facebook account.
7. Click Edit in the Password section to change your Facebook password.

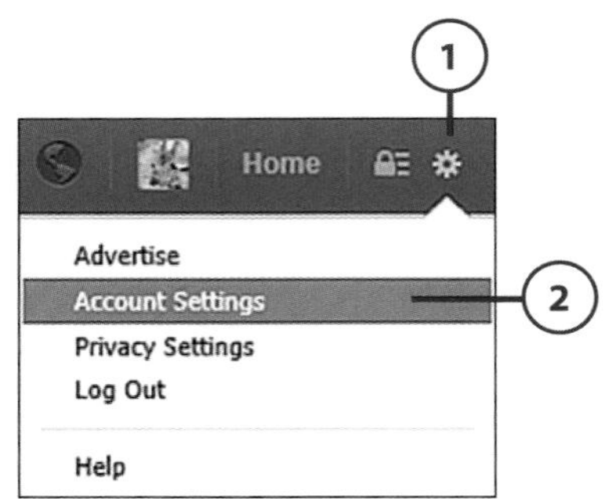

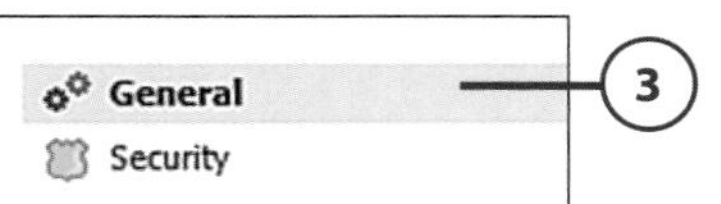

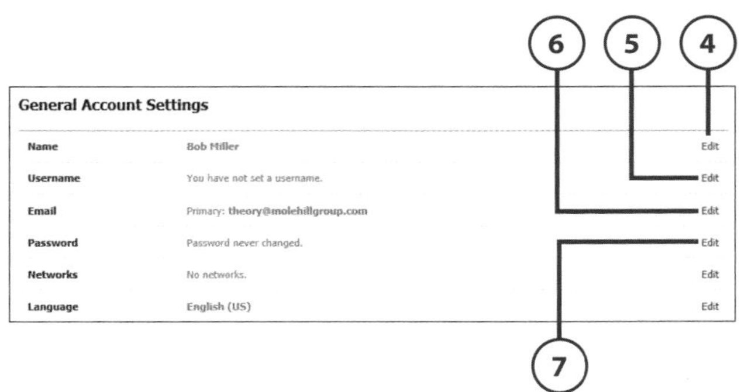

Changing Passwords

It's a good idea to change your Facebook password every month or two. This decreases the possibility of your account password being hacked.

8. Click Edit in the Networks section to manage any school or work networks you have.

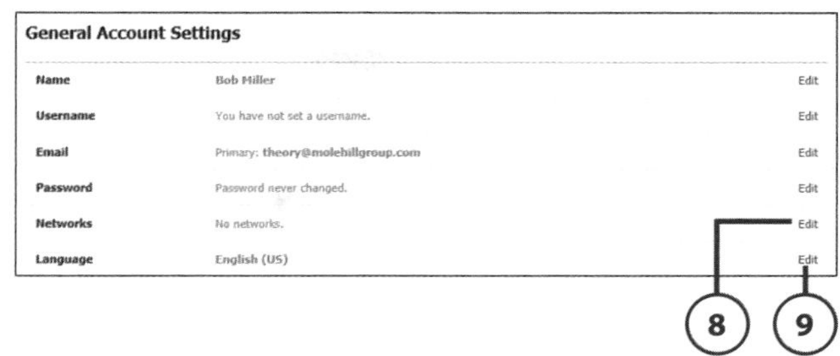
General Account Settings

Name	Bob Miller	Edit
Username	You have not set a username.	Edit
Email	Primary: theory@molehillgroup.com	Edit
Password	Password never changed.	Edit
Networks	No networks.	Edit
Language	English (US)	Edit

Networks

A Facebook network is like a group for people who attended a specific school or worked at a given company. To join a network, you must have an official email address from that school or company. (For example, if you work at 3M and have a yourname@3m.com email address.) If you do have the proper email, you're automatically a member of that network.

---

9. Click Edit in the Language section to change the language in which you read Facebook.

Configure Security Settings

To change settings related to your system security, select the Security tab. You can also deactivate your Facebook account from this page.

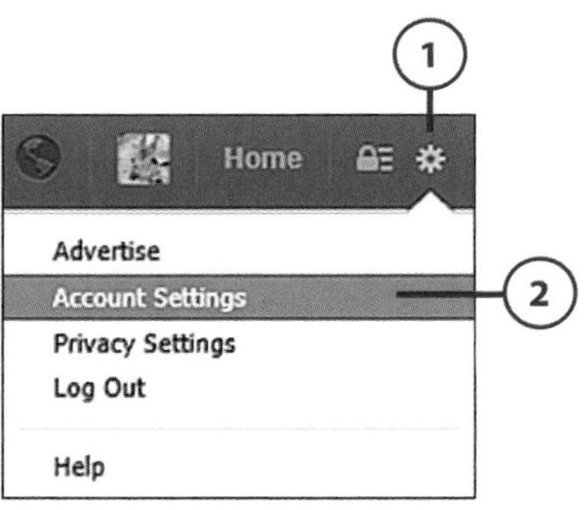

1. Click the Gear button on the far right of the Facebook toolbar to display the menu of options.
2. Click Account Settings to display the Account Settings page.
3. Click the Security tab in the left column to display the Security Settings.

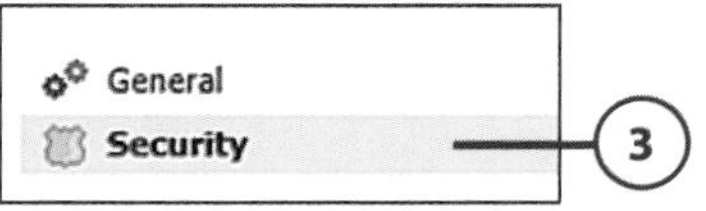

4. Click Edit in the Security Question section to set a security question to be used if you can't remember your password. (If you've already set your security question, this option does not appear.)
5. Click Edit in the Secure Browsing section to browse Facebook over a secure Internet connection (safer when entering personal information).
6. Click Edit in the Login Notifications section if you want to be notified when your Facebook account is accessed from a computer or mobile device that you haven't used before.
7. Click Edit in the Login Approvals section to require a security code if someone tries to access your Facebook account from an unknown browser.
8. Click Edit in the App Passwords section to manage passwords you use for various Facebook apps.
9. Click Edit in the Trusted Contacts section to set some of your friends as "trusted contacts" who can help you reset your password if you can't log in.

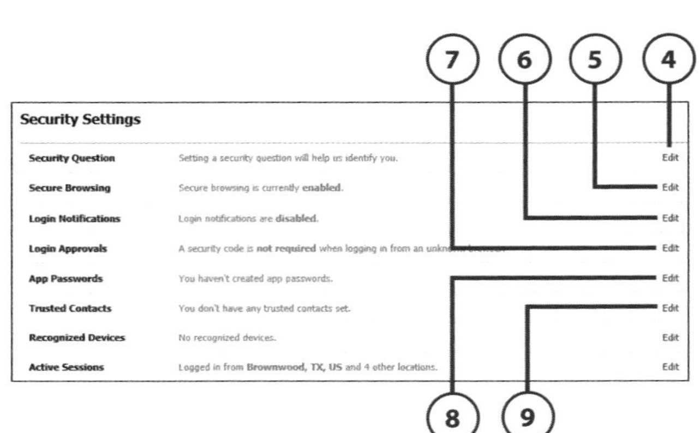

10. Click Edit in the Recognized Devices section to manage mobile devices you use to access Facebook.
11. Click Edit in the Active Sessions section to view the most recent locations from which you've logged into Facebook.

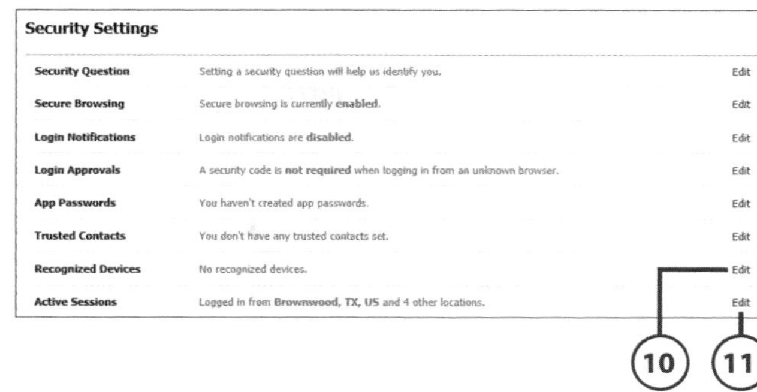

Active Sessions

If you think someone else has been logging into your Facebook account without your knowledge, use the Active Sessions list to compare Facebook's login records with what you know you've done.

Configure Privacy Settings

Chapter 18, "Keeping Private Things Private," covers several of Facebook's privacy settings. You can access many of these same settings from the Account Settings page.

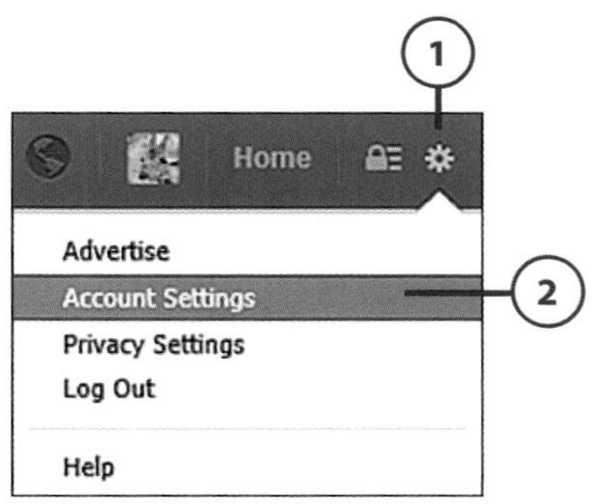

1. Click the Gear button on the far right of the Facebook toolbar to display the menu of options.
2. Click Account Settings to display the Account Settings page.
3. Click the Privacy tab in the left column to display the Privacy Settings and Tools.

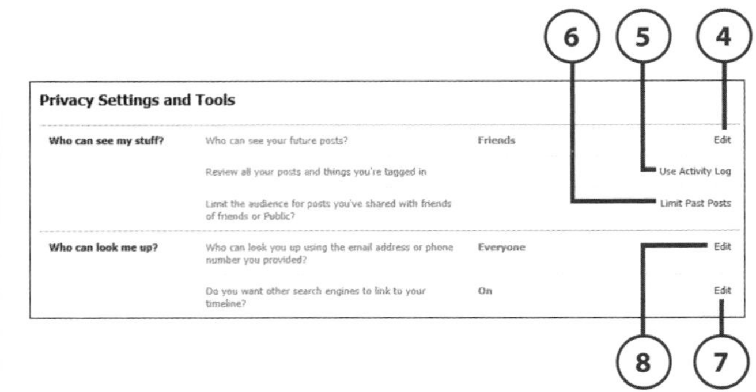

4. Click Edit in the Who Can See Your Future Posts? section to configure who can view your status updates.
5. Click Use Activity Log to use the Activity Log to review all your posts and items in which you've been tagged.
6. Click Limit Past Posts to limit viewing of your previous posts to only those people on your friends list.
7. Click Edit in the Do You Want Other Search Engines to Link to Your Timeline? section to limit who can look you up on Facebook via email address or phone number.
8. Click Edit in the Who Can Look You Up… section if you don't want your Facebook information searchable via Google and other search engines.

Configure Timeline and Tagging Settings

To determine who can add things to or see items on your Timeline, use the Timeline and Tagging page.

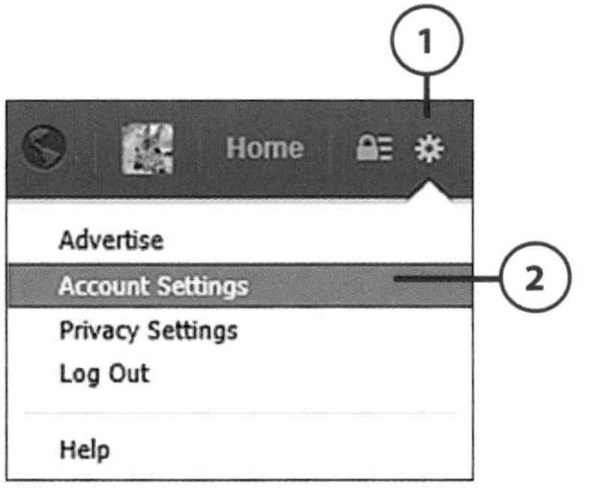

1. Click the Gear button on the far right of the Facebook toolbar to display the menu of options.
2. Click Account Settings to display the Account Settings page.

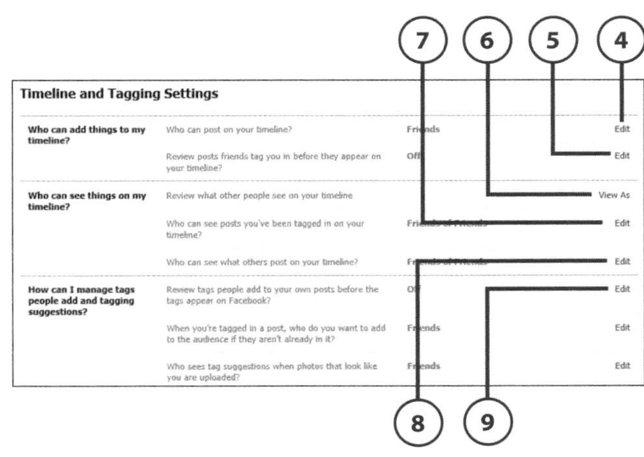

3. Click the Timeline and Tagging tab in the left column to display the Timeline and Tagging Settings.
4. Click Edit in the Who Can Post on Your Timeline? section to control who can post messages to your Timeline page.
5. Click Edit in the Review Posts Friends Tag You in Before They Appear on Your Timeline? section to manually approve any posts or photos in which you've been tagged.
6. Click View As in the Review What Other People See On Your Timeline section to display your Timeline as it's seen by other users.
7. Click Edit in the Who Can See Posts You've Been Tagged In On Your Timeline? section to determine who can see posts or photos in which you've been tagged.
8. Click Edit in the Who Can See What Others Post on Your Timeline section to determine who can see posts that others make on your Timeline.
9. Click Edit in the Review Tags People Add to Your Own Posts Before the Tags Appear on Facebook to manually approve any tags that people add to your posts or figures.

10. Click Edit in the When You're Tagged in a Post, Who Do You Want to Add to the Audience If They're Not Already In It? section to display items in which you've been tagged to other users.

11. Click Edit in the Who Sees Tag Suggestions When Photos That Look Like You Are Uploaded? section to determine who can see your name in the tag selections for pictures they've uploaded.

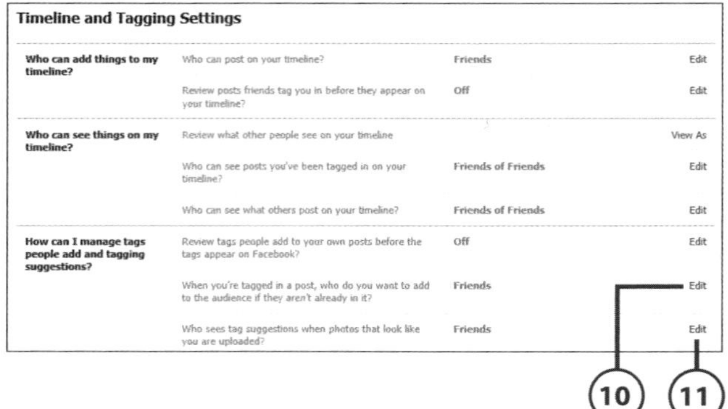

Manage Blocked Users

Facebook enables you to block users who are annoying you; when someone is blocked, they're added to your Restricted list and nothing they write ever gets to you. You can also block messages from annoying apps. Just use the Blocking page.

1. Click the Gear button on the far right of the Facebook toolbar to display the menu of options.
2. Click Account Settings to display the Account Settings page.
3. Click the Blocking tab in the left column to display the Manage Blocking page.
4. Click Edit List in the Restricted List section to remove people from your Restricted list.

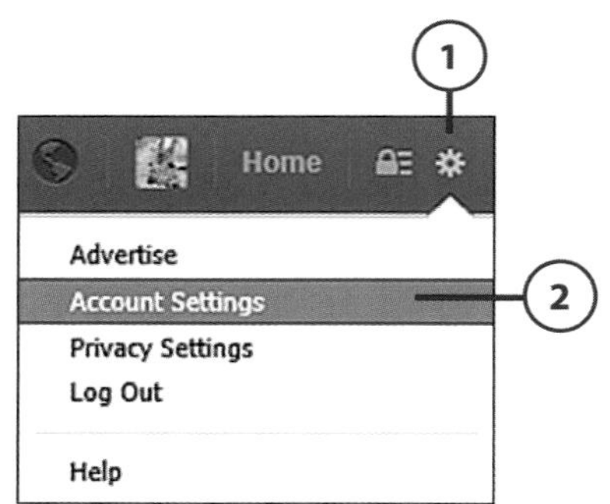

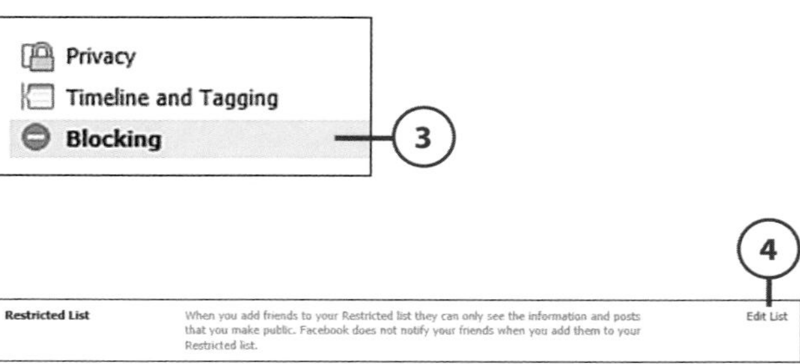

5. Add a user to the Restricted list by entering his or her name into the Block Users box and then clicking the Block button.
6. Block app invitations from a specific user by going to the Block App Invites section, entering his or her name into the Block Invites From box, and pressing Enter.
7. Block event invitations from a specific user by going to the Block Event Invites section, entering his or her name into the Block Invites From box, and pressing Enter.
8. Keep a given app or game from contacting you on Facebook by going to the Block Apps section, entering the name of that app into the Block Apps box, and pressing Enter.
9. Unblock an app you've previously blocked by going to the Block Apps section and clicking Unblock for the given app listed there.

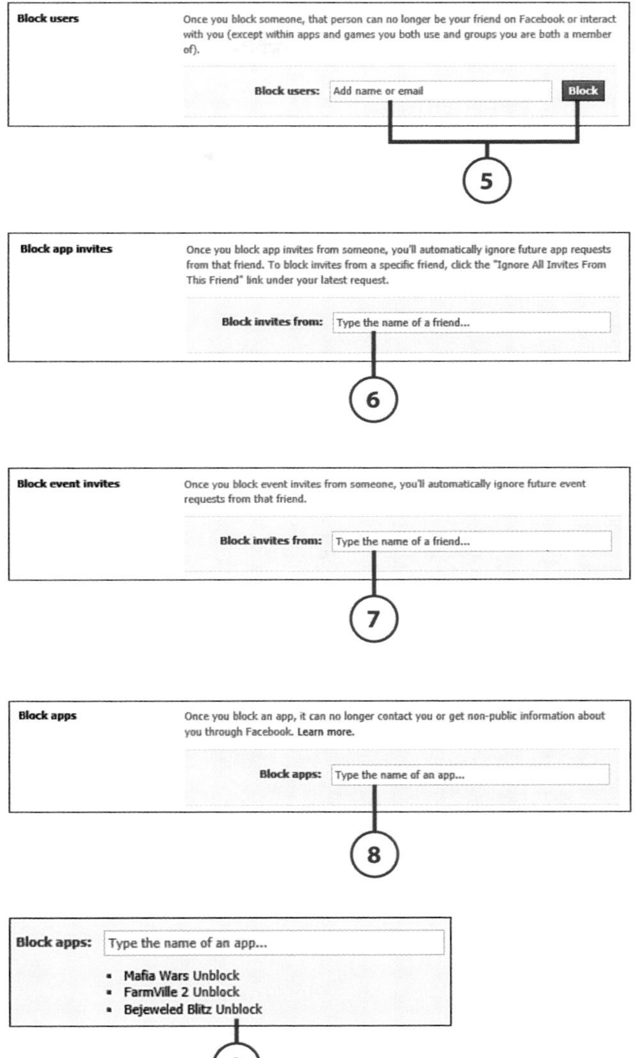

Configure Notifications

Facebook gladly notifies you of all sorts of activity related to your account—when a friend makes a post, when you get tagged in a post or photo, or even when someone posts to one of the groups to which you belong. You can opt to get notified on Facebook or via email or text message.

1. Click the Gear button on the far right of the Facebook toolbar to display the menu of options.
2. Click Account Settings to display the Account Settings page.
3. Click the Notifications tab in the left column to display the Notifications Settings page.
4. Click View in the On Facebook section to turn off the sound Facebook makes when you receive a new notification.
5. Click Edit in the Email section to determine what types of notifications you receive via email.
6. Click View in the Push Notifications section to view which apps can send notifications to your mobile phone.
7. Click Edit in the Text Message section to determine what types of notifications you receive via text message to your mobile phone.

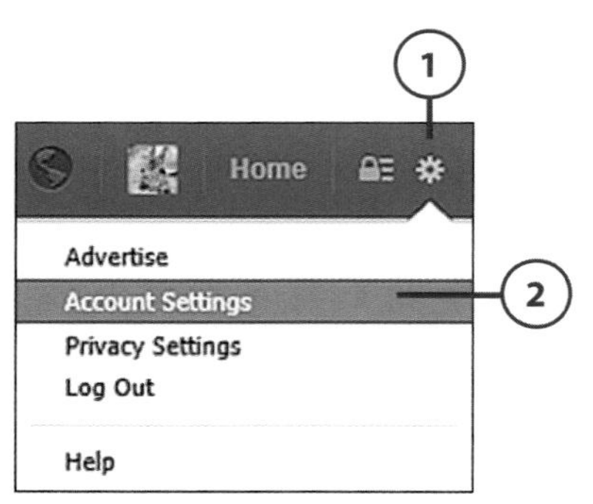

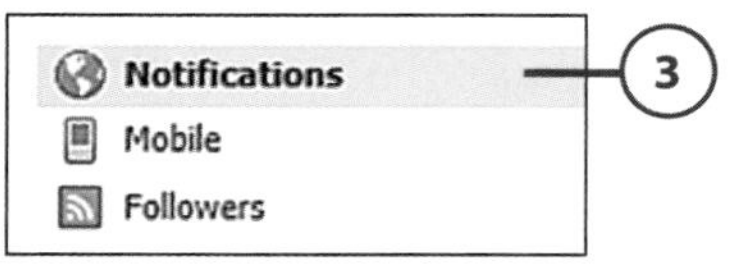

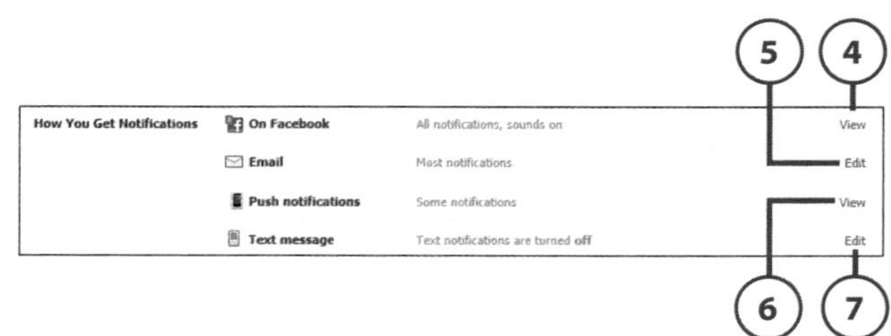

8. Click Edit for activities listed in the What You Get Notified About section to determine which activities you receive notifications about.

Configure Facebook for Mobile Use

Many users, especially younger ones, opt to send new status updates to Facebook via text message from their phones. To do this, you must register your mobile phone number with Facebook.

1. Click the Gear button on the far right of the Facebook toolbar to display the menu of options.
2. Click Account Settings to display the Account Settings page.
3. Click the Mobile tab in the left column to display the Mobile Settings page.
4. Click the Add a Phone button to display the Activate Facebook Texts dialog box to register your mobile phone with Facebook.

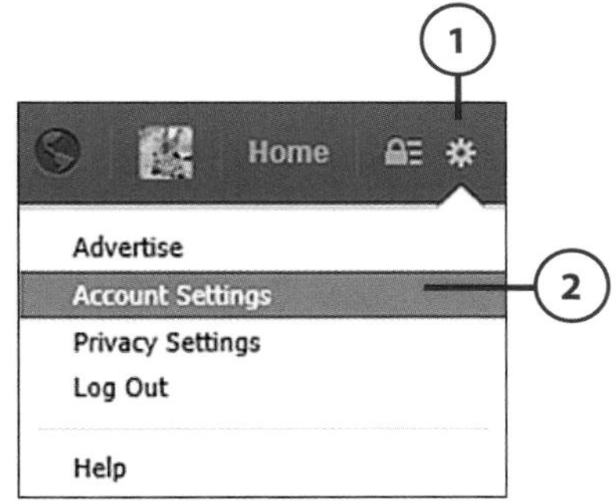

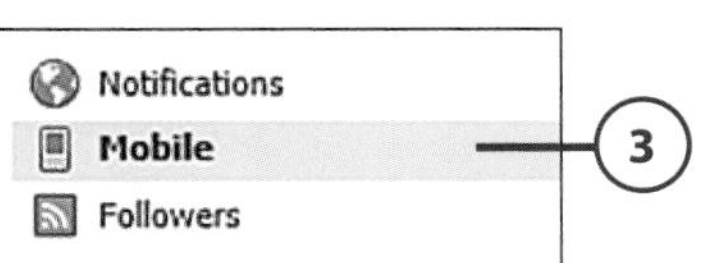

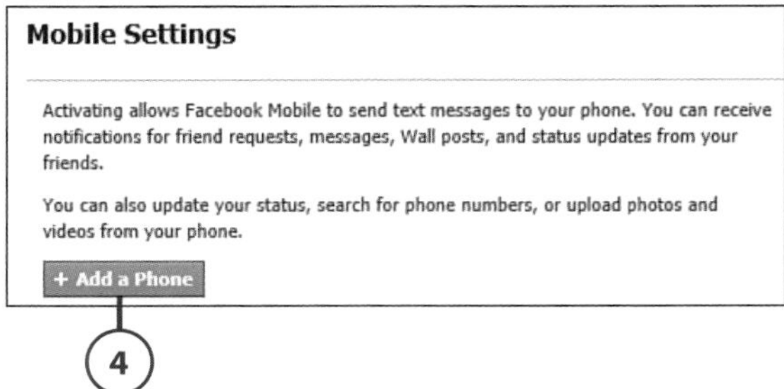

5. Select the country of your mobile phone carrier from the Country/Region list.
6. Select your mobile phone carrier from the Mobile Carrier list.
7. Click the Next button.
8. From your mobile phone, text the letter F to 32665 (FBOOK).

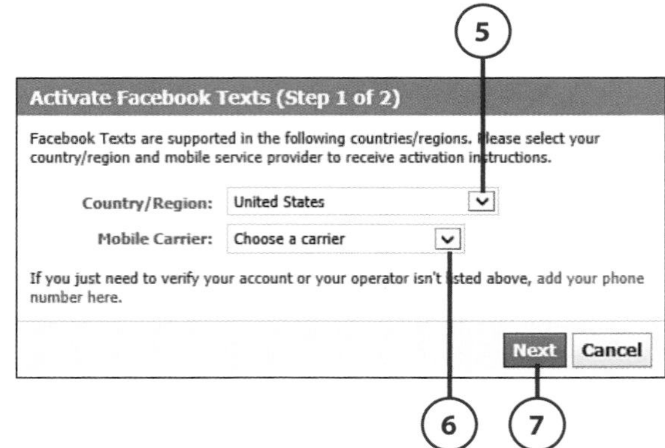

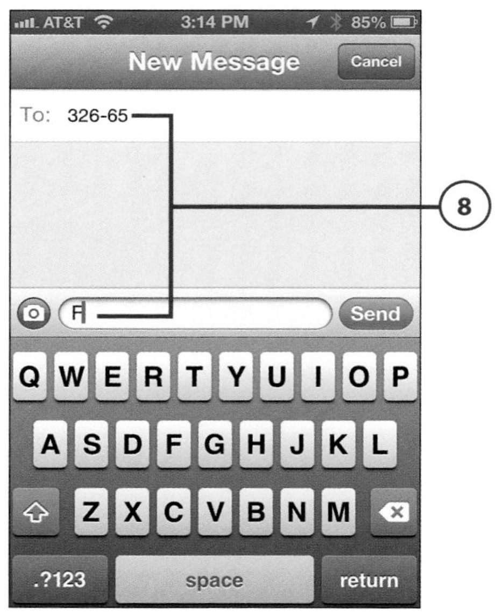

9. Facebook sends a confirmation code via text message to your mobile phone.
10. Enter that code into the Confirmation Code box.
11. Uncheck the Share My Phone Number with My Friends box if you don't want your Facebook friends to see your mobile phone number.
12. Uncheck the Allow Friends to Text Me from Facebook box if you don't want friends to text you via Facebook.
13. Click the Next button to display the Mobile Settings page.
14. Click Edit in the Text Messaging section if you've already registered your mobile phone number and want to change it.
15. By default, Facebook texts you when anyone posts a message for you from his mobile phone. To not receive these texts, click Edit in the Facebook Messages section and make a new selection from the Text Me list.
16. Click Edit in the Daily Text Limit section and choose a quantity to limit number of daily text messages that Facebook can send you.
17. To send a status update via text message, text the message to the phone number displayed in the Post-By-Email Address section.

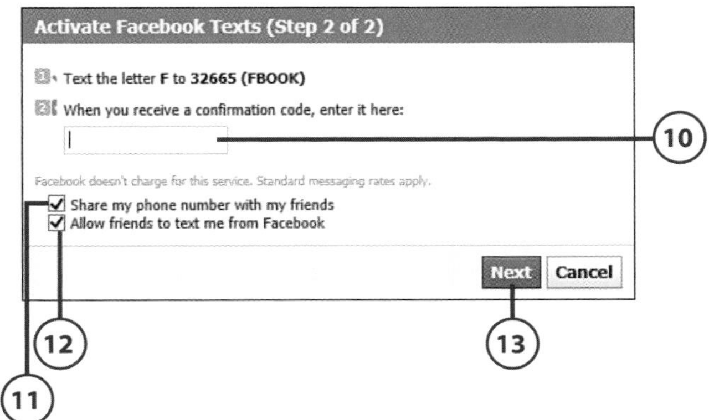

Manage Following and Followers

If you have a lot of people who want to read your status updates but you don't necessarily want to read theirs, you can activate Facebook's Following feature. With Following activated, others can opt to follow your posts without having to be on your friends list.

Following

Following is best suited for public people or organizations with a large number of fans or customers, not for regular individuals.

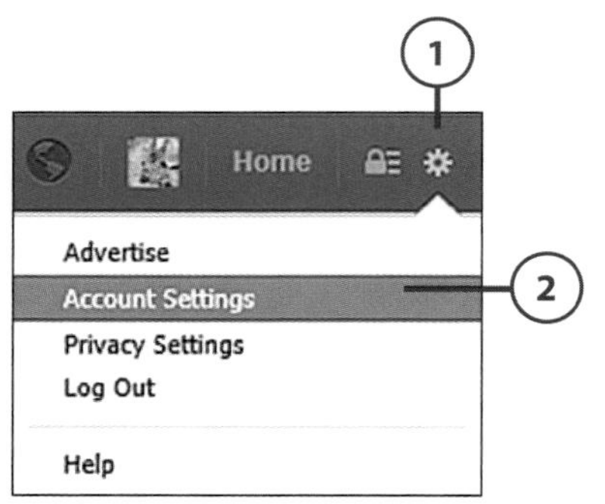

1. Click the Gear button on the far right of the Facebook toolbar to display the menu of options.
2. Click Account Settings to display the Account Settings page.

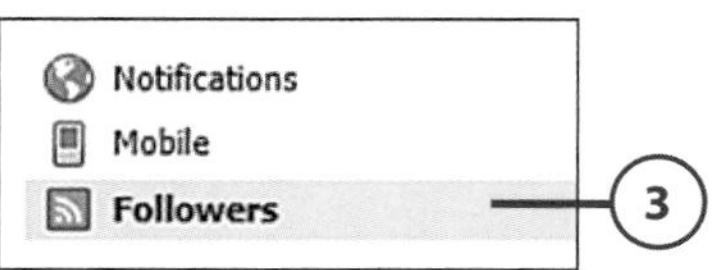

3. Click the Followers tab in the left column to display the Follower Settings page.
4. Check the Turn On Follow box. This expands the page to display more options.

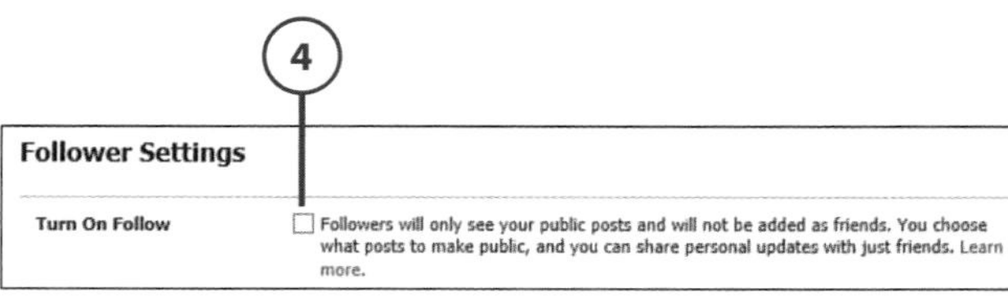

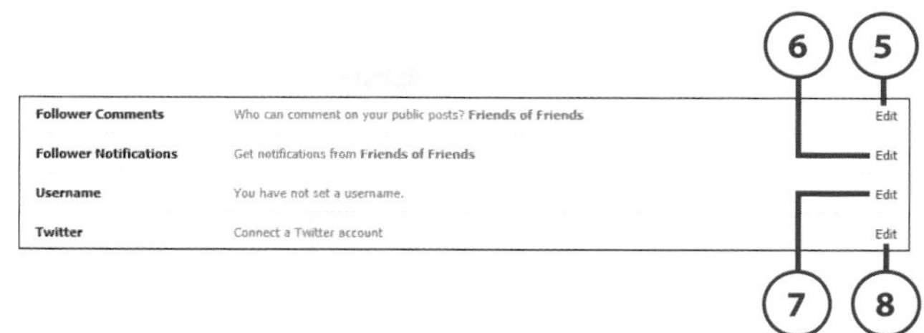

5. Click Edit in the Follower Comments section to determine whether or not followers can comment on your posts.
6. Click Edit in the Follower Notifications section to receive notifications when people who aren't your friends start following you.
7. Click Edit in the Username section to change the username that followers see.
8. Click Edit in the Twitter section to connect your Facebook account to your Twitter account, so that one post goes to both social networks.

Manage Apps and Games

If you use a lot of Facebook apps or games, you can edit how those apps interact with your Facebook account. You can even delete unused apps, if you want, so they won't bother you with unwanted notifications and such.

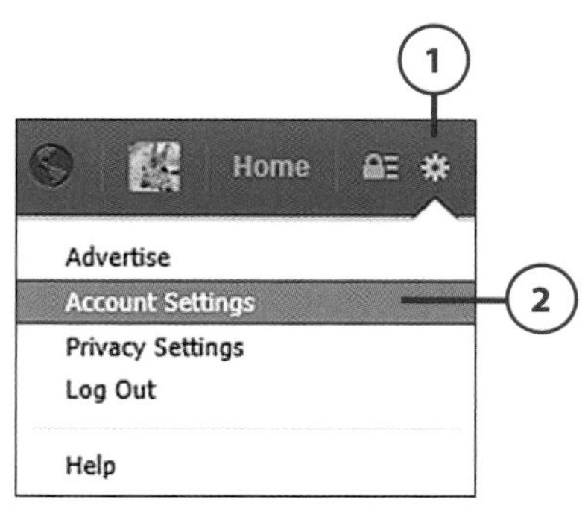

1. Click the Gear button on the far right of the Facebook toolbar to display the menu of options.
2. Click Account Settings to display the Account Settings page.

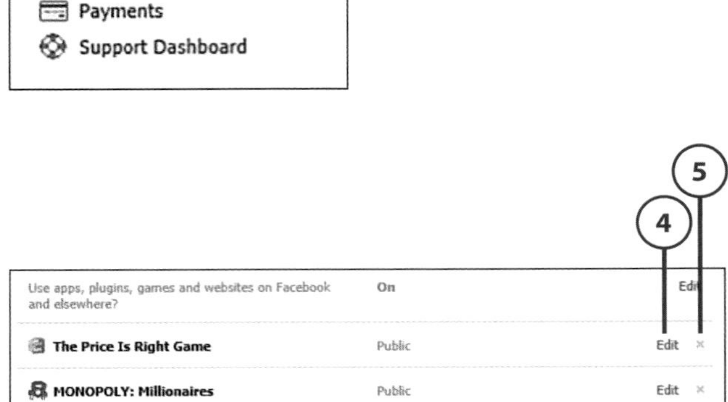

3. Click the Apps tab in the left column to display the App Settings page.
4. Click Edit next to the app's name to edit the settings for a given app.
5. Click the X next to an app's name and, when prompted, click the Remove button to delete that app.
6. Click Edit in the Apps Others Use section to limit which information about you that your friends' apps can use. The section expands to include a list of items; uncheck those you don't want to share.

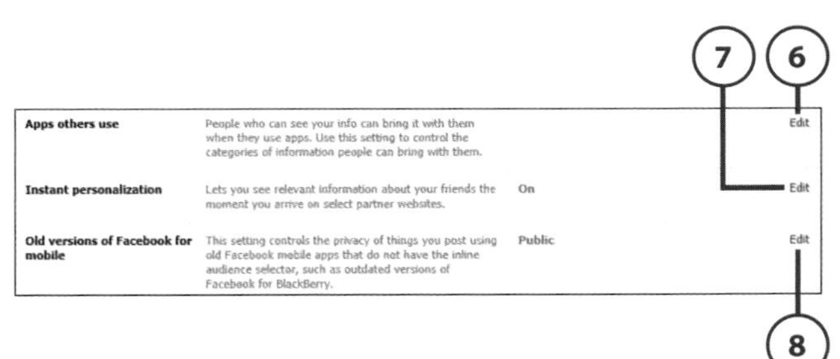

7. Some websites use your friends' Facebook data to present a more personalized experience when you visit their sites. To turn off this sharing of data (which some find a bit creepy), click Edit in the Instant Personalization section and then uncheck Enable Instant Personalization on Partner Websites.
8. Click Edit in the Old Versions of Facebook for Mobile if you're using an older version of Facebook's mobile app and want to better control the privacy of the information posted there.

Configure Ad Settings

Some advertisers like to use information you provide to Facebook to provide more personal ads to your friends. These ads typically say something like "John Doe likes this page" or product or whatever. Some people don't like being used by advertisers without just compensation (which they don't provide); for this reason, Facebook enables you control how advertisers can use your information.

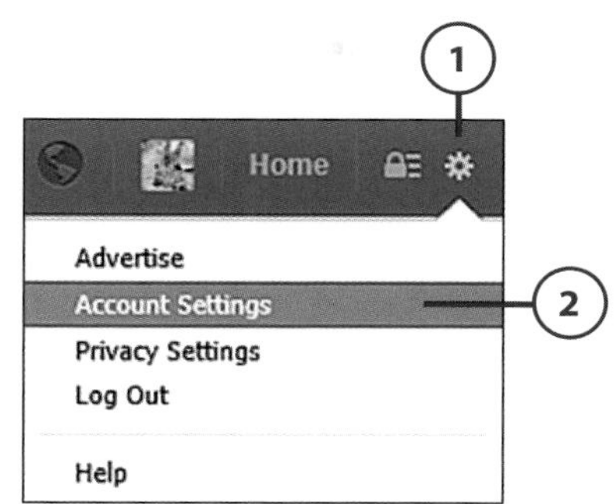

1. Click the Gear button on the far right of the Facebook toolbar to display the menu of options.
2. Click Account Settings to display the Account Settings page.

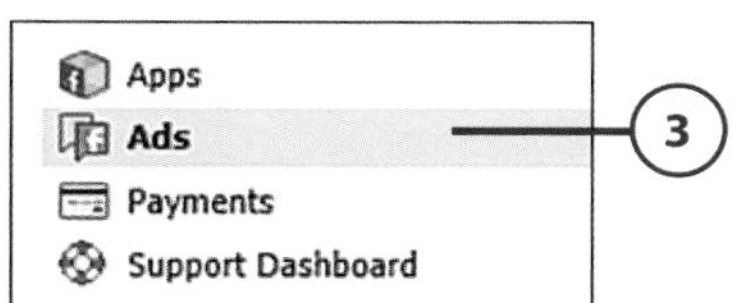

3. Click the Ads tab in the left column to display the Facebook Ads page.
4. At present Facebook does not let third-party advertisers use your name or picture in their non-Facebook ads. If Facebook changes this policy, you can tell Facebook *not* to use your information in this manner by clicking Edit in the Third Party Sites section and then selecting No One from the list.

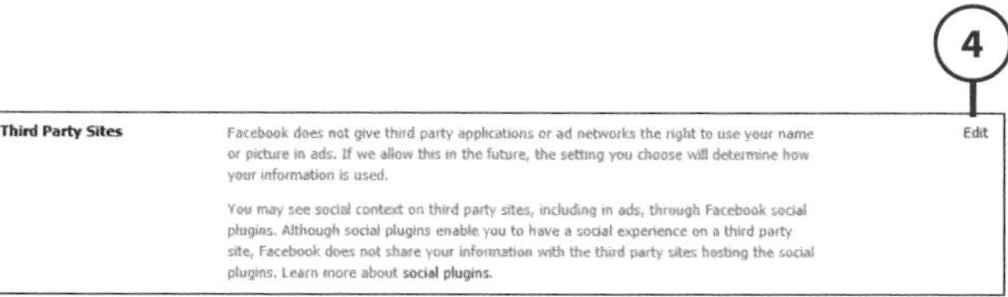

5. To prohibit advertisers from linking your name to their products in Facebook ads presented to your friends, click Edit in the Ads & Friends section and then select No One from the list.

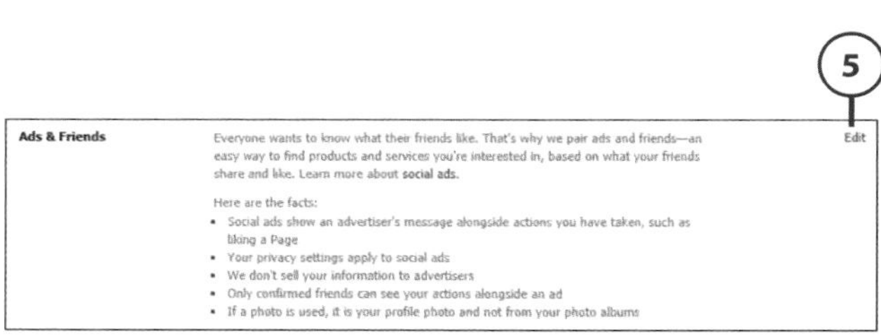

Manage Facebook Payments

Some Facebook apps and games accept Facebook Credits as currency for buying new game levels and such. You can manage your Facebook Credits on the Payments tab.

No More Credits

Facebook is phasing out Facebook Credits for in-app and in-game payments, in favor using of standard credit card payments. It's likely that this configuration option will disappear over time.

1. Click the Gear button on the far right of the Facebook toolbar to display the menu of options.
2. Click Account Settings to display the Account Settings page.
3. Click the Payments tab in the left column to display the Payments Settings page.
4. Click view in the Subscriptions section to view any recurring subscription payments you've set up.
5. Click View in the Purchase History section to examine your recent purchase history.
6. Click Edit in the Payment Methods section to manage your payment methods (credit card and so forth).
7. Click Edit in the Preferred Currency section to change the currency you use.

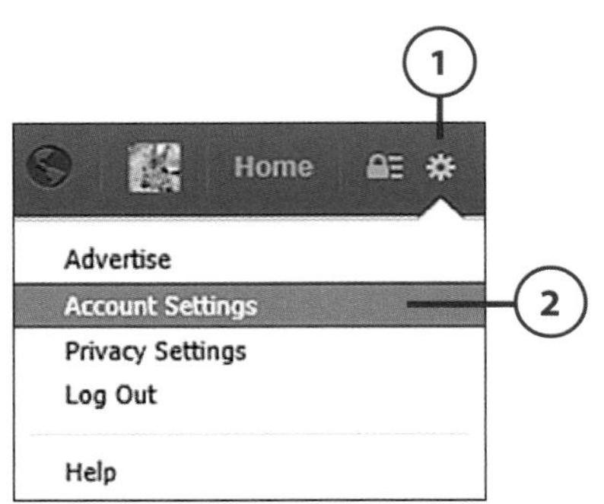

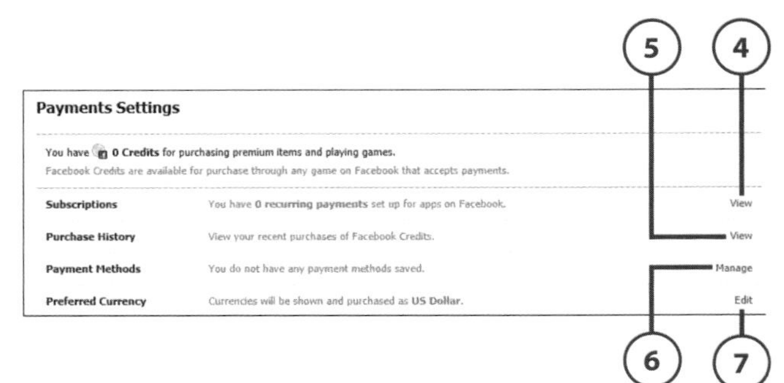

Leaving Facebook

If you ever choose to leave Facebook, you have two options. You can deactivate your account, which temporarily hides your account information from others, or you can delete your account, which permanently removes your account information.

Deactivate Your Account

Deactivating your account is meant as a temporary solution that you can undo at any future point. When you deactivate your account, Facebook doesn't actually delete your account information; it merely hides it so others can't view it. Because your account information still exists, it's simple enough to reactivate a deactivated account.

1. Click the Gear button on the far right of the Facebook toolbar to display the menu of options.
2. Click Account Settings to display the Account Settings page.
3. Click the Security tab in the left column to display the Security Settings page.
4. Scroll to the bottom of the page and click Deactivate Your Account to display the Are You Sure You Want to Deactivate Your Account? page.

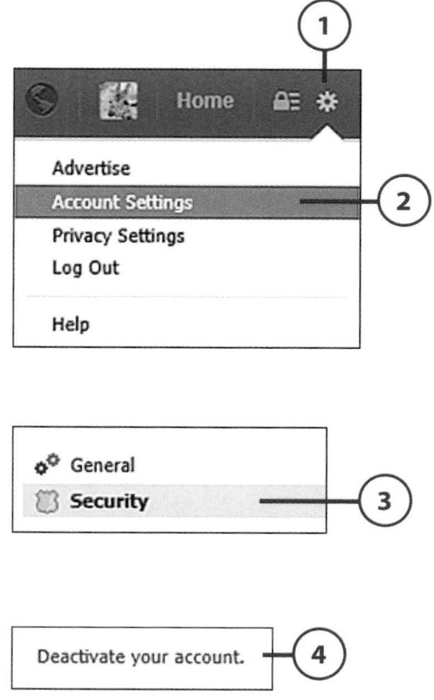

5. Scroll to the Reason for Leaving section and select just why it is you're leaving. This is a requirement; you have to tell Facebook something here.
6. Check the Email Opt Out box if you don't want to be hounded by Facebook to venture back into the fold.
7. Click the Confirm button to deactivate your account.

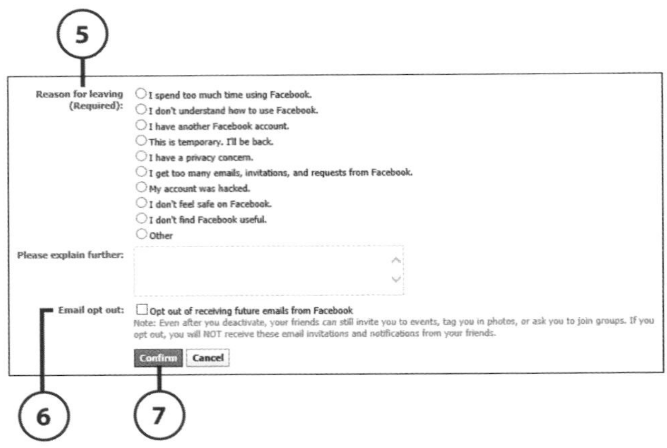

They'll Miss You!

Facebook really, really doesn't want to see you leave, so it tugs at your heartstrings by showing you pictures of some of your Facebook friends with the messages "Bob will miss you," "Dinah will miss you," and so forth. If you truly want to leave, resist the urge to change your mind.

Permanently Delete Your Facebook Account

If you're absolutely, positively sure you'll never want to be a Facebook user again—and you want more reassurance that your personal data has been wiped—then you want to permanently delete your account. This is more difficult to do than deactivating your account for the simple reason that your Facebook account is likely connected to lots of other websites.

It's Not All Good

It's Final

Deleting your Facebook account is final; all your status updates and other information will be permanently erased. If you later want to rejoin Facebook, you'll have to start completely from scratch.

1. Go to each website you've linked to your Facebook account and disconnect the link—that is, create a new login ID that is not related to your Facebook ID. Do *not* log into these sites with your Facebook account!
2. Log in to your Facebook account and then go to Facebook's Delete My Account page (www.facebook.com/help/delete_account). You have to enter this URL directly into your web browser; there's no link to this page from within Facebook.
3. Click the Delete My Account button to display the Permanently Delete Account dialog box.
4. Enter your Facebook password into the Password box.
5. Enter the displayed characters into the Security Check box.
6. Click the Okay button.

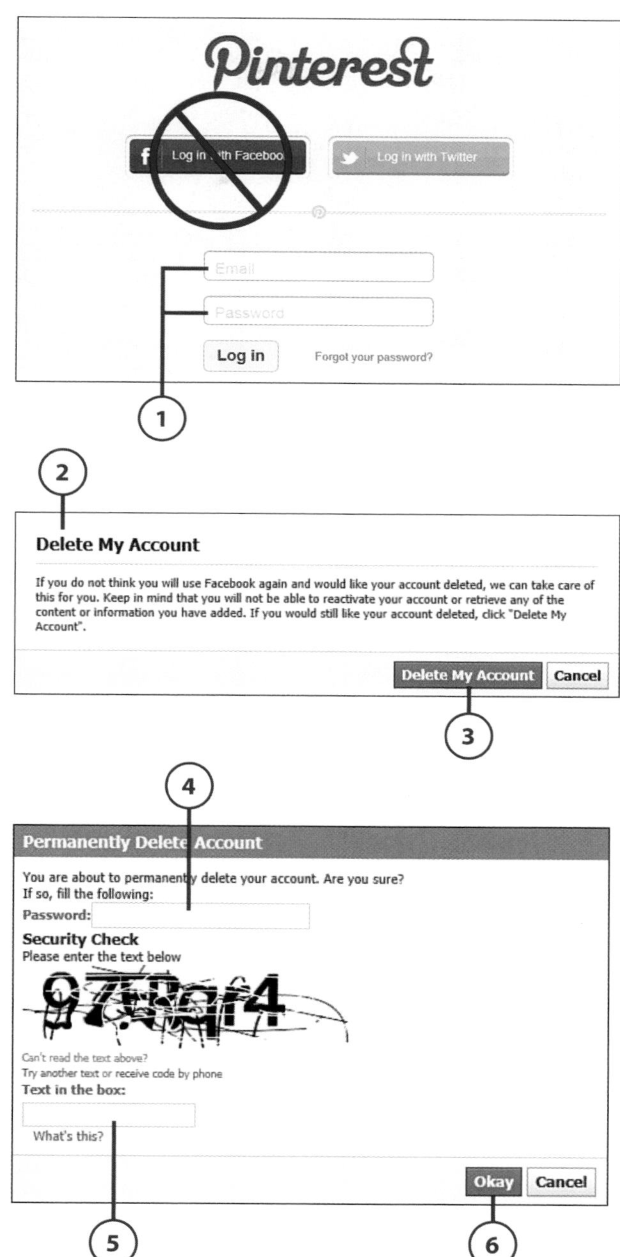

It's Not All Good

14 Days

When you follow this procedure, Facebook will delete your account—so long as you don't log back in to Facebook for the next 14 days. Any interaction with your Facebook account during this 14-day period reactivates your account. This also means not logging into any other websites connected to your Facebook account, or clicking the Facebook Like button on any other website.

Dealing with Death

Here's a question none of us want to face but all of us will have to: What happens to your Facebook account when you die?

The legal status of one's online accounts is a growing issue as online users age. After all, only you are supposed to have access to your online accounts; only you know your password to get into Facebook, Twitter, or even your online banking site. And if you aren't able to get online, because you're dead, how can your accounts be put on hold or deleted?

Facebook, fortunately, has considered this situation and offers several options for accounts belong to deceased members.

Memorialize an Account

If your spouse or another loved one has passed away, Facebook offers two options. You can memorialize his account, or you can simply remove it from the Facebook site.

If you choose to memorialize the deceased's account, Facebook retains that person's Timeline page but locks it so that no one can log into it, and so no new friends can be accepted. Current friends, however, can share memories of the deceased on the memorialized timeline, and all existing content remains available for friends to view. (Who can view it depends on the Timeline's existing privacy settings.)

Anyone can report a deceased user to Facebook, and thus begin the memorialization process.

1. From your web browser, go to www.facebook.com/help/contact/305593649477238 to display Facebook's Memorialization Request page.
2. Enter the full name of your loved one into the Full Name of Deceased Person box.
3. Enter any of the email addresses used by this person into the Email Addresses Listed on the Account box.
4. Enter the URL of the deceased person's Timeline page into the Web Address (URL) of the Timeline You'd Like to Report box.

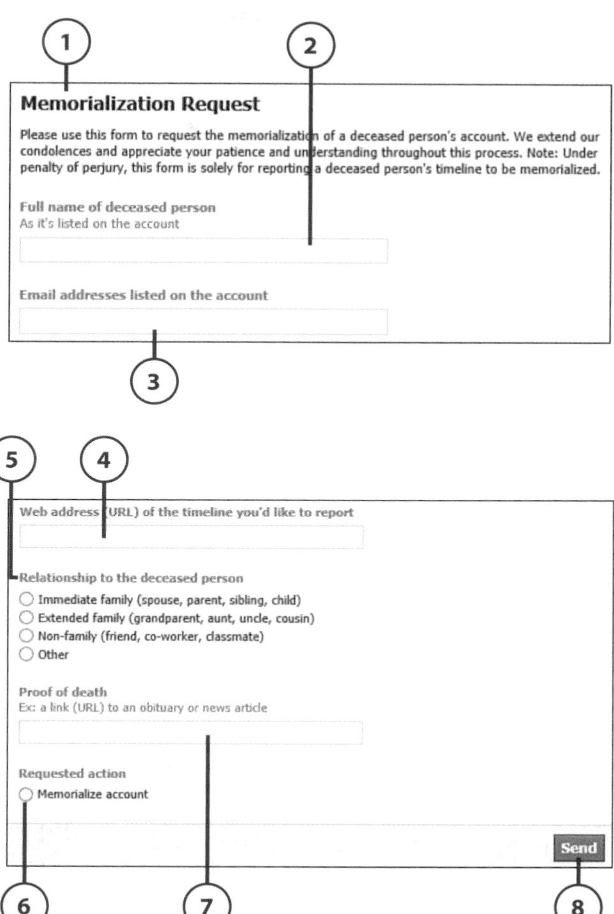

Timeline URL

You can find the URL of the person's Timeline page by opening that page in your web browser and then copying the address that appears in your browser's address box.

5. Go to the Relationship to Deceased Person section and check how you're related—Immediate Family, Extended Family, Non-Family, or Other.
6. Enter a link to any online article or website reporting this person's death into the Proof of Death box. You can link to this person's online obituary or memorial page from the attending funeral home.
7. Check the Memorialize Account option.
8. Click the Send button.

It's Not All Good

Mistaken Memorialization

What do you do if someone memorializes your account—either on purpose or by mistake—and you're not dead yet? You need to contact Facebook via a special form to tell them you're still alive and want to continue using your account. You won't be able to log into Facebook if your account is in a memorialized state, so go to www.facebook.com/help/contact/292558237463098 and fill out the form there.

Remove an Account

If you'd rather not have a loved one's Facebook account memorialized, you can ask Facebook to remove the person's account from the site. Believe it or not, this is a more involved process than memorializing the account.

In preparation for this process, you need some proof of the person's death, typically a copy of the death certificate. This documentation needs to be scanned into your computer as an image file that you can upload to Facebook when required.

1. From your web browser, go to www.facebook.com/help/contact/?id=228813257197480 to display the Special Request for Deceased Person's Account page.
2. Enter your name into the Your Full Name box.
3. Enter the name of the deceased person into the Full Name on the Deceased Person's Account box.

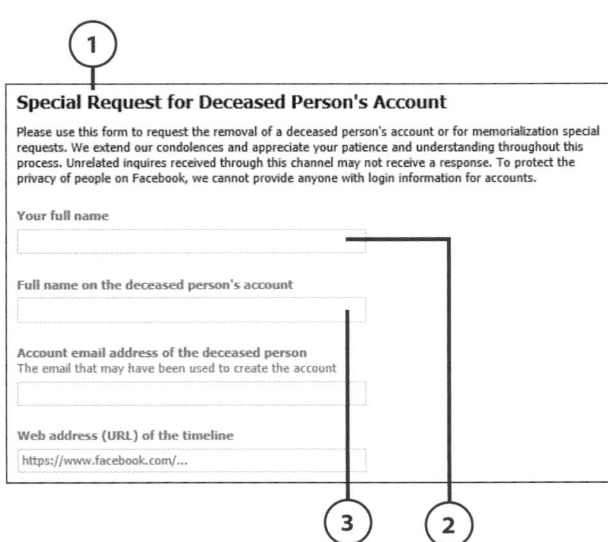

4. Enter the email address used by the deceased person (if you know it) into the Account Email Address of the Deceased Person box.
5. Enter the URL of the deceased person's Timeline page into the Web Address (URL) of the Timeline box.
6. Go to the Relationship to the Person section and check how you're related—Immediate Family, Extended Family, Non-Family, or Other.
7. Go to the How Can We Help You? section and select the Please Remove This Account option.
8. Go to the Please Provide Verification That You're an Immediate Family member section and click the Upload button to display the Upload a File dialog box.
9. Click the Choose File button and select the file for the death certificate or other document.
10. When you return to the Special Request for Deceased Person's Account page, enter any additional comments or requests into the Additional Information box.
11. Click the Send button.

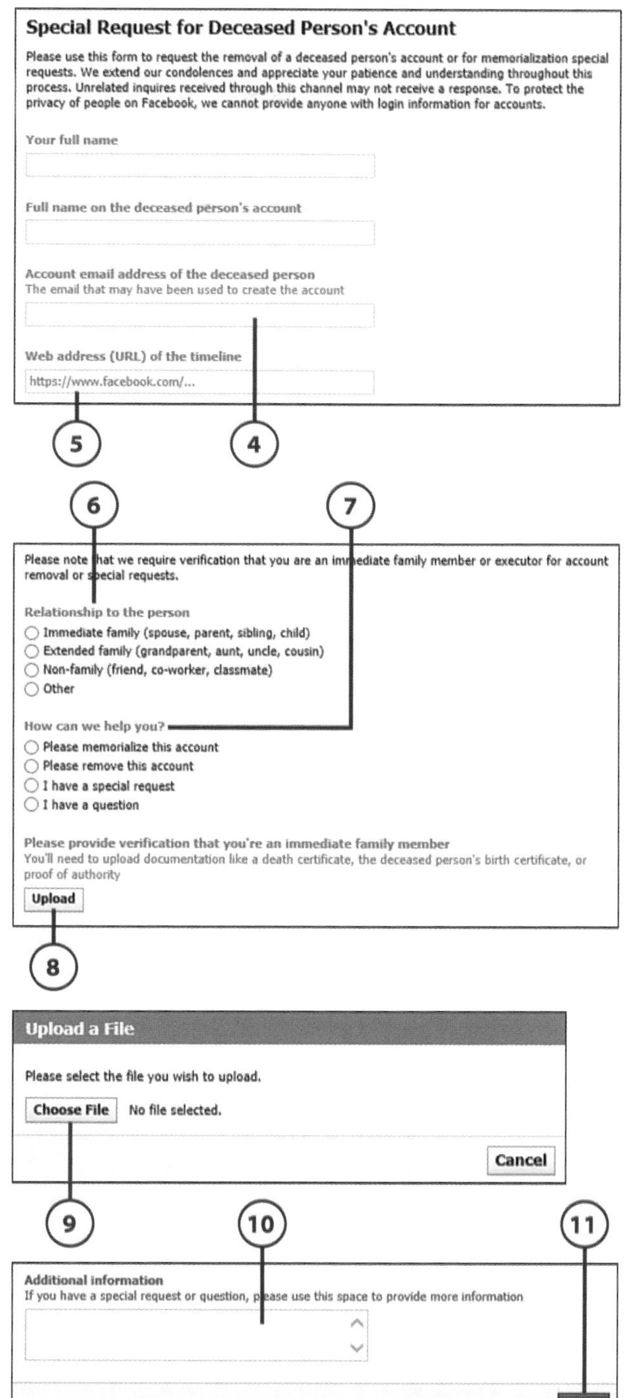

Download Content from a Deceased Person's Account

Most Facebook users put a large chunk of their lives online, in the form of photos, videos, and such. Rather than abandon those photos and other content when a loved one dies, you can request to download that content for your own use.

Due to privacy concerns, which continue after a person's death, this process is somewhat involved. You need to have a copy of your driver's license or other government-issued ID scanned into your computer to upload to Facebook when asked; you also need to scan a copy of the deceased person's death certificate.

1. From your web browser, go to www.facebook.com/help/contact/398036060275245 to display the Requesting Content from a Deceased Person's Account page.
2. Check Yes that you're an authorized representative of the deceased person. The page expands.
3. If the person is a minor, check Yes. Otherwise, check No. The page expands.

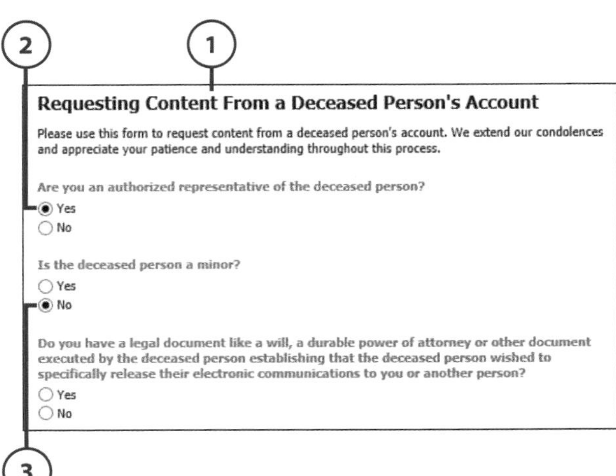

Requesting Content From a Deceased Person's Account

Please use this form to request content from a deceased person's account. We extend our condolences and appreciate your patience and understanding throughout this process.

Are you an authorized representative of the deceased person?

- (•) Yes
- ( ) No

Is the deceased person a minor?

- ( ) Yes
- (•) No

Do you have a legal document like a will, a durable power of attorney or other document executed by the deceased person establishing that the deceased person wished to specifically release their electronic communications to you or another person?

- ( ) Yes
- ( ) No

4. When you're asked if you have a will or power of attorney that specifically addressed this person's Facebook account, click Yes if you do and No if you don't.
5. If you checked Yes, send a certified copy of that document and a court order referencing the disclosure of this and other electronic content to the following address:

   Facebook Security
   1601 Willow Road
   Menlo Park, CA 94025
6. If you checked no, check the disclaimer box at the bottom of the page. The page expands.
7. Enter your name into the Your Full Name box.
8. Enter your street address into the Your Mailing Address box.
9. Enter your email address into the Your Email Address box.
10. Click the Upload button under the Photocopy of Your Government-Issued ID section. The Upload a File dialog box displays.
11. Click the Choose File button and select the file for your scanned-in ID.

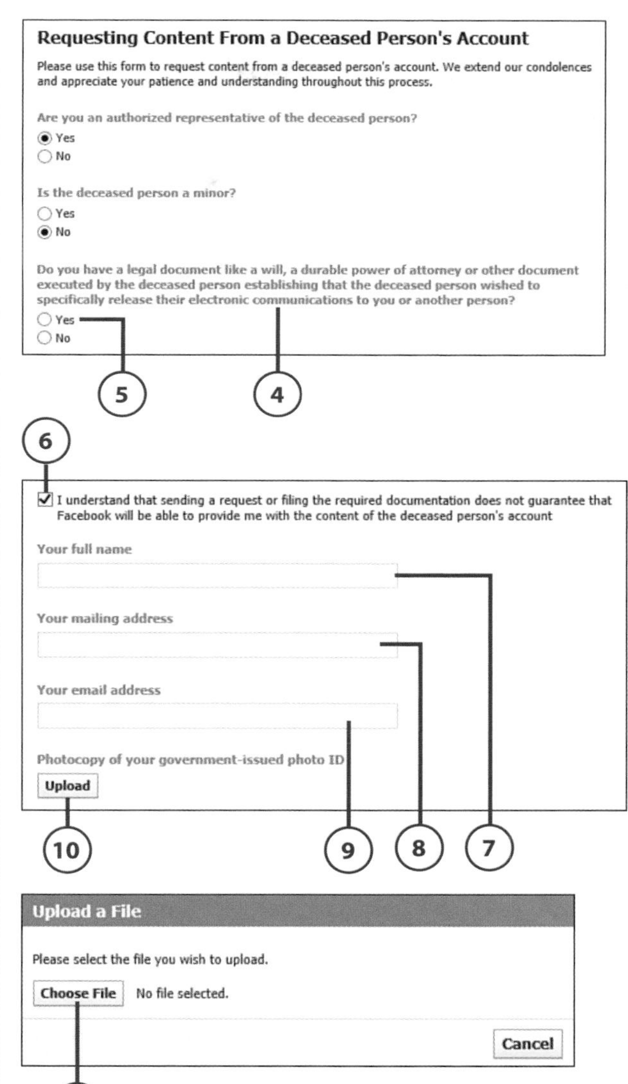

(12) When you're returned to the main page, enter the deceased person's email address or URL of his Timeline page into the Email Address of the Deceased Person That Is Associated with Their Facebook Account or a Link (URL) to Their Timeline box.

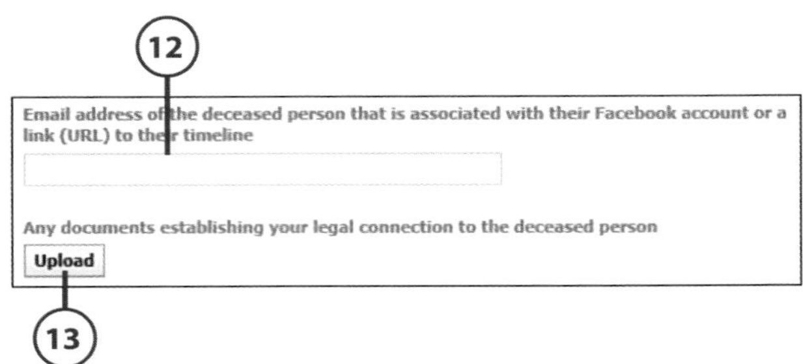

(13) Go to the Any Documents Establishing Your Legal Connection to the Deceased Person and click the Upload button to display the Upload a File dialog box.

Upload a File
Please select the file you wish to upload.
Choose File No file selected.
Cancel
14

(14) Click the Choose File button and select the file that contains said documents.

Copy of the deceased person's death certificate
If the death certificate is not in English, please provide an accurate, notarized translation
Upload
15

(15) When you're returned to the main page, go to the Copy of the Deceased Person's Death Certificate section and click the Upload button to display the Upload a File dialog box.

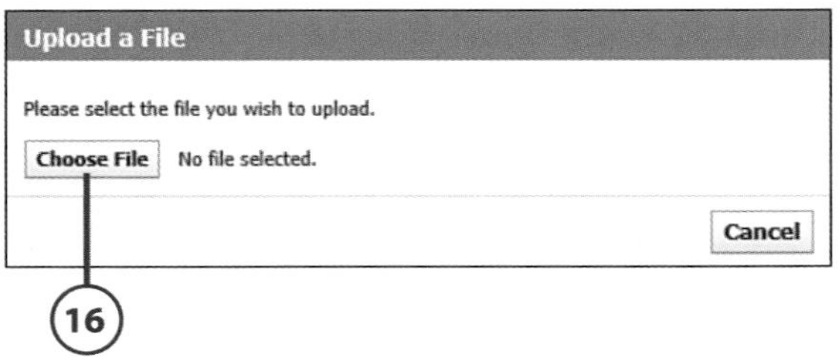

(16) Click the Choose File button and select the file for the scanned-in death certificate.

(17) When you're returned to the main page, click the Send button. Facebook now evaluates your request and will eventually respond with further instructions.

It's Not All Good

Incapacitated Users

The situation is less clear if you're still alive but incapacitated, without the ability to sign onto Facebook on your own behalf. At present Facebook offers no formal process for a spouse or other family member to access an incapacitated user's account. The best thing to do, if you can, is have the person give you his password and then then log onto his account yourself, on his behalf. You can then delete or deactivate the account, as per the incapacitated user's request.

If your loved one is unable to provide you with his Facebook password, the situation is much more murky. You can try contacting Facebook on the behalf of your loved one, but it's unclear whether Facebook has the right to let you access that person's account. It's worth trying, however.

To contact Facebook about this or other issues, email info@facebook.com or call 800-608-1600.

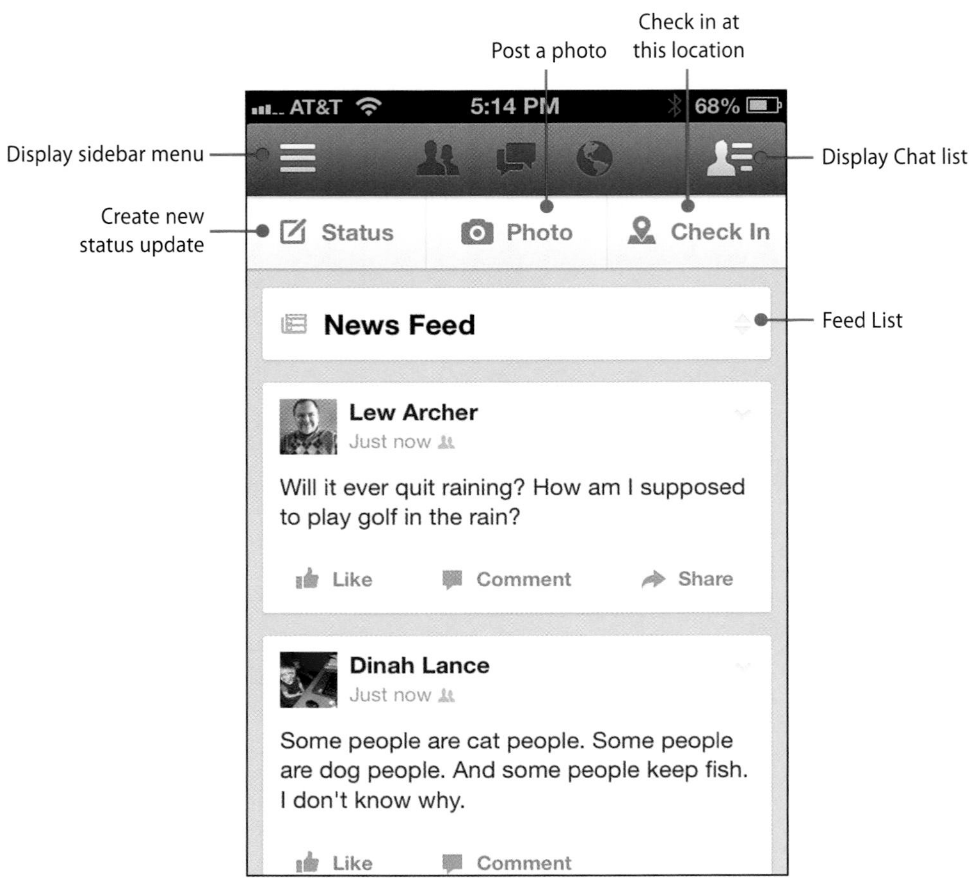

Check in at
this location
Post a photo
AT&T
5:14 PM
68%
Display sidebar menu
Display Chat list
Create new
status update
Status
Photo
Check In
News Feed
Feed List
Lew Archer
Just now
Will it ever quit raining? How am I supposed to play golf in the rain?
Like
Comment
Share
Dinah Lance
Just now
Some people are cat people. Some people are dog people. And some people keep fish. I don't know why.
Like
Comment

In this chapter you find out how to use Facebook on your smartphone or tablet.

- → Comparing Facebook on Different Devices
- → Using Facebook's iPhone App

20

Using Facebook on Your iPhone or iPad

More and more of us are using our phones and tablets to access the Internet. It's convenient to check in on the Web while we're on the go.

For that reason, Facebook has developed apps for the iPhone, iPad, and other popular smartphones and tablets. You don't have to wait until you get home to check your Facebook News Feed—or post a status update or photo!

Comparing Facebook on Different Devices

Chances are you have at least one mobile device that can connect to the Internet. That might be an iPhone or Android phone, or an iPad or other tablet. Fortunately, Facebook has apps to run on just about any type of mobile device.

App Stores

Look for the Facebook app for your device in your device's app store. For example, if you have an iPhone or iPad, look for the Facebook app in the Apple App Store on your device.

Facebook on the iPhone

The most popular mobile device is Apple's iPhone. It's the single most popular smartphone today, and it's used by many as a kind of mobile computer to access the Internet on the go.

The iPhone's Facebook app looks a lot like Facebook's website. There's a toolbar at the top of the screen, and a sidebar menu you access by sliding the main screen to the right.

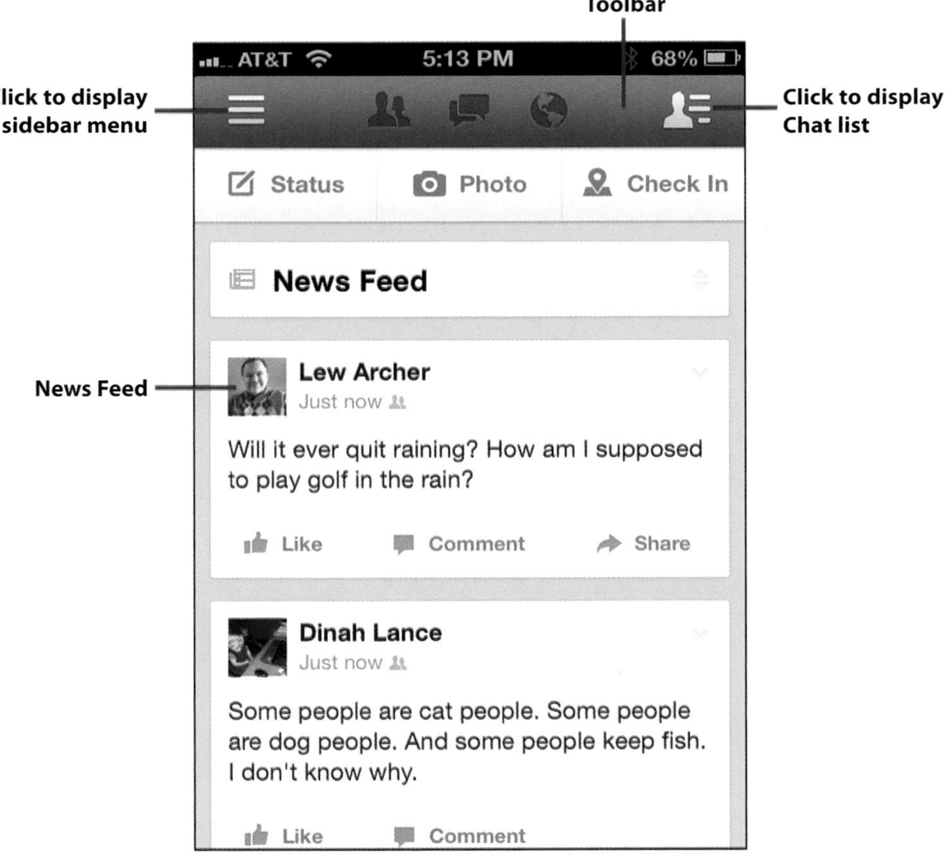

Facebook on the iPad

The Facebook app for the iPad is almost identical to Facebook's iPhone app. The big difference is that the larger screen of the iPad enables you to see more options without having to slide the News Feed to the side. In particular, the Chat list is always visible on the right side of the screen.

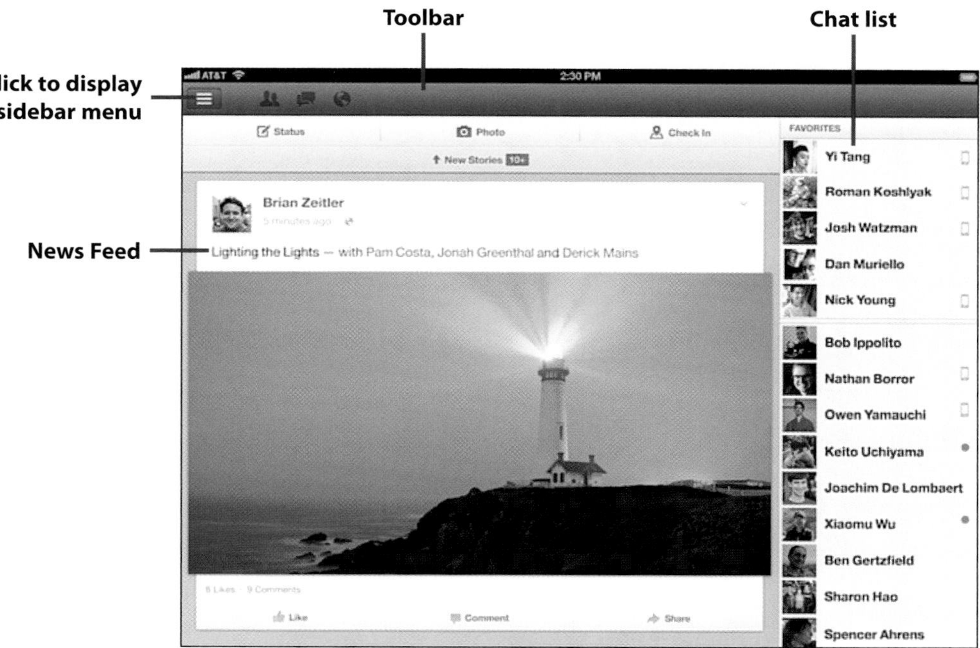

Facebook on Android Devices

If you have an Android phone or tablet, you can install Facebook's Android app. It functions very similarly to Facebook's iPhone and iPad apps.

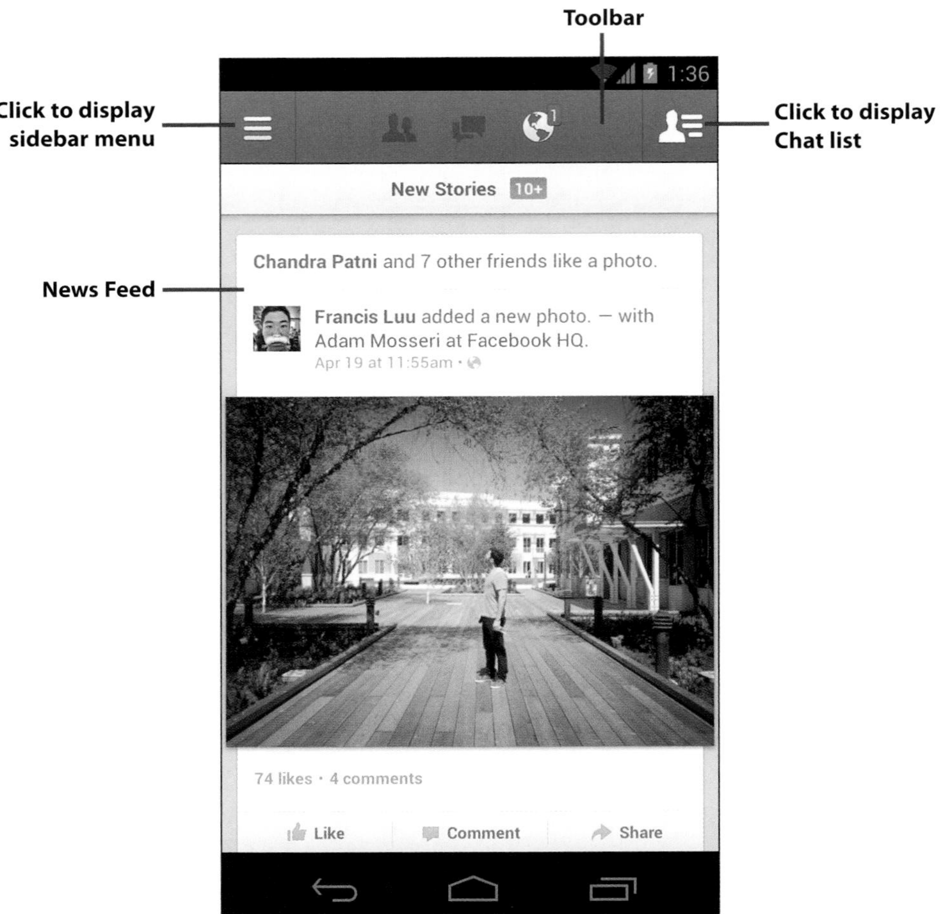

Facebook Home on Android Phones

If you're really, really, *really* into Facebook, and you have an Android phone or tablet, there's another option available. Facebook Home is a group of apps that take over your Android device and turn it into an all-Facebook, all-the-time device. When you install Facebook Home, you see the Facebook Cover feed instead of your phone's normal home screen; this displays pictures and status updates from your friends, one screen at a time. In addition, Facebook notifications pop up no matter what else you might be doing on your phone, Facebook messages are integrated into your phone's text messages, and there's a special "chat heads" feature that lets you continue chatting with your Facebook friends while you use your phone for other tasks.

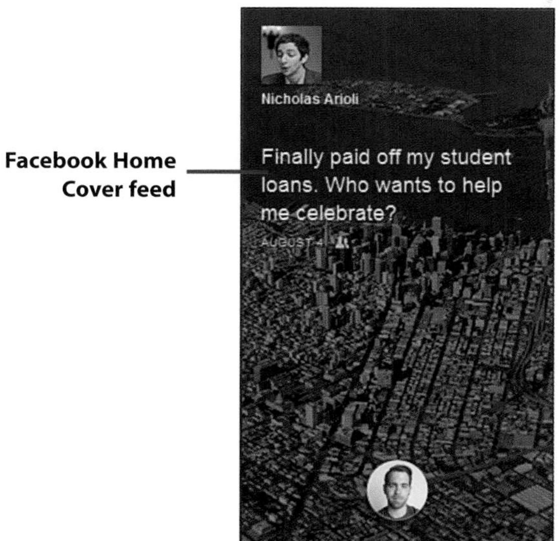

Facebook Home is definitely for Facebook "power users"—people who sign into Facebook first thing in the morning and stay signed in until they go to sleep at night. If you can't go 10 minutes without checking your Facebook feed, Facebook Home is worth considering. For the rest of us, however, Facebook Home is overkill, especially in the way it hijacks all of your phone's operations. I'd say that Facebook Home probably isn't a good choice for most seniors—although some of your grandkids might like it.

Android Only

Facebook Home is available from the Google Play Store for selected Android phones, and it comes preinstalled with the HTC First phone. At present it is not available for Android tablets or for Apple's iPhone or iPad.

Facebook on Other Mobile Devices

Facebook also offers apps for other mobile devices. There are Facebook apps for Android, Blackberry, INQ, Nokia, Palm, Sidekick, Sony Ericsson, and Windows Mobile devices. You can also connect your web-enabled phone directly to Facebook's mobile website, at m.facebook.com, which offers functionality similar to Facebook's device-specific apps.

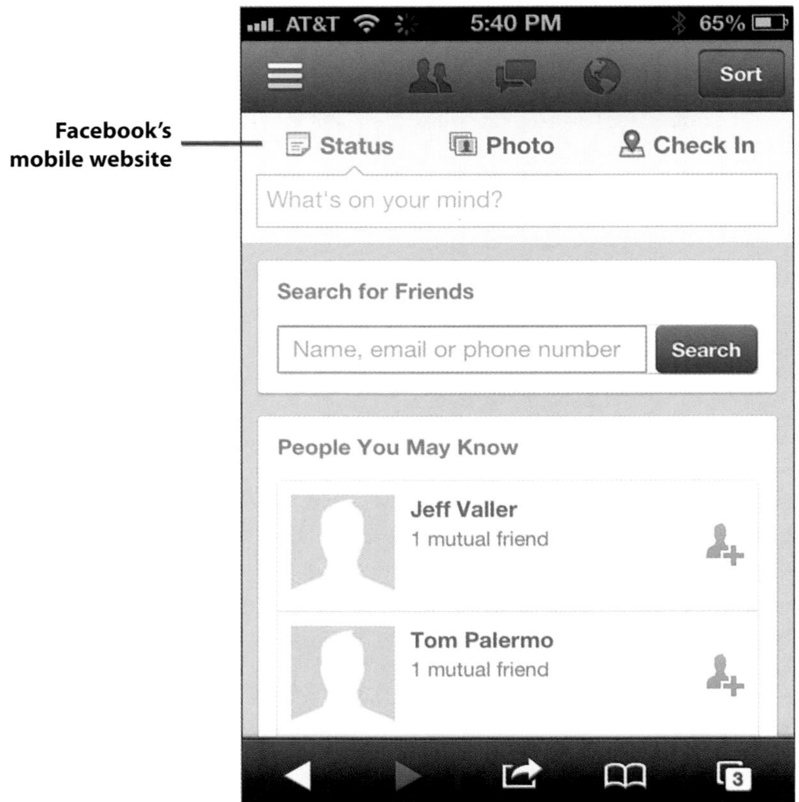

Using Facebook's iPhone App

Because the Facebook app is pretty much the same on different mobile devices, this chapter uses Facebook's iPhone app as a general example. You can find the Facebook app in Apple's iPhone App Store; just search the store for "Facebook" and then download the app—it's free.

Logging In

The first time you launch the Facebook app, you need to enter your email address and password to log in to the Facebook site.

View the News Feed—and Other Feeds

When you first open the Facebook app you see the News Feed screen. You can display other feeds on this screen, such as the Most Recent, All Friends, Following, Photos, Music, Groups, and Games feeds.

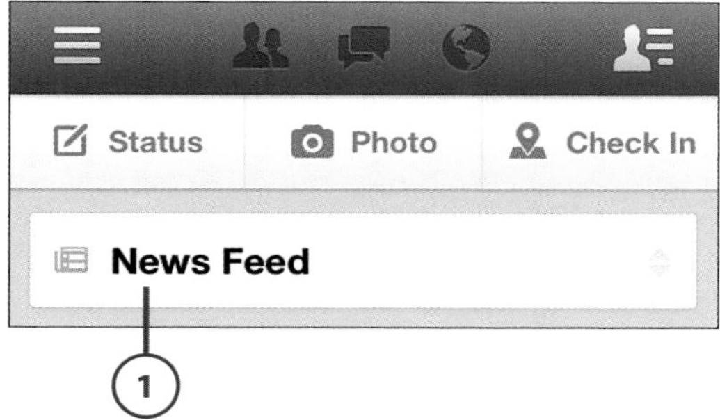

1. Scroll to the top of the page and tap News Feed to display the Feed List.
2. Tap the down arrow to display more feeds.
3. Tap the feed you want to view.

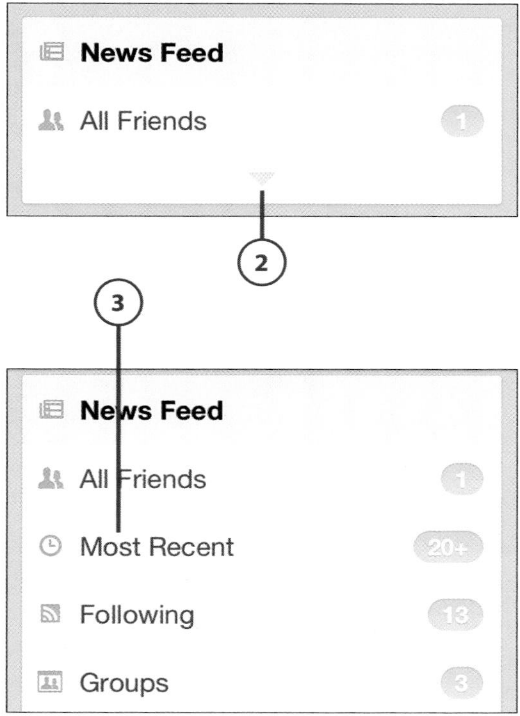

Refresh

To refresh the News Feed, scroll to the very top of the page, and then pull the page down. You should see an Updating message while the feed is being refreshed.

4. To view a poster's Timeline page, tap that person's name.
5. If a post contains a link to another web page, tap the link to open the linked-to web page in a new screen.

6. If a post has a picture attached, tap the picture to view it fullscreen.
7. To "like" a post, tap Like.
8. To comment on a post, tap Comment to display the Comment screen.

Comments

To read other comments, tap the Comments (word balloon) icon.

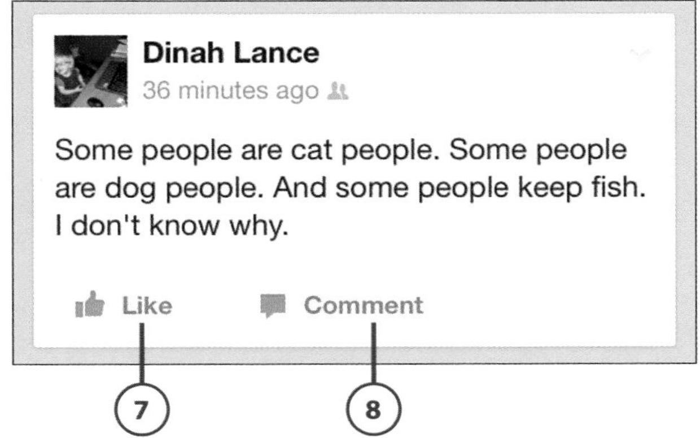

9. Use the onscreen keyboard to type your comment.
10. Tap the Post button.

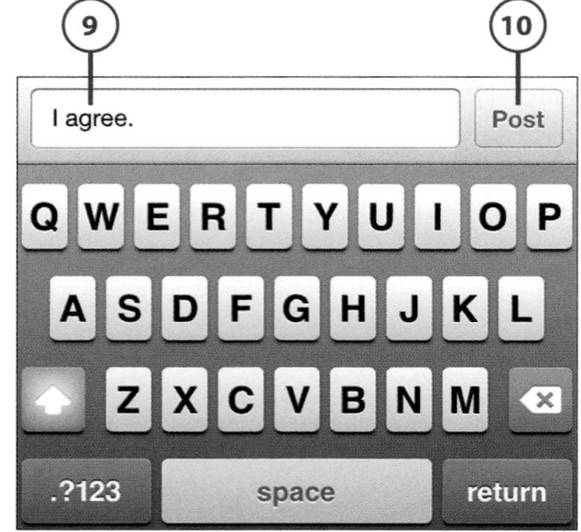

Use the Sidebar Menu

In Facebook's iPhone app, the sidebar menu is hidden from view by default. To access other parts of the Facebook site, you need to display and use the sidebar menu.

1. Tap the Menu button on the toolbar or slide the News Feed screen to the right to display the sidebar menu.
2. Tap your name to display your Timeline page.
3. Tap News Feed to redisplay the News Feed screen.
4. Tap Messages to read or write private messages.
5. Tap Local Search to see interesting places near your current location.
6. Tap Events to view upcoming events.

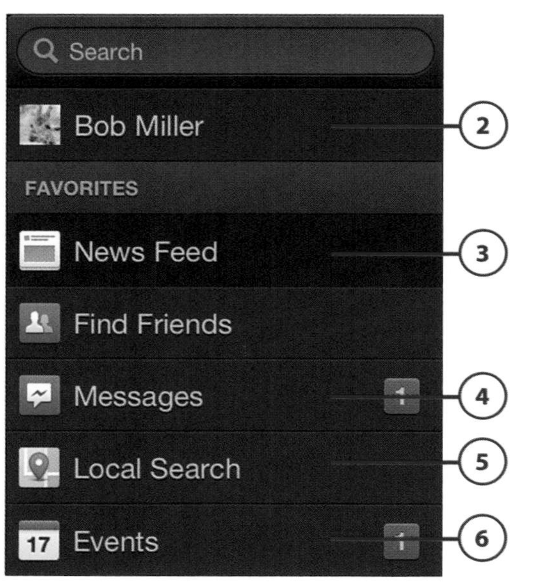

7. Tap Groups to see all the groups you belong to, or tap any group name to view that group's feed.
8. Tap Apps to view and access your installed apps and games.
9. Tap App Center to visit the Facebook App Center.

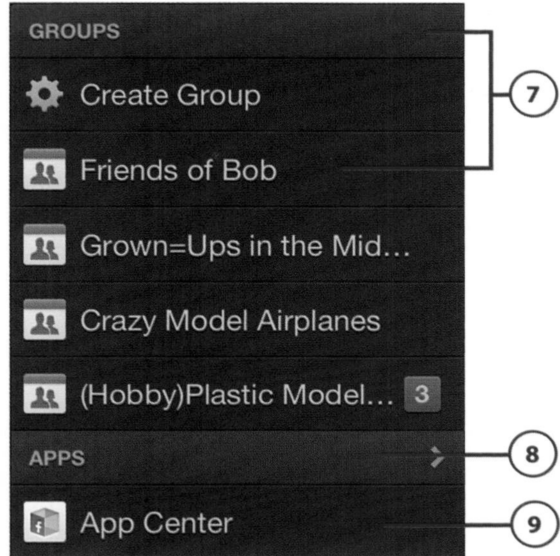

Post a Status Update

The Facebook app on the iPhone enables you to easily post status updates from wherever you happen to be at the time. It's a great way to let your friends know what you're doing and where you are.

1. Scroll to the top of the main screen and tap the Status button to display the Update Status screen.

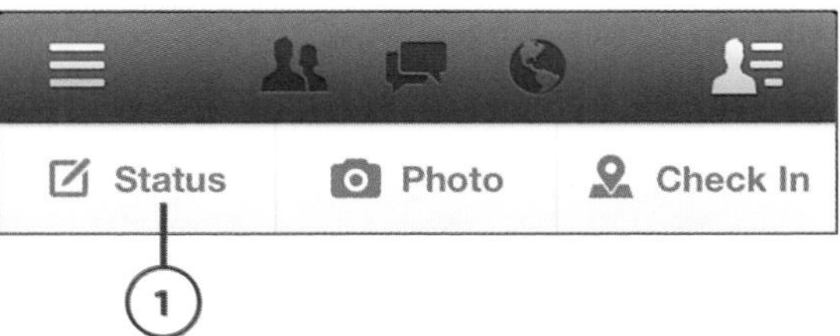

2. Use the onscreen keyboard to enter the text of your message.
3. To tag a person you're with in your post, tap the With? button to display your friends list.
4. Tap to select one or more people you're with.
5. Tap the Done button to return to the Update Status screen.

Searching for People

If you have a large list of friends, use the Search box at the top of the With? screen to more easily select a specific person.

6. To add a location to this post, tap the Where Are You? button to display a list of nearby locations.
7. Tap your current location to return to the Update Status screen.

Finding a Location

If your location is not automatically listed, you can enter the name of your location into the Search box.

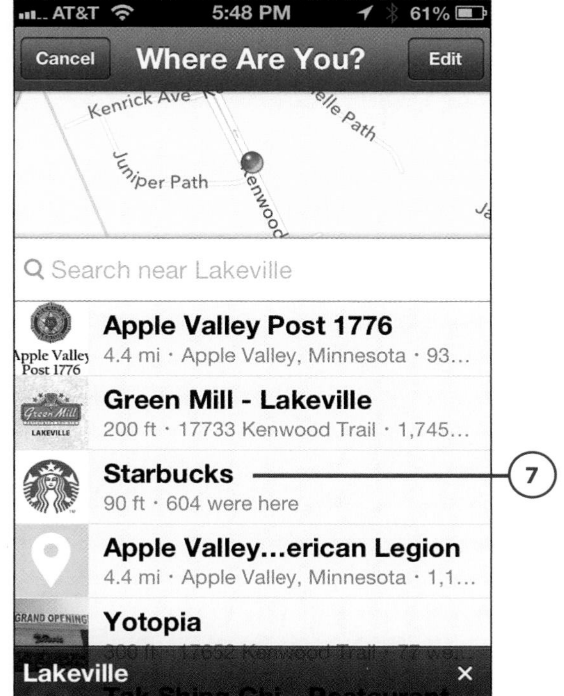

8. To determine who can view this post, tap the Privacy button to display a list of options.
9. Tap one of the available options: Public, Friends, and Only Me. (You can also select one of your personalized friends lists, if you have any.)
10. Tap the Post button to post your status update.

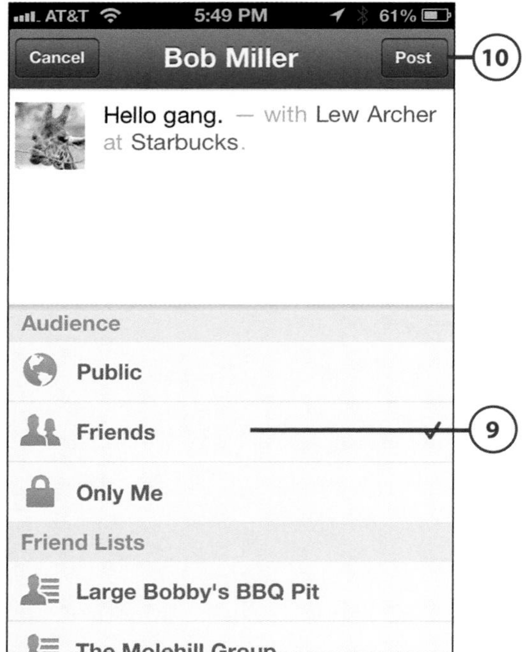

Take and Post a Picture

With the Facebook iPhone app you can post pictures directly from your smartphone. You can post pictures already stored in your Photos library, or you can take a new picture with your iPhone's built-in camera.

>>>Go Further

MAKING MOVIES

Follow this same process to take and post videos to Facebook. When you get to the camera screen to take a photo, tap the switch in the lower-right corner to switch from still camera to video camera mode.

1. Scroll to the top of the main screen and tap the Photo button to display the Camera Roll screen.
2. Tap the Camera button to switch your phone to camera mode.

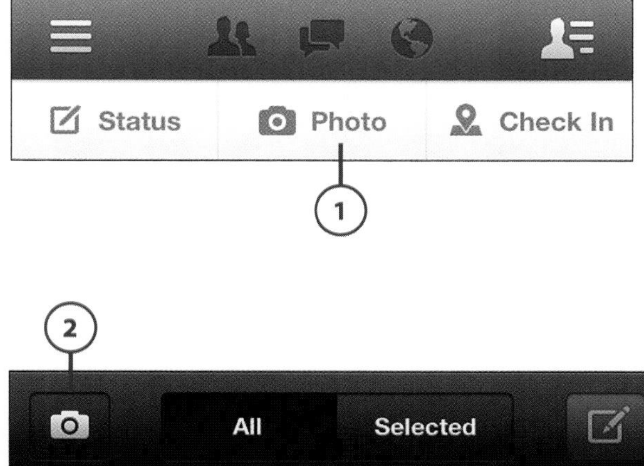

3. Tap the Camera button to snap a picture.

Self-Portraits

To take a picture of yourself, tap the button at the top right of the camera screen. This switches the iPhone to the self-facing camera, aimed right at your smiling face.

---

4. Tap the thumbnail at the lower right to display the editing screen.
5. Make any edits to the picture you want and then tap the Post button on the lower right to display the Update Status screen with the photo attached.

6. Complete the status update by adding a text message, people you're with, where you are, and privacy settings.
7. Tap the Post button to post the photo.

>>>Go Further

CAMERA APP

Apple also lets you post pictures to Facebook directly from your iPhone's built-in Camera app. After you take a photo, tap the Share button and then tap the Facebook icon. When the Update Status screen appears, add a message and complete the status update as normal to post the photo to your Facebook feed.

Post a Picture from Your Camera Roll

You can also post photos that you've already taken and stored in your iPhone's Camera Roll. The process is similar to posting a newly taken photo.

1. Scroll to the top of the main screen and tap the Photo button to display the Camera Roll screen.
2. Tap the picture you want to post; this displays the editing screen.
3. Make any edits to the picture you want and then tap the Post button on the lower right to display the Update Status screen with the photo attached.

4. Complete the status update by adding a text message, people you're with, where you are, and privacy settings.
5. Tap the Post button to post the photo.

Check In from Your Current Location

Because you're likely using the Facebook iPhone app while you're out and about, you can use the app to let your friends know where you are. You update your location via the Check In feature, which posts a quick and easy update with your current location entered.

It's Not All Good

Beware Stalkers

Using the Check In feature to broadcast your current location can alert any potential stalkers where to find you—or tell potential burglars that your house is currently empty. Because of the potential dangers, think twice about using this feature.

1. Scroll to the top of the main screen and tap the Check In button to display the Where Are You? screen.
2. Tap your current location in the list.
3. Alternatively, enter your current location into the Search box if it isn't in the list. The Update Status screen displays with a new status update started for you.
4. Complete the status update by adding a text message if you like, as well as people you're with and privacy settings.
5. Tap the Post button to post your location.

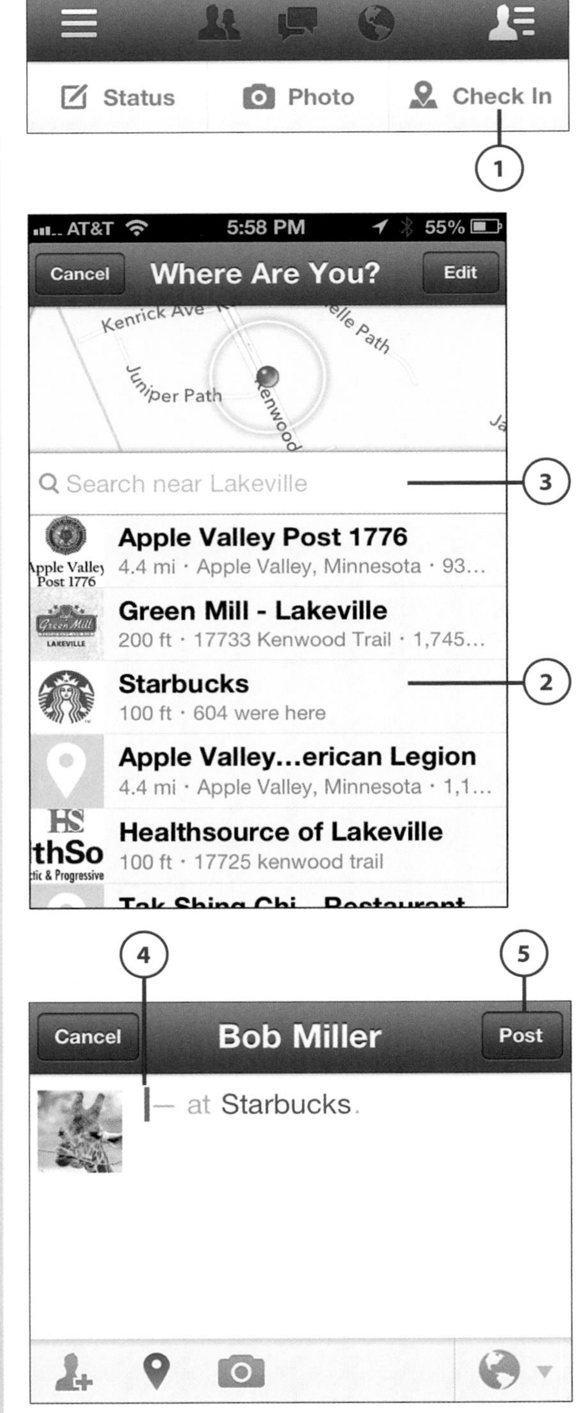

No Message Necessary

You don't have to enter a text message with your check-in status. If you don't enter any text, your status update simply reads "At location," such as "At Times Square."

View a Friend's Timeline

You can view any person's Timeline page on your iPhone, just as you would on your computer. Note, however, that the iPhone timeline is a little different than the one you see on your (larger) computer screen; the information has been rearranged to fit better in the palm of your hand.

1. Tap your friend's name in a status update to display his or her Timeline page.
2. Your friend's basic information is displayed at the top of the page. Tap About to display more personal information.

Contact a Friend

If your friend has listed contact information (email address, website URL, or phone number), tap that item on the Info page to initiate contact.

3. Tap the Message button to post a message on your friend's timeline page.
4. Tap Photos to view your friend's photos.
5. Scroll down the screen to view your friend's status updates and life events.

Check Your Messages

You can use your iPhone to check your Facebook messages while you're on the go. If you have private messages from other users, they show up in your Facebook inbox.

1. Tap the Menu button on the toolbar to display the sidebar menu.
2. Tap Messages.

New Messages

You can also access new messages by tapping the Messages icon on the toolbar.

3. You now see a list of messages, grouped by sender. Tap a person's name to view all messages (including chats) from that user.

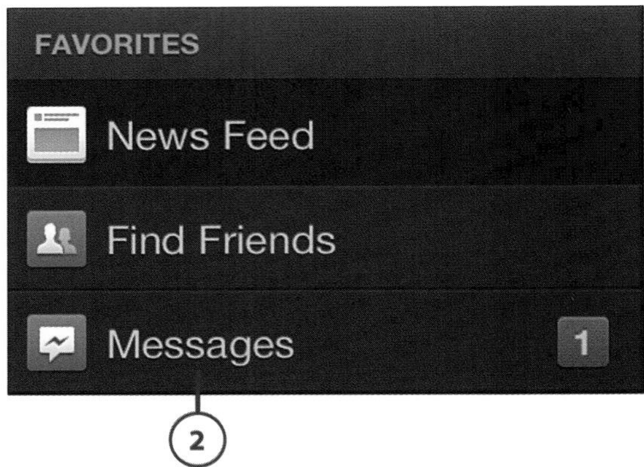

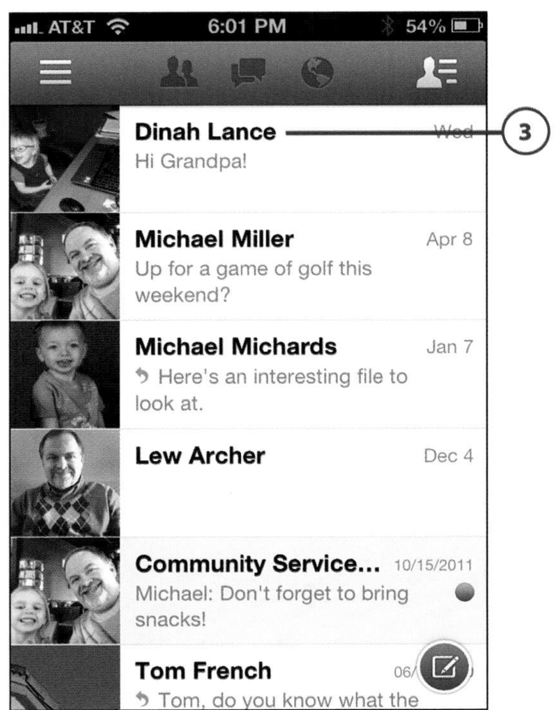

4. Enter text into the bottom text box to reply to the latest message from this person.
5. Tap the Send button to send your reply.

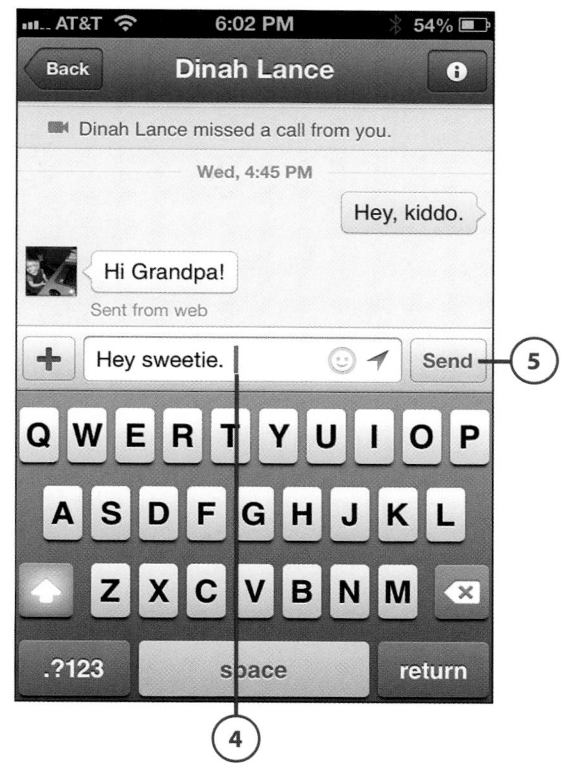

Other Messages

The Messages screen also displays other information. To view notifications from pages you've liked, tap the Other button. To see which of your friends are currently online, tap the Online button.

Chat with Friends

If you need to send an instant message to one of your Facebook friends, you can do that from your iPhone, too. All you have to do is access Facebook's mobile chat feature.

1. Tap the Chat button on the toolbar to display the Chat list.

2. Tap a person's name to initiate a chat session.

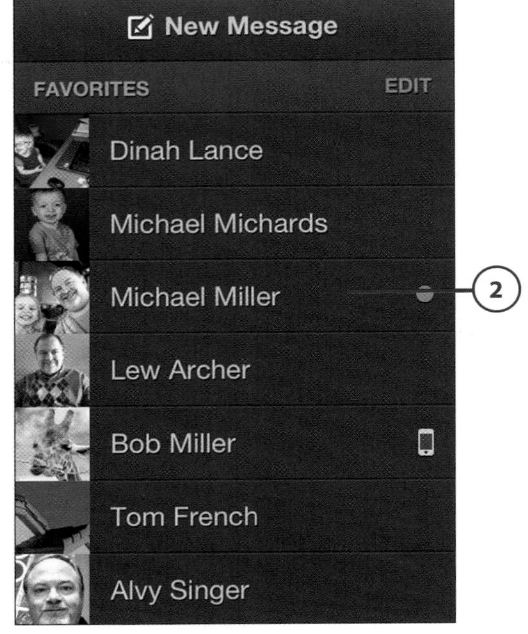

Green Dots

Friends who are available for chat have a green dot next to their names in the chat list. Friends who are online via their mobile phones have a phone icon next to their names.

3. Use the onscreen keyboard to enter your initial message.
4. Tap the Send button.
5. Your ongoing conversation displays in the top of the window.

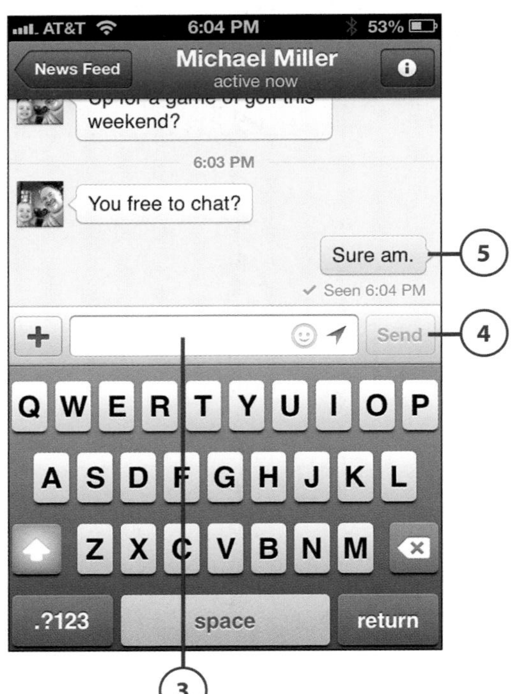

>>>Go Further

FACEBOOK ON THE GO

Mobile phone usage, especially to access Facebook, differs significantly by age. Younger users are much more likely to use their smartphones for Facebook than are older users. Seniors are the least likely age group to access Facebook via mobile.

This might change over time, as more of us become more comfortable using our iPhones and Android phones to do more than just text and make phone calls. Then again, people our age don't feel the same urge to constantly update our friends on our comings and goings, which the younger generation is seemingly compelled to do. We're okay with waiting until we get home to post a new status update or read our News Feeds.

That said, you can do just about everything on Facebook's mobile app that you can with your computer using the Facebook website. If you need to keep in touch or post an update while you're on the go, there's no reason not to pull out your iPhone and do just that.

Index

Symbols

A

B

C

D

G

H

I

J - K - L

M

O - P

R

S

U

V

W

X - Y - Z

Safari
Books Online

FREE Online Edition

Your purchase of ***My Facebook® for Seniors*** includes access to a free online edition for 45 days through the **Safari Books Online** subscription service. Nearly every Que book is available online through **Safari Books Online**, along with thousands of books and videos from publishers such as Addison-Wesley Professional, Cisco Press, Exam Cram, IBM Press, O'Reilly Media, Prentice Hall, Sams, and VMware Press.

Safari Books Online is a digital library providing searchable, on-demand access to thousands of technology, digital media, and professional development books and videos from leading publishers. With one monthly or yearly subscription price, you get unlimited access to learning tools and information on topics including mobile app and software development, tips and tricks on using your favorite gadgets, networking, project management, graphic design, and much more.

Activate your FREE Online Edition at informit.com/safarifree

STEP 1: Enter the coupon code: IZGJGWH.

STEP 2: New Safari users, complete the brief registration form. Safari subscribers, just log in.

If you have difficulty registering on Safari or accessing the online edition, please e-mail customer-service@safaribooksonline.com

Adobe Press

Cisco Press